Parry Sound

D1637207

PARRY SOUND

Gateway to Northern Ontario

Adrian Hayes

Natural Heritage Books
Toronto

Dedicated to the memory of former Parry Sound North Star *columnist*
Hugh Francis Dent (December 7, 1915–March 9, 1986)

Published by Natural Heritage/Natural History Inc.
P.O. Box 95, Station O, Toronto, Ontario, Canada M4A 2M8
www.naturalheritagebooks.com

Cover photographs, *clockwise from bottom*: W. Beatty store; loading lumber, Bay
Street wharf, 1898; Parry Sound, west along Seguin Street, *courtesy of the Parry
Sound Public Library Historical Collection*; Minnewawa Grove, *courtesy of Frances Marion
Beatty*. Back cover, *clockwise from top left*: The *Island Queen V*; Waubuno Park; looking
north on James Street, *courtesy of Adrian Hayes*.

Design by Blanche Hamill, Norton Hamill Design
Edited by Catherine Leek and Jane Gibson
Printed and bound in Canada by Hignell Book Printing, Winnipeg, Manitoba

The text in this book was set in a typeface named Perpetua.

Library and Archives Canada Cataloguing in Publication

Hayes, Adrian
Parry Sound : gateway to Northern Ontario / Adrian Hayes.
Includes bibliographical references and index.
ISBN 1-896219-91-8
1. Parry Sound (Ont.)—History. 2. Parry Sound (Ont.)—Biography. I. Title.
FC3099.P29H39 2005   971.3'15   C2004-905803-7

Natural Heritage / Natural History Inc. acknowledges the financial support of
the Canada Council for the Arts and the Ontario Arts Council for our publishing
program. We acknowledge the support of the Government of Ontario through
the Ontario Media Development Corporation's Ontario Book Initiative.
We also acknowledge the financial support of the Government of Canada
through the Book Publishing Industry Development Program (BPIDP)
and the Association for the Export of Canadian Books.

Contents

       the Inevitable Murder

17   The Politics of Policing   158

18   There Were Once Three Theatres   172

19   HMCS *Parry Sound*   181

20   A Memorial to the Forest Rangers   186

21   Hockey Heroes   190

22   The Bulldozing of History   201

23   Parry Sound Today   207

     Notes   216

     Bibliography   240

     Index   241

     About the Author   254

Acknowledgements

It is with a great deal of pleasure that I acknowledge the assistance given to me during the years that I worked on this project.

I fondly remember the many hours that I spent during the 1980s at the home of the late Marion and Reginald Beatty reading the correspondence of Marion's grandfather, William Beatty Jr., the founder of Parry Sound. Mrs. Beatty graciously allowed me to make copies of the numerous Beatty family photographs that appear in this book.

Many years ago, Dave Thomas began borrowing and copying old photographs of Parry Sound for his immensely popular slide presentations. Through Mr. Thomas's efforts, duplicates of many of these images are now in the Archives of Ontario, accessible to researchers like myself. In some cases the original photographs no longer exist.

I am grateful to Laurine Tremaine and Becky Smalldon of the Parry Sound Public Library, who frequently assisted my research by looking up information in the microfilm of the *Parry Sound North Star* and e-mailing it to me. I also appreciate the assistance given to me by the staff at the Parry Sound municipal office, particularly Rebecca Johnson and Ruth Rosewell.

Archivist Wayne Crockett was extremely helpful in directing me to Ministry of Municipal Affairs records relating to Parry Sound at the Archives of Ontario.

Thank you to Jim Hanna, former editor of the *North Star*, for his constant encouragement and help, as well as current editor Mark Ladan. I deeply regret that Peter McVey, former curator of the West Parry Sound District Museum, and E. Roy Smith did not live to see the publication of this book.

Finally, thanks to my wife, Jessie, who allowed me to spend numerous Friday nights at the Archives of Ontario and weekends in Parry Sound. Last but not least, thanks to Frank Doherty and Millie Madigan, who gave me a bed and opened their home to me during my visits.

Introduction

For decades after Parry Sound's incorporation as a town, the residents battled to overcome one setback after another in their quest to maintain economic prosperity. Everyone from the lumber company directors to the mill hands and local merchants knew that the supply of trees was not limitless and the town's sawmills would eventually close. An editorial that appeared in the *Parry Sound North Star* in September 1892, is inspirational and, oddly, prophetic. The newspaper's editor, William Ireland, wrote that the townsfolk had to create a future for their community by attracting other industries:

> Instead of waiting to see what will turn up to take the place of the sawmill, steps should be taken toward the establishment of industries that are best suited to a successful growth here. Foremost among the industries which may be said to be indigenous of the soil may be ranked a tannery because the supply of tanbark available is almost inexhaustible and the means of bringing in hides is easy and cheap. A furniture factory would also find an abundance of the finest raw material from which to draw its supplies. No better point could be found for a blast furnace when the railway opens up the iron mines between here and Ottawa. There will also be a good opening for a woolen factory and carding mill, sash, door and planing mill, foundry, cheese factory and a number of minor industries.[1]

In addition to the creation of a board of trade, the editorial also proposed that the town needed to look into establishing a hydroelectric plant. "By this means all our factories could be built along the water-front of the bay or sound and could be driven by electricity generated by water power at the falls up the Seguin River and transmitted by wires where required." A group of eight local businessmen led by Conger Lumber Company president William Henry Pratt incorporated the Parry Sound Electric Light Company Limited in November 1895, which the municipality acquired in May 1901.[2]

Parry Sound's business leaders also firmly believed that the town required a railway connection as ice closed the harbour during the winter months. The day before the *North Star* editorial appeared, a representative of the Department of Railways and Canals inspected the first 20 miles of a railway financed and controlled by local entrepreneurs to link the town to the Northern and Pacific Junction Railway at Scotia Junction. However, in 1895, the line was diverted away from the town by a new owner, John Rudolphus Booth of Ottawa. Booth's decision was of monumental importance as a new railway community sprouted and thrived at Depot Harbour on Parry Island, which became the Georgian Bay terminus of a rail system that extended all the way to Vermont. Parry Sounders inevitably felt their community had been robbed of its destiny and vowed not to let it happen again.

Parry Sound council passed a bylaw in August 1900 to grant the James Bay Railway a $20,000 bonus to construct a spur line into the town and, six years later, the politicians acquiesced to every demand made by the Canadian Pacific Railway, including the closure of numerous streets. The resulting influx of railway labourers was largely responsible for an increase in the town's population from 2,773 in 1904 to a total of 3,819 in 1908, although it dropped significantly afterwards. During the boom, the *North Star* commented that "the growth of the place is greatly retarded owing to the scarcity of buildings. It would be a good investment for anyone to put up a number of houses for rent, as rents are very high and empty houses impossible to find."[3] The newspaper also noted "we now have 13 teachers on the school staff with every room containing more scholars than the regulations allow, and more scholars being added to the rolls continually. Another teacher should be added to the staff almost immediately but there is no room available."[4]

Apparently taken aback by the sudden growth, council introduced numerous bylaws to regulate everything from the operation
of bowling alleys, billiard rooms, theatres and roller-skating rinks
to the sale of milk and cigarettes. Council also passed bylaws creating a board of police commissioners to supervise the town's single
constable, Octave Julien, and curtail noise from whistles, hoot-
ers and bells, the sounds of which were all signs of a busy, healthy
industrial centre. One reader of the *North Star* complained council was composed of too many old-timers who wanted the
community to remain a quaint rural village:

> What will be the use of Parry Sound seeking or inviting any
> large manufacturing concern to settle in its midst where maybe
> some hundreds of hands are employed if a whistle to call those
> hands in must only be blown once? Promptness and being on
> time is essential, and it is unfair to employees and unreasonable
> to expect that real men of enterprise would be tied down by
> such an old-fashioned bylaw as our latest is.[5]

In September 1907, council agreed to a 15-year, $30,000 loan
to Shortells Limited to build a $50,000 charcoal and wood alco-
hol plant in the town that would result in the employment of at
least 25 on-site workers and another 400 to 500 in the forest
felling maple trees and transporting the cordwood. When the

Prior to the First World War, the Algoma Lumber and Chemical Company
Limited constructed a wood alcohol and chemical plant on the waterfront
after receiving generous incentives from the municipality. *Courtesy of the
Parry Sound Public Library Historical Collection, Album I #42.*

bylaw authorizing the loan failed to pass in an October 7 referendum of Parry Sound ratepayers, Shortells began negotiating unsuccessfully with other Georgian Bay communities to obtain a bonus. Although the company purchased property in Parry Sound from the William Beatty Company Limited and workmen cleared the site and blasted out rock for the foundations in March 1908, the factory never materialized.[6] Likewise, the Provincial Smelting and Refining Company Limited failed to construct an iron ore smelter that was to have had a monthly payroll of at least $20,000.[7]

The board of trade and the Parry Sound council became almost reckless in their attempts to attract industries and a bylaw passed in September 1909 authorized an interest-free $30,000 loan to the Algoma Lumber and Chemical Company Limited to construct a $75,000 wood alcohol and chemical plant employing an average of 50 labourers and never less than 20.[8] Council passed an even more generous bylaw in February 1912 to grant a $25,000 bonus to the Standard Chemical, Iron & Lumber Company of Canada Limited to erect a smelter employing an average of 60 workers on a six-acre site purchased by the municipality for $4,750. In the bylaw, the town also agreed to acquire the waterlot directly in front of the property, construct a 600-foot wharf costing $30,000 and provide the company with an interest-free, $25,000 loan repayable over 20 years.[9] The two bylaws also guaranteed both companies greatly reduced assessments on their properties for a period of ten years.

The chemical plant and the smelter both proved to be abysmal failures that cost taxpayers a great deal of money. Although the chemical plant operated intermittently until 1921 (the longest shutdown appears to have been 17 months), the site of the inactive smelter reverted to the municipality early in 1918 after Standard Chemical defaulted on its loan repayments. Apparently, the original plan had been to fuel the smelter with inexpensive charcoal produced at the Algoma Lumber and Chemical Company plant. When this process did not work, hotter-burning coke had to be shipped in along with the iron ore from Lake Superior, adversely affecting cost efficiency.

The outbreak of the First World War had an immediate impact upon the Parry Sound area. In January 1913, workers for Canadian Explosives Limited had begun constructing a dynamite plant on a 5,000-acre site north of town to serve the mines at Sudbury, Cobalt and Porcupine, as well as the proposed Georgian Bay Canal, which, if it had been built, would have required more explosives than were needed for the blasting of the Panama Canal.[10] Production of commercial dynamite at Nobel ceased in August 1914 and construction began on a large munitions plant to manufacture cordite, a smokeless explosive used in military ammunition. The first line began operation in December 1914 and, by August 1915, upon completion of the second cordite and guncotton lines, total daily output reached 40,000 pounds. Nobel had a huge workforce and the population of Parry Sound increased to almost 4,000 in 1915.

At the request of the Canadian government, Canadian Explosives Limited constructed a cordite plant on vacant company-owned land. Operating under the name British Cordite Limited, the plant started operation in August 1916 with a huge production quota of 80,000 pounds of cordite a day.[11] The population of Parry Sound surged to more than 6,000 in 1916, with many workers boarding with local families and taking special CPR trains to and from Nobel.

The Armistice in 1918 resulted in tough times for Parry Sound as Nobel reduced its workforce to 60 and then shut down entirely between 1922 and 1926. During the war, the Parry Sound Lumber Company had ceased to operate and the final sawmill in the community, the Conger Lumber Company, burned on September 21, 1921. Convinced that increasing the output of the municipality's hydro-generating facilities would attract industry, local ratepayers supported a bylaw to raise $150,000 for a massive construction project.

"Let us not build any castles in the air as to what Nobel will bring us," insisted the *North Star*. "Nobel was built as a war measure industry and could not be operated on a peace basis except at a great loss. Let us go after something concrete and not waste our time looking to Nobel for our growth."[12] While some small manufacturers did commence operations, the population of Parry Sound did not exceed 3,500 during the 1920s.

Top: Looking north up James Street from the intersection with Seguin Street in the early 1920s. The municipality tried spreading slag on the main streets in the spring of 1919, but business owners soon complained the dust was ruining their merchandise. The first street paving was completed in 1928. *Bottom*: A 1920s view of the north side of Seguin Street looking towards the bridge. A fire in April 1954 destroyed eight businesses in this block as well as the Masonic Hall on the northwest corner of Seguin Street and Miller Street. *Both photographs courtesy of the Parry Sound Public Library Historical Collection*, top, *Album I #97*, bottom, *Album II #100*.

Immediately after the war, the *North Star* touted tourism as a viable industry, but council and the board of trade did not really run with the idea. Perhaps, there's no better evidence of Parry Sound's failure to acknowledge itself as a tourist destination than the annual returns filed by successive municipal clerks to the Ministry of Municipal Affairs. The question on the return was: "If municipality is a summer resort, give extra summer population." This request went unanswered for decades until clerk John Cranston Campbell finally wrote "12,000" on the 1961 return.[13] In 1919, the *North Star* wrote:

Speaking of industries, there is an industry right at hand. This is the tourist industry. Here is an industry that is so indigenous to our town and district that it is developing in spite of our apathy and indifference to its worth and value to us. However, it would develop much more rapidly if we studied its needs and made an organized effort.[14]

Although the Belvidere Hotel and the Rose Point Hotel had been catering to summer visitors since the 1880s and the huge American cruise ships *South American* and *North American* began visiting Parry Sound shortly after the First World War, it was really during the Depression that residents began to appreciate tourists, particularly those travelling by automobile. As unemployment soared, the Ontario government embarked on numerous highway improvements as relief projects, which in turn increased automobile traffic to Parry Sound. The *North Star* reported in January 1935 that over 700 men were doing roadwork north of Parry Sound; a year later a gravel highway existed as far as Pointe au Baril and there was talk of it being extended all the way to Sudbury.[15]

In 1929, roads were little improved since the Free Grant and Homestead Act had enticed settlers into Muskoka and Parry Sound districts some 50 years earlier with promises of free farmland. The pavement on Highway 11 ended at Washago and from there the most direct path to Parry Sound, over rough dirt and gravel roads, meandered through Gravenhurst, Bracebridge, Beatrice, Utterson and Rosseau. A decade later, the pavement extended to

Top: A 1930s view from the water tower of downtown Parry Sound. The roof visible in the lower right corner is that of the old curling rink.
Bottom: Looking west along Seguin Street in Parry Sound. The electric welcome sign was erected in the spring of 1930. *Both photographs courtesy of the Parry Sound Public Library Historical Collection,* top, *Album III #26,* bottom, *Album II #85.*

Bala on a less circuitous route, up the west side of Lake Muskoka. By 1942, the pavement went as far as Nobel, largely due to the start of the Second World War and a shift from workers' dependence on trains to automobiles.

The Second World War and the conversion of the Canadian Industries Limited (CIL) plant at Nobel to the wartime production of military explosives, once again, caused the population of Parry Sound to jump to almost 6,500 in 1942. At the request of the government,

CIL established a subsidiary company called Defence Industries Limited on the old British Cordite site. TNT and cordite production began in 1940 and continued until the end of the war, at one time employing 4,100 workers. Although Parry Sound's population decreased after the war to 4,439 in 1946, this was still significantly higher than it had been in 1939. In January 1950, the Ontario Municipal Board approved the annexation of a portion of McDougall Township containing a large number of homes built by Wartime Housing Limited for workers employed at Nobel.[16]

Numerous manufacturing plants have opened and closed in Foley and McDougall since the Second World War, but Parry Sound has been largely unsuccessful in attracting industry. A. V. Roe of Canada Limited and later Orenda Engines Ltd. employed about 225 workers at Nobel doing testing and research on jet engines until the government scrapped the CF-105 Avro Arrow in 1959. Between 1964 and 1978, Rockwell International Corporation operated a manufacturing plant for car parts in Foley that employed close to 300 workers. While CIL invested almost $7 million in the late 1970s to build a new cap sensitive slurry explosives plant at Nobel, a significant decline in demand for the product led to a complete closure in 1985, affecting the remaining 50 workers at the site.[17]

In the early 1970s, the municipalities of Parry Sound, McDougall and Carling together purchased a 1,000-acre site north of town on Highway 69 for an industrial park, and retired high school teacher and former Parry Sound councillor Donald Ritchie Sr. became economic expansion officer for the area in May 1981. Since Premier William Davis officially opened the industrial park in July 1979, numerous tenants have come and gone. "The people of Parry Sound haven't worked hard enough to bring industry in here," Mayor Wilfred Hall told the *Parry Sound Beacon Star* in 1982. "I think they've been too passive. This town has got everything it needs to go ahead with finding industry—all we need is the will. To bring industry in here, we really have to sell our small-town life—the good life."[18]

Abbreviations

AO	Archives of Ontario
CIL	Canadian Industries Limited
CPR	Canadian Pacific Railway
CRF	Community Reinvestment Fund
CXL	Canadian Explosives Limited
DIL	Defence Industries Limited
IOOF	Independent Order of Odd Fellows
LAC	Library and Archives Canada
LACAC	Local Architectural Advisory Committee
NHL	National Hockey League
OHA	Ontario Hockey Association
OHF	Ontario Heritage Foundation
OPC	Ontario Police Commission
OPP	Ontario Provincial Police
PUC	Public Utilities Commission
RCMP	Royal Canadian Mounted Police
SCA	Simcoe County Archives

Parry Sound

It is up to our people to do things instead of day dreaming of what may or may not happen. A town is prosperous just in proportion to the activity of its citizens. Towns do not generally grow and expand because of local advantages or geographical position, or from other reasons. It is generally the push and pluck of the citizens which makes towns and cities expand.

— PARRY SOUND NORTH STAR, September 15, 1904

William Beatty Jr.:
The Founder of Parry Sound

IT IS HARD TO IMAGINE, but less than a century and a half ago the whole of Northern Ontario was a vast area inhabited only by the Aboriginal Peoples. Mineral deposits such as those found in the Sudbury Basin were known to exist, but remained inaccessible. The same was true of the vast stands of white pine. The signing of the Robinson Huron Treaty in 1850 and the extension of the Northern Railway to Collingwood in 1855, however, made the north shore more appealing to businessmen.

One of these entrepreneurs was William Beatty Jr., the founder of Parry Sound. During the early years, he devoted much of himself to make sure the tiny community at the mouth of the Seguin River had every opportunity to grow and prosper.

William Beatty Jr. was born January 19, 1835, in Stonyford, County Kilkenny, in the Republic of Ireland. His family emigrated to Upper Canada in 1836 and settled in Thorold, where William Sr. erected a tannery and, several years later, two sawmills on the Welland Canal.[1] William Jr. was educated at the local schools before he attended Victoria College in Cobourg, where he received a BA (1860), MA (1863), and LLB (1864). In 1865, he was elected to the university's board of regents and sat on that body for the next quarter of a century.

Despite his academic abilities and aptitude for law, William had become involved with his brother James Hughes Beatty and their father in the lumber business. In the summer of 1863, they travelled up the north shore of Lake Huron in search of timber limits.

William Beatty Jr. In October 1966, Minister of Education Bill Davis officially opened a school named in honour of William Beatty Jr., two years after the province unveiled a historical plaque in front of the municipal office recognizing the role of the Beatty family in the founding of Parry Sound. *Courtesy of Frances Marion Beatty.*

On Parry Sound, at the mouth of the Seguin River, they came upon an unused sawmill built by William Milnor Gibson and James Alexander Gibson, two sons of David Gibson, the superintendent of colonization roads for Canada West. The Gibson brothers originally acquired two berths[2] of 50 square miles each in April 1856, but they surrendered one back to the Crown shortly after. The second berth was renewed repeatedly and worked until the limit was forfeited to the Crown in December 1862 for partial non-payment of stumpage and ground rent dues. Sporadic records indicate that in 1861 the Gibsons cut 5,214 white pine sawlogs of 12 feet in length.[3]

The Beattys were immediately taken with the possibilities of the land holding and, in 1864, they obtained a Crown lease to the timber rights on 234 square miles surrounding the mill site in the projected townships of Carling, McDougall, Foley, Conger and Cowper. In that year, a ground rent of $117 was paid and the lease was maintained at comparable rates until 1867, when another 50 square miles were leased on Moon River in Freeman Township.[4]

The yearly output of the sawmill under the Beattys is unknown, but in the 1871 manuscript census it is recorded that 32,000 pine sawlogs had produced 3.2 million board feet of lumber, lath and shingles worth $30,000. Eighty men were employed with yearly aggregate wages amounting to $18,000.[5]

Although all three Beattys were partners in the J. & W. Beatty and Company, which was formed to exploit the timber limits, it was William Jr. who took the most interest in the operations.[6] The Parry Sound Road, surveyed by John Stoughton Dennis in 1863, was completed by William four years later, making the outpost accessible by land from the Muskoka Road to the south.

The resident manager of J. & W. Beatty and Company was Nathaniel Parker Wakefield, the husband of Beatty boys' sister Rosetta. He became Parry Sound's first postmaster on September 1, 1865 and received an appointment as Crown land agent for the northern part of Simcoe County on September 20, 1866.[7]

James worked closely with his father in the family tanning business and travelled extensively in search of leather supplies and retail outlets. A prominent businessman in Thorold, he served several terms as a councillor and reeve. James and William Sr. also formed the Northwest Transportation Company in 1865 to operate the *Waubuno*, built at Port Robinson by Melancthon Simpson. This 193-ton steamer transported passengers and supplies from the Northern Railway's railhead at Collingwood to Parry Sound and Thunder Bay, becoming the primary commercial vessel on the upper Great Lakes.

Nathaniel Wakefield, husband of William Beatty Jr.'s sister Rosetta, was resident manager of the J. & W. Beatty and Co. operations at Parry Sound until his death on June 8, 1869. He was appointed the first postmaster on September 1, 1865. *Courtesy of Ruth Houldcroft.*

In May 1867, J. & W. Beatty and Company purchased 2,198 acres of Crown land at the mouth of the Seguin River in McDougall Township for a townsite; in October 1869, the first official town plan was completed by Peter Silas Gibson. William Jr. made the emerging community extremely attractive to potential settlers and, as early as 1869, Parry Sound could boast the services of Dr. Alex

Stephens, as well as the only schoolteacher in the entire district, Edmund Forsyth. There was also a gristmill, a weekly newspaper (the *Northern Advocate*, founded by Thomas McMurray) and a stage-coach service to Bracebridge, operated by the Beattys. Beatty quickly earned the title "Governor" for his leadership and attention to the needs of the settlers.

A devout Methodist, William had conducted services as a lay minister from as early as the fall of 1864. Two years later, he donated the materials for the village's first church. During the summer months he held outdoor prayer meetings—in an attempt to convert the Natives—and he attracted worshippers from the entire Georgian Bay area. In August 1872, he wrote to his future wife, Isabella Eliza Bowes of Toronto:

> Our camp meeting began yesterday as announced and a fleet of Indian boats from the north arrived about noon. They presented a beautiful appearance as they came sailing down the bay to the camp ground harbour.
>
> The Indians immediately commenced putting up their tents, and very soon the forest presented quite an animated aspect. Large additions will be made tomorrow when the steamer Waubuno arrives bringing the Indians from Christian Island and a large number of others from Toronto, Collingwood and other places.
>
> The camp ground at night is one of the most solemn and impressive scenes which can possibly be witnessed anywhere, the camp fires and lamps illuminating the forest, and the large assembly of worshippers uniting in praise and prayer in God's own temple....[8]

William also helped establish a public library as early as 1869. He was an educated, well-read man and did his utmost to assist others to increase their knowledge, if they desired to do so. The *Northern Advocate* termed the new library "handsome" and wrote of Beatty's donation:

> It is gratifying to mark the interest which employers are taking in those under them, and we have a noble instance of this in the

case of Mr. Beatty of this village. Employers cannot tell the results which may flow from following this course. Many a dull lad has been stimulated to activity, many a natural genius has been drawn out, many a rough stone has been polished and gone out into the world, and made their mark there, who would, in all probability, have been lost to the world, had it not been for the encouragement they received from those in whose employment they were engaged....[9]

In 1867, Beatty competed in the first federal general election for the riding of Algoma, which included Parry Sound. Unable to get a boatload of supporters to Sault Ste. Marie before the polls closed, he lost by a mere nine votes. In a campaign poster from this contest, Beatty expressed his support of Confederation and the acquisition of the North-West Territories from the Hudson Bay Company, a monopoly he steadfastly opposed. He upheld a more liberal policy of immigration and settlement and was opposed to any policy that would inevitably put land in the hands of speculators. He also advocated a change in mining policy to encourage the exploitation and development of the country's mineral wealth.

Another chief concern was education, which he considered "of prime importance." He promised to use his influence to secure grants so settlers in new areas could afford teachers and their children would receive the same level and quality of education as those in the older sections.[10]

In 1867, Beatty was elected as a Reformer to the Ontario legislature for Welland. The major achievement of the first session, in 1868, was the passage of the Free Grant and Homestead Act. Beatty spoke in favour of the bill and suggested practical amendments—one, which was incorporated, stated that timber rights on free land should be granted only after the settler had fulfilled a stringent set of regulations and received a patent.[11] In March 1871, he lost his seat, largely because of his support for the coalition government of John Sandfield Macdonald.

After his defeat in the provincial election of 1871, Beatty retired as an active participant in politics. In September 1872, he wrote to Isabella: "I feel a sense of sweet satisfaction that I am free of

The J. & W. Beatty and Co. store in Parry Sound in 1869. It also served as the customs and post offices. This postcard was made from a Duncan Fraser Macdonald glass negative, now in the Archives of Ontario. *Courtesy of the Parry Sound Public Library Historical Collection.*

political life, and that I had firmness to resist all temptation to re-enter it."[12] He never entered any municipal, provincial or federal election again.

Some time after Beatty's defeat, the partnership of J. & W. Beatty and Company was dissolved. In December 1871, the three part-ners sold the sawmill and a portion of the property at the mouth of the Seguin River to Hugo Burghardt Rathbun and Edward Wilkes Rathbun of Trenton for $125,000.[13] The Rathbuns immediately resold the property to Anson Greene Phelps Dodge, John Clau-son Miller and others who formed the Parry Sound Lumber Company in 1872.[14]

The reasons for the sale of the mill by the Beattys remain unclear, but presumably James was the instigator. The *Waubuno* had appar-ently whetted his appetite for the shipping business and, in 1870, he formed a partnership, known as J. & H. Beatty and Company with his cousin Henry Beatty.[15] They commissioned the con-struction of the sidewheel steamer *Manitoba* and leased the propeller-driven *Acadia*. The ships operated out of Sarnia and trav-elled north to Lake Superior.

William Beatty, who had witnessed the ravages caused by alcohol in other lumbering centres, was determined that the young settlement should become a respectable village. Many of the early settlers in this company town supported his temperance position. In the summer of 1872, the residents of McDougall Township, in which Parry Sound was located, voted to keep the township dry, under the provisions of the Duncan Act.[16]

In addition, from the time that Beatty obtained sole ownership of the townsite in December, anyone who bought town land from him had to agree to a clause prohibiting the sale, barter or exchange of liquor on the premises. The force behind the document was that Beatty or his descendants could repossess the land of violators. The so-called "Beatty Covenant" remained in effect in Parry Sound until 1950.

On December 9, 1873, Beatty married Isabella, the daughter of merchant and former Toronto mayor John George Bowes. They occupied what, at that point, was Parry Sound's largest and most prestigious dwelling, Minnewawa Grove, and raised a family which

The Beatty family, *from left to right*: Adelaide Mary Harriet Beatty, William Beatty Jr., Frances Isabel Margaret Beatty, Anna Georgina Bowes Beatty, William James Bowes Beatty, Isabella Eliza Beatty and Rosetta Victoria Alice Beatty, foreground. *Courtesy of Frances Marion Beatty.*

came to include four daughters and a son, William James Bowes Beatty.

Beatty's primary occupation after the dissolution of the Beatty firm was the proprietorship of the general store established in 1863. He did, however, continue to venture in and out of the lumbering industry and other enterprises. In 1874, he built the Seguin Steam Mills at the foot of Bay Street. The sawmill was 40 by 80 feet, and a 60-horsepower steam engine was capable of producing 40,000 feet of lumber, 10,000 feet of shingles and 5,000 feet of lath per day. Beatty sold the mill to J.C. Miller and the Parry Sound Lumber Company for $22,800 in October 1881.[17]

William Beatty also retained his interest in the *Waubuno*, which the family had continued to operate after 1871. It served as the lifeline of the north shore until the introduction in 1876 of the *Northern Belle* by Thomas and John Joseph Long of Collingwood. The competition between the vessels soon led to a merger under the name of the Georgian Bay Transportation Company Limited and Beatty obtained a share in the new venture.[18] The tragic sinking of the *Waubuno* in a fierce storm in November 1879 resulted in the company being at the centre of several contentious lawsuits for negligence.

Although it was finally exonerated, disasters continued to plague the company. In May 1882, the *Manitoulin*, built to replace the *Waubuno*, was destroyed by fire and in September the *Asia* sank, losing more than 100 lives. In 1885, the directors sought a surrender of the provincial charter and the remaining ships were absorbed into the federally incorporated Great Northern Transportation Company Limited (the White Line), of which James H. Beatty was the primary stockholder.[19]

One of the first to recognize the tourist potential of the Parry Sound area, William Beatty incorporated the Parry Sound Hotel Company in 1881, with himself as president.[20] The company constructed the imposing three-storey Belvidere Hotel, which overlooked Georgian Bay. The hotel opened on Dominion Day 1883 and catered to summer visitors until its destruction by a fire in 1961.

Beatty was also one of the organizers of the Parry Sound Colonization Railway, incorporated in 1885 to construct a line from

Minnewawa Grove, home of the Beatty family, circa 1900. The house, 30 Church St. today, originally stood on a five-acre lot. When the Canadian Pacific Railway was purchasing land in 1906, this was one of four houses moved to accommodate the tracks and station. Following the sale, William Beatty Jr.'s widow and her daughters moved to Toronto, returning to Parry Sound only during the summers. *Courtesy of Frances Marion Beatty.*

the Northern and Pacific Junction Railway westward to Parry Sound. He served as vice-president of this venture until it was taken over by John Rudolphus Booth, the Ottawa lumber baron, and his Canada Atlantic Railway in 1893.

After the sale of the Seguin Steam Mills to the Parry Sound Lumber Company in 1881, it would appear that Beatty was engaged in the lumber industry primarily as a jobber. This situation changed in December 1890, when he took possession of a sawmill only recently erected by his cousin Robert Banning Armstrong. He operated the sawmill on the outer harbour for several years and invested heavily in improving the machinery. Early on the morning of July 22, 1893, the facilities caught fire and, while the newly organized volunteer fire brigade rushed to the scene and managed to prevent the spread of the flames to the mill yard and docks, the mill was a total loss, incurring damages in the neighbourhood of $10,000. The ever gracious Beatty placed a card of thanks in the *North Star,* thanking the fire fighters for their valiant efforts and offering testimony to the efficiency of the town's new waterworks system.[21]

William Beatty Jr. died in Parry Sound on December 2, 1898, after a lingering illness. The *North Star* best captured the grief felt by local residents:

> In him the poor had a friend who did more than console them with kind words. He daily practised the golden rule, and his lovable and gentle disposition endeared him to all who loved righteousness and truth. Truly he earned the endearing title of 'Governor' which was universally accorded him.... His reputation extended far beyond the borders of the town and district where his life's work has been spent, and wherever he was known he was loved and respected.[22]

Beatty left Minnewawa Grove to his widow Isabella, and a sizable bequest to St. James' Methodist Church in Parry Sound. Once the funeral expenses and his debts were paid, the remaining estate was to be divided, with half going to Isabella and the rest to be dispersed among his five children as each reached the age of 25. His will stipulated that his heirs could carry on his business or wind it up.[23]

At the time of William Beatty Jr.'s death, his son was just 14 years old and hardly able to assume control of the management of his father's business affairs. It appears, initially, that Isabella tried to continue operating the estate with the help of the second-eldest daughter, Anna Georgiana Bowes Beatty (Bobelle), and advice from her brothers-in-law, James H. Beatty and John David Beatty. In a letter John advised Isabella:

> Bobelle will have the run of the business so well in hand that she will not feel the extra responsibility—she must not worry over her work and must not overwork herself and should make herself as comfortable as possible while doing her office work...I hope she finds no trouble with the books and accounts. If she does have her write to me and I will explain matters to her....[24]

William Beatty Wakefield Armstrong, a second cousin to the Beatty girls, became the manager of the William Beatty estate in 1900. He was the son of John Armstrong of McKellar and had originally

Left: William James Bowes Beatty
served as a councillor in 1908 and
mayor from 1921 to 1923. According to the *North Star*, he was the first
person born in Parry Sound to be
elected to council. His son, William
Sidney Beatty, took over managing
the Beatty store in 1938 after his
father suffered a stroke. *Courtesy of
Frances Marion Beatty.*
Below: The residence of William
James Bowes Beatty at 25 Waubeek
St. It was inherited in 1946 by his
son, and stayed in the family until
1960. *Courtesy of the Parry Sound Public Library Historical Collection, Maurice
Brais #97.*

moved to Parry Sound in 1895 to be manager of the Parry Sound
Electric Light Company, leaving that employment to study law
under solicitor Walter Lockwood Haight. He had then become
the manager of the Peter estate in 1898, following the death of
lumberman William Peter.

Top: The William Beatty Company store, circa 1918. *Bottom:* The William Beatty Company Ltd. store in 1933. *Both photographs courtesy of Frances Marion Beatty.*

The William Beatty Company Limited was incorporated in June 1904, with members of the immediate family as directors, to provide for the management of the general store and coal business. John D. Beatty was the president of the company, while Isabella held the office of vice-president and her daughter Frances was secretary-treasurer. William and Bobelle rounded out the board of directors. The total authorized capitalization was $60,000, although only 400 shares of $100 each were actually issued. Isabella held $19,800, while Frances, Bobelle and Adelaide each held $4,000. The president held one token share, as did young William, although shares worth $8,000 were held in trust for the boy and would be turned over to him upon his 25th birthday.[25]

William graduated from business studies at Albert College in Belleville and became manager of the general store at the corner of James and Seguin streets. In January 1906, he married Sidna Hume Brown and the couple made their home at 25 Waubeek Street, where they raised children Frances Marion, Eleanor Georgina and William Sidney. Isabella assumed the presidency of William Beatty Company Limited following the death of John D. Beatty in 1911 and William became vice-president. He later became president.

In April 1914, a second company, William Beatty Lands and Timber Limited, was incorporated to handle the sale of the property and timber left by William Beatty Jr. The company had an authorized capitalization of $100,000 divided into 1,000 shares of $100 each, but of this amount only 800 shares were issued with Isabella subscribing to $40,000 and her five children each taking $8,000. By then, William was president of the company and his sister Frances was secretary-treasurer.[26,]

The William Beatty Company Limited is still an active company, headed today by president James Andrew Beatty, a great-grandson of William Beatty Jr. Although the company no longer operates a general store at the corner of James and Seguin streets, the Beattys still own the building, which is now home to several retailers. The structure standing at 35 Seguin Street is probably Parry Sound's oldest commercial building. William Beatty Lands and Timber Limited also remains an active company.

2

The Miller Family, More Timber Rights and a Tragic Event

I F ANY FAMILY CAN BE SAID to rival the Beattys in importance to the early development of Parry Sound, it would be the Millers. Today, there is little to show that they were ever in Parry Sound, apart from the name of a downtown street and a family plot in Hillcrest Cemetery. But more than a century ago, hundreds of labourers depended upon the Millers for their livelihood.

In the fall of 1872, the partners of J. & W. Beatty and Company agreed to sell their sawmill and 234 square miles of timber limits in the surrounding townships of Carling, McDougall, Foley, Conger, Cowper and Freeman to Hugo Berghardt Rathbun and Edward Wilkes Rathbun of Mill Point in Hastings County. Originally from Aurora, New York, Hugo Rathbun had established a sawmill in 1848 at Mill Point and, when his son joined the business, it became known as H.B. Rathbun & Son. During the mid-1860s the operations grew as timber limits were secured in areas north of the Bay of Quinte.[1]

At the first Crown timber auction involving limits in the districts of Parry Sound and Muskoka, held on November 23, 1871, the Rathbuns purchased rights to limits totalling 47 square miles in the townships of Ferguson, McKellar and Hagerman for bonus payments totalling $8,970.[2] By a deed dated one month later, the partnership of William Beatty Sr., William Beatty Jr. and James Hughes Beatty sold its sawmill, timber limits and all of the property on the Parry Sound townsite bounded on the north by Bay

Street, on the west by Seguin Street and on the south by the Great North Road, to H.B. Rathbun & Son.

The particulars of the agreement between the Beattys and the Rathbuns were worked out quite some time prior to the auction of the Crown limits and the signing of the deed in December. Within a matter of days after the auction, however, Anson Greene Phelps Dodge of Keswick approached the Rathbuns regarding the resale of the properties to him.

Dodge was the "black sheep" son of respected New York City businessman and philanthropist William Earl Dodge. With reckless abandon, he assembled an empire of lumber companies during the early 1870s that included sawmills at Byng Inlet, Collingwood, Muskoka Mills, Port Severn and Waubaushene. On June 14, 1872, the House of Commons passed a special statute naturalizing Dodge and, in the election of July 20, he became the Conservative MP for the riding of York.[3]

In a written agreement with the Rathbuns, Dodge agreed that John Clauson Miller would have the same relationship with him that he would have had with the Rathbuns.[4] In another agreement, concluded on the same day between Dodge and Miller, the latter agreed to immediately pay $12,000 to Dodge and, in return, he would receive 288 shares of $100 each in capital stock in a company to be formed to operate the Parry Sound sawmill and work the former J. & W. Beatty and Company timber limits. A further 712 shares were to be held in trust for Miller by John Crawford of Toronto and would be gradually turned over to him as he made instalment payments over the next three years, with the final one being in January 1875.[5] By the schedule of payments, Miller would come to own a one-third interest in the new company, but, in the event he defaulted, he would lose $12 of stock for every $5 he failed to pay.

J.C. Miller's grandfather had come to North America as a British soldier under General John Burgoyne and was taken prisoner at the battle of Stillwater in the American Revolution. After the hostilities, he migrated north to Upper Canada and settled on a farm in Yonge Township in Leeds County, where John's father, Samuel, was born in 1796.[6]

Anson Greene Phelps Dodge. The District Court of the United States for the Southern District of New York adjudicated Anson Greene Phelps Dodge as bankrupt on November 15, 1873. After his son's failure in Canada, William Earl Dodge sent Anson to the southern U.S. to manage the Georgia Lands and Timber Company. Anson G.P. Dodge passed away in Chicago on May 28, 1918, at the age of 85. *Courtesy of F. Daniel Welsch.*

John Clauson Miller was born on the same farm on December 16, 1836, and was educated at the local public schools before marrying Adelaide Augusta Chamberlain of Farmersville (now Athens, Ontario) on August 2, 1859. He became a merchant at Seeley's Bay and acted for a time as deputy sheriff for the United Counties of Leeds and Grenville.[7] Miller then moved to Toronto where he was employed by the Ontario Crown Lands Department as of March 1868. Although initially classified as a clerk, with an annual salary of $1,200, and later as chief clerk, Miller acted as superintendent of the Woods and Forests Branch until he resigned in December 1871 because of a partial loss of vision.[8]

The Parry Sound Lumber Company was incorporated by provincial statute on March 2, 1872, with Anson G.P. Dodge as president, Barrie lawyer Dalton McCarthy Jr., QC, as vice-president, and three New York City businessmen rounding out the board of directors.[9] J.C. Miller was the mill manager and shortly became the secretary-treasurer as the number of shares held by him increased.

By the fall of 1872, Anson G.P. Dodge was in deep personal debt. In September, John Bell, solicitor for H.B. Rathbun & Son, wrote to McCarthy advising him that his clients had not yet received the $20,000 bonus promised to them for acting as intermediaries in the transaction with the Beattys, which had been due in June.[10] Dodge had also not been making the payments on a mortgage held by the Beattys on the mill property. Bell feared that his clients were open to a lawsuit because the Rathbuns had originally signed the mortgage and were thus responsible for the payments.

At this point William Earl Dodge began to advance large sums to his son to assist in the solvent liquidation of his debts and liabilities and, in return, Anson transferred his interest in several lumber companies to his father. By a May 1873 agreement, Anson agreed to sell his two-thirds interest in the Parry Sound Lumber Company for two-thirds of the purchase price paid by the Rathbuns to the Beattys.[11] By a December 1874 agreement, the senior Dodge undertook to guarantee the company's debts up to $125,000 with the Royal Canadian Bank for a period of two years.[12]

W.E. Dodge replaced Anson as president of the company while McCarthy and Miller continued to act as vice-president and secretary-treasurer. Dodge, however, rarely ventured into Ontario and McCarthy held a power of attorney for him as well as a proxy for use at meetings of the board of directors.[13] These meetings were usually held in Barrie at the law offices of McCarthy, Pepler and Boys.

In the late summer and fall of 1874, the Parry Sound Lumber Company demolished the former Beatty sawmill and erected the wooden shell of a much larger mill on the same site.[14] Throughout the winter, work was carried out to equip the structure with the most modern cutting implements capable of producing 11 million feet of lumber annually.

On February 2, 1875, J.C. Miller was elected as the Liberal MPP for Muskoka/Parry Sound. He was devoted to addressing the needs and concerns of the homesteaders. In January 1877, Miller introduced a radical amendment to the Free Grant and Homestead Act that suggested a resident of a free grant location be able to sell his land provided he had cleared, fenced and cultivated at least one acre. The purchaser would have to complete the improvement stipulations of the act and the patent would be granted five years from the date of the original grant.[15] The bill had widespread support among settlers in the districts of Parry Sound and Muskoka, but was defeated during its second reading.

On January 8, 1876, a notice appeared in the *Ontario Gazette* that the Parry Sound Lumber Company intended to apply to the Lieutenant-Governor for letters patent under the provisions of the

Former merchant and Ontario Crown Lands Department clerk, John Clauson Miller became secretary-treasurer and then president of the Parry Sound Lumber Company. He was also MPP for Muskoka-Parry Sound. *Courtesy of AO/David L. Thomas Collection, C-253 Tray 1-42.*

Ontario Joint Stock Companies Act of 1874.[16] On January 26, 1876, a meeting of the company board of directors, at which only Miller and McCarthy were present, passed a bylaw authorizing the application. At a shareholders meeting held immediately afterwards, the same two men ratified the decision.[17]

Once the new Parry Sound Lumber Company was incorporated on April 1, 1876, it assumed all the rights, obligations and properties of the old company.[18] It had an authorized capitalization of $300,000, and the board of directors consisted of W.E. Dodge, J.C. Miller and Theodore William Buck. McCarthy was no longer associated with the company as a shareholder, but he still acted as the company's solicitor. After McCarthy's death on May 11, 1898, his firm of McCarthy, Osler, Hoskin and Harcourt continued to represent the Parry Sound Lumber Company.[19]

According to two contemporary sources published in 1878, the partnership between Miller and W.E. Dodge ended in 1878 when Miller purchased the two-thirds interest in the Parry Sound Lumber Company held by Dodge.[20] As the transfer would have been in the form of stock shares, there is no documentation for the transaction in land records. There are also no surviving company records from this period, such as a stockbook. How Miller was able to pay Dodge remains a mystery.

The earliest available annual return of the Parry Sound Lumber Company is that for the year ending December 31, 1878, which was not filed with the office of the provincial secretary of Ontario until two years later.[21] Miller held $285,000 in stock. The other directors were Alex Campbell and Thomas McCracken, two Toronto bankers who together held $11,000. Harvey Mixer, Dalton McCarthy and

Anson G.P. Dodge each held ten shares valued at $1,000 and T.W. Buck held five shares.

Construction began on the stone foundations of the elegant Pine Lodge during the summer of 1880. It was to become the Miller family residence, the site of the former Parry Sound District Hospital. By September, the frame was being raised and the *North Star* predicted it would be the finest house in the district.[22] Late in 1881, the female members of the Miller family relocated from Toronto and the Pine Lodge became a cultural and social centre of the village, frequently serving as the setting for parlour concerts.

John Bellamy Miller took over as president of the Parry Sound Lumber Company in 1884.
Courtesy of AO / David L. Thomas Collection, C-253 Tray 1-43.

Miller's only son, John Bellamy Miller, joined the Parry Sound Lumber Company as a clerk in 1880, rising quickly to vice-president. Like his father, he was born in Leeds County (July 26, 1862) and was educated at the Toronto Model School and then Upper Canada College.[23] On October 3, 1883, he married Hannah Pollock Hunter, the only daughter of Robert Hunter of the Toronto publishing firm of Hunter, Rose & Co. They had two sons, John Clauson Miller and Henry Hayburn Miller, born in 1884 and 1886.[24]

The Parry Sound Lumber Company expanded when J.C. Miller acquired William Beatty Jr.'s Seguin Steam Mills at the foot of Bay Street, a sizable piece of the waterfront, Bob's Island and the waterfront lot between the island and the mainland in October 1881.[25] Miller filled in the waterlot, creating great piling grounds, and dramatically expanded the Beatty mill. Whereas the sawmill had a maximum capacity of five million feet annually under Beatty, it could now cut 11 million feet.

Although J.C. Miller was re-elected in the June 1879 election, he later resigned to run in the federal election of June 1882, which

The Parry Sound Lumber Company mill, looking north, circa 1890. The Miller family home, Pine Lodge, is visible to the left. *Courtesy of the Parry Sound Public Library Historical Collection, VF II.*

he lost by a margin of three votes to William Edward O'Brien of Shanty Bay. Following his political defeat, Miller's health began to fail and he was diagnosed with tuberculosis. In November 1883, Miller travelled with his wife to California to recuperate in the milder climate. He died at Colton on April 2, 1884. When his remains were returned to Parry Sound for interment in May, the village witnessed the largest funeral procession in its short history. Over 800 mourners participated.[26]

There are indications that the Parry Sound Lumber Company was in financial difficulty at the time of J.C. Miller's death. Early in February 1884, Crown wood ranger Duncan Fraser Macdonald recorded in his pocket journal that he had heard, while in Bracebridge, that the company "was in deep water and trouble."[27] That month J.C. Miller concluded an agreement with William Henry Pratt of Rosseau and Augustus Nathaniel Spratt of Alpena, Michigan, to sell the newly developed steam sawmill at the foot of Bay Street. J.B. Miller closed the deal in April 1884.[28]

The financial troubles of the Parry Sound Lumber Company persisted, and it was forced to offer collateral by way of a December 1884 mortgage to cover the $166,532 in notes held by the

Hannah Pollock Miller with sons Henry Hayburn
and John Clauson. *Courtesy of AO/David L. Thomas
Collection, C253 Tray 1-44.*

Ontario Bank. The money was due to be repaid in full by March
17, 1885, but clearly the Parry Sound Lumber Company was incapable of doing this, and a second mortgage in January 1885
indefinitely extended the length of time before repayment.
Although a small portion of the money had been repaid to the
bank by this point, the liabilities now stood at $158,610.[29]

The finances of the Parry Sound Lumber Company deteriorated
during the next decade and the amount of money owed to the
Ontario Bank increased. A November 1889 mortgage offered the
company's holdings as collateral on $202,011 in notes held by the
bank. A fourth mortgage, dated November 1893, once again
extended the time in which the bank was to be repaid the $308,722
it was now owed.[30]

Top: Parry Sound Lumber Company workers sorting logs in June 1898.
Bottom: Loading lumber onto the Parry Sound Lumber Company steamship
Seguin at the Bay Street wharf in September 1898. *Both photographs courtesy
of the Parry Sound Public Library Historical Collection / John Bellamy Miller*, top,
#6, bottom, #302.

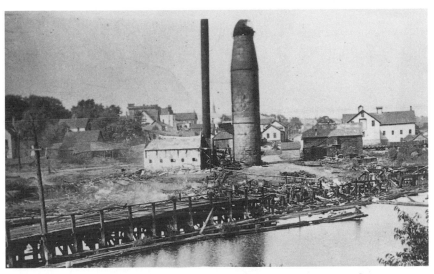

The Parry Sound Lumber Company's sawmill at the mouth of the Seguin River was destroyed by fire on the morning of Tuesday, September 1 1, 1 9 1 7. *Courtesy of AO / David L. Thomas Collection, C253 Tray 2-32.*

The main sawmill of the Parry Sound Lumber Company continued to operate under the presidency of J.B. Miller, but the lumber concern became secondary to other business ventures. The Polson Iron Works of Toronto had been incorporated by provincial letters patent to take over the business of William Polson and to continue the manufacture of boilers and steam vessels. By 1 8 9 2, Miller was the second largest investor after Polson and was a member of the board of directors.[31]

J.B. Miller's life centred so much around Toronto that he purchased a residence at 4 3 1 Jarvis Street for his wife, Hannah, and the two boys. His mother, Mrs. J.C. Miller, and his sister, Addie, continued to reside at Pine Lodge in Parry Sound while the Parry Sound Lumber Company was under the management of vice-president John McClelland. Miller and his family still came north to spend the summer months at Pine Lodge, however, and it was during one of these visits that tragedy struck.

On August 2 5, 1 8 9 3, Hannah Miller, her two sons, Addie and her companion, a Miss Cunningham, rowed to Sloop Island for a day of relaxing in the sun. While the women and Henry were on the shore, nine-year-old John Clauson played with a toy schooner in the water.

Unknown to the party, the sandy beach only extended a few feet from shore before dropping off sharply. The boy fell into deep water and drowned, as did Hannah when she tried to rescue him.[32]

Miss Cunningham rowed to Rosetta Island, where McClelland and the crew of the Parry Sound Lumber Company tug *Minnehaha* were working. Although everything possible was done to resuscitate the victims, they had been submerged too long. A funeral service was held at Pine Lodge on August 27, after which the bodies were conveyed to Toronto via the *Manitou* for a second funeral and interment at Mount Pleasant Cemetery on the following morning.[33]

In 1894, Addie and Mrs. Miller moved out of Pine Lodge to take up residence in Toronto and the building was purchased by Dr. John R. Stone, who converted it into Parry Sound's first hospital.[34] On September 22, 1897, J.B. Miller married Jessie Thomson, daughter of John Thomson, a former partner of W.E. Dodge in the Longford Lumber Company in Orillia. They had a daughter, Margaret.[35]

Although J.B. Miller was no longer residing in Parry Sound, he still remained a part of the community and made frequent trips northward to oversee the operations of the Parry Sound Lumber Company. He was a member of the Parry Sound Rifle Association and a senior officer with the 23rd Northern Pioneers, the local militia unit headquartered in Parry Sound. Although not a curler, he was also a supporter of the Parry Sound Granite Club, incorporated in 1898. In January 1901, he donated the prestigious Miller Cup as the prize in a bonspiel held annually until 1953.[36]

The earliest 20th century corporate record still in existence for the Parry Sound Lumber Company is the annual return filed with the provincial secretary of Ontario in 1906. At that time the directors were president J.B. Miller, vice-president John McClelland, secretary-treasurer William Buchan Tindall and Dr. Theodore Chamberlain, a brother to Mrs. J.C. Miller. Out of an authorized capitalization of $300,000, the J.C. Miller estate held $223,700 in shares while J.B. Miller held $75,100. All of the directors resided in Toronto.

The final regular meeting of the directors of the Parry Sound Lumber Company took place in April 1910.[37] Shortly afterwards, *Canada Lumberman* magazine reported that the directors of the company had decided to dispose of the sawmill, planing mill, box factory and the Crown timber limits. An auction was to be held in the rotunda of the Toronto Board of Trade building in December. The reason given for the sale was that J.B. Miller and the other directors were too busily engaged in other ventures and could no longer devote the necessary time to the business.[38]

The Parry Sound Lumber Company's box factory burned April 25, 1911, and the sawmill sat idle until destroyed by fire on September 11, 1917. The *North Star* reported, in January 1918, that the 120-foot high sawdust burner had been purchased by the Pembroke Lumber Company, while the boilers went to various other parties.[39] The board of directors did not formally meet again until December 1930, at which time they passed a bylaw authorizing an application to the provincial-secretary to surrender the company's charter.[40] The patent was duly cancelled on March 16, 1931, two months after an advertisement appeared in the *North Star* stating that all of the company's properties were for sale "at very low prices."

J.B. Miller had been largely instrumental in the formation of the Canadian Lumberman's Association, serving as vice-president in 1909–10 and as president in 1910–11. Also, in 1910, he was appointed to a directorship of the Dominion Forestry Association and became president of that body in 1916.[41] With regards to his business interests, he was president of the Polson Iron Works of Toronto Limited, the Polson Dry Dock and Shipping Company and the Consumers Box Company until his retirement in 1919. He died at Toronto on September 2, 1941, and was interred in Mount Pleasant Cemetery beside his first wife and their son John Clauson.

3

Patrick McCurry:
Judge and Entrepreneur

IN 1868 THE LEGISLATURE OF ONTARIO assented to the passage of the Free Grant and Homestead Act, adapted from the system which was opening the American Midwest. In the Muskoka-Parry Sound region, between Georgian Bay and the upper Ottawa River, Crown land formerly held for sale was offered as free grants in bundles of 100 acres. The homesteader, after five years of residence, provided he had built a shelter and cleared a portion of his land, would have clear title to the farm. For half a dollar an acre he could also purchase a second lot. The government did much to help the homesteader, and colonization roads, branching off from the southern roads, were pushed north toward the Canadian Shield. Grants for implements and livestock supplemented earlier provisions and the grant of 100 acres was increased to 200 in 1869.

The legislation created an influx of settlers into the southwestern District of Parry Sound, who demanded the extension of the institutions of Simcoe County into the frontier. There was an urgent need for a register of deeds to record the grants as each claim matured after the passage of five years from the date of the original location. There was also a need for a magistrate to dispense justice, as wherever there are people there will be conflicts.

An Ontario statute, which received royal assent in December 1869, provided for the appointment of a registrar of deeds, justices of the peace and a stipendiary magistrate for the District of

Parry Sound.[1] The act also allowed for the establishment of a division court, where the magistrate would be required to travel the circuit and hold court in each of the divisions at least once every three months. This magistrate would receive an annual stipend of $1,000 and was prohibited from practising as a lawyer while holding the position of Crown adjudicator.

Construction began on the Parry Sound courthouse in 1871, the first of a series of northern courthouses built under the direction of the Department of Public Works and designed by architect Kivas Tully.[2] The building was a modest frame structure with a

Patrick McCurry dispensed justice in the Parry Sound area for 44 years as a stipendiary magistrate and District Court judge. He was also involved in numerous business ventures, including the Parry Sound Colonization Railway. *Taken from the Parry Sound Directory, 1898–99.*

second floor courtroom and a jail and registry office occupying the lower floor. At this time the new magistrate, who would represent law and order in Parry Sound for the next four decades, arrived to assume his responsibilities.

Patrick McCurry was born in Belfast, Northern Ireland, on April 1, 1838, and came to Upper Canada with his parents in 1842. The McCurry family settled at Guelph and young Patrick received his early education there at the common school, finishing at St. Michael's College in Toronto. Called to the bar in 1864, he practised in Guelph for a period of about seven years. Also in 1864, he married Emily M. Foley, daughter of Michael M. Foley, former postmaster-general in the Brown/Dorian government of the Province of Canada. They had at least five children: Katherine Barbara, James Hamilton, Mary, Constance and Henry.[3]

As the magistrate for the District of Parry Sound, McCurry was the judge in the division courts, but he was not a member of the bench. The court of appeal for cases arising in the division courts under McCurry was the Court of General Sessions of the Peace for the County of Simcoe. As magistrate and an ex-officio justice of the peace, McCurry travelled extensively around the district dispensing justice. Although his position obligated him to prosecute those breaking the Duncan Act in McDougall Township, he did not personally oppose the consumption of alcohol. Thus, it would appear that the new magistrate was not of the same moral fibre as William Beatty Jr.

McCurry was also a businessman and he was impressed by the financial gains to be made in the lumber industry. Immediately upon his arrival, he began trying to interest prominent businessmen from the Guelph area in the establishment of a lumber company. McCurry also had other ulterior motives for attracting lumbermen. He calculated that he could make a considerable amount of money by retaining full land-granting privileges in a prosperous community and selling off property, in much the same way as Beatty did.

McCurry took the first steps toward the realization of this dream on December 24, 1872, when he, in partnership with Robert Pauncefort Carrington, purchased the homestead of Joseph Hunt in Foley Township for $2,000.[4] This 179-acre township lot, located at Lot 150 on Concession A, bordered directly on the Beatty holdings at the mouth of the Seguin River and thus offered an excellent mill location. Six months later, McCurry and Carrington sold the first parcel of waterfront property to the principal partners of the Guelph Lumber Company. In the following month, provincial land surveyor Henry White surveyed the company town, then known as Carrington.[5]

By the late 1870s, the Guelph Lumber Company was cutting 11 million board feet of saw logs annually, employing 70 men at the mill and a further 160 men felling trees during the winter. The company held the rights to 250 square miles of timber limits in the townships of Monteith, Shawanaga, Spence, McKellar, Ferguson, Hagerman, Christie, Humphrey and Foley, as well as an extensive lumber yard at Sarnia, supplying the western peninsula of Ontario, and another at Emerson, Manitoba.[6]

The village of Parry Harbour, circa 1879, as sketched by Seymour Richard George Penson. *Taken from the* Guide Book & Atlas of Muskoka and Parry Sound Districts.

A post office named Parry Harbour opened under postmaster Martin Rose on November 1, 1876.[7] By the end of the decade the village included a sawmill, planing mill, shingle mill, two hotels, a store, schoolhouse, two blacksmith shops, a wagon and carriage shop and a telegraph office. Patrick McCurry, a devout Roman Catholic, donated property in Parry Harbour to the Diocese of Peterborough for the construction of a frame church in 1879. The Guelph Lumber Company provided the materials and the labour was provided by the men of the mission, which consisted of 25 Catholic families.[8]

Unfortunately, the Guelph Lumber Company entered the already glutted lumber market at the height of a depression that began in the fall of 1872 and, as early as December 1875, most of the company's holdings were mortgaged to the London and Canada Loan and Agency Company.[9] The company was forced to take out a second mortgage on January 4, 1878, to act as collateral security on notes held by the Ontario Bank totalling $232,663.[10] The Ontario Bank assumed the mortgage held by the London and Canada Loan and Agency Company to obtain clear title in January 1880 and foreclosed on the Guelph Lumber Company.[11] On June 24, 1880, the company's holdings were placed on the auctioneer's block at F. W. Coate & Co. in Toronto but apparently no one wanted them.[12] Not until May 1883 did the Midland and North Shore Lumber Company purchase the mill facilities from the Ontario Bank for $107,000.[13]

John Clauson Miller hired William Rabb Beatty, who came from the same area in Leeds County, to be the Parry Sound Lumber Company's mill manager in the mid-1870s. He was elected MPP for Parry Sound in June 1894 after serving on the McDougall and Parry Sound councils. Beatty died in Revelstoke, B.C., in February 1905 while attempting to rescue several people from a burning boarding house. *Taken from the Parry Sound Directory, 1898–99.*

Patrick McCurry's participation in the creation of Parry Harbour was frowned upon by many leading citizens in nearby Parry Sound and it came back to haunt him in 1888, when an Ontario statute created the United Provisional District of Muskoka and Parry Sound.[14] Under the new legislation there would now be a sheriff in each of the two districts, as well as a district court and a surrogate court, but only a single district judge having jurisdiction in both areas. McCurry campaigned vigorously to secure the appointment.

Among the papers of Prime Minister John A. Macdonald in Ottawa is one extremely enlightening letter from William Rabb Beatty, mill manager of the Conger Lumber Company in Parry Sound at the time, as well as a fanatical member of the Orange Order. Beatty was a former councillor and reeve of McDougall, as well as president of the local Conservative association in Parry Sound. At a later date in 1894 he would become the MPP for Parry Sound. Beatty wrote:

> He is not in a moral sense fit for the position, which can be proven, and had it not been for his co-religionist's influence there is not the slightest doubt in the world, but the Ontario government would have dismissed him long ago. Should it be the misfortune of these Districts to have Mr. Patrick McCurry as their District Judge where there is such a large Protestant element I am afraid that the result of such an appointment would

prove fatal to the government candidate in the next election.

I have no doubt that our worthy member, Col. William E. O'Brien, will be able to enlighten you on McCurry's political, moral, and social standing in the District. Politically, he has always in an underhanded manner used his influence with those that he could sway to oppose the Conservative candidate in every election that has been held in the District since he has been in it....[15]

With such a blistering indictment against him, it is no wonder that McCurry was passed over for the district judgeship. Instead, the appointment went to William Cosby Mahaffy, who operated out of the Muskoka courthouse in Bracebridge. Mahaffy was born at Bond Head, Ontario, in March 1848, and raised in an Irish, Protestant, and extremely Orange household. He was educated at the Barrie High School and Upper Canada College. Mahaffy had established his own firm in Bracebridge in 1877 after practising law with George Robb in Toronto.[16]

The territorial districts of Parry Sound and Muskoka were divided and each became a separate judicial district in 1898. By this time the Conservative government in Ottawa had given way

Looking east along the Parry Sound Road in Parry Sound's east ward, circa 1910. *Taken from the Parry Sound Public Library Historical Collection, VFV(a).*

to Prime Minister Wilfrid Laurier's Liberals and, in Ontario, the Liberals under Arthur Sturgis Hardy won the provincial election of March 1898. Thus, even though he was still sitting as MPP for Parry Sound, William Rabb Beatty now had little influence to prevent the appointment of McCurry as district judge, which was to a large degree a patronage reward for his long-time loyalty to the Liberal Party.

Patrick McCurry retired from the bench in 1914, having reached the age limit of 75 years, and died in Parry Harbour on August 7, 1919. In his will, written in October 1918, McCurry left his entire estate to be divided equally between his unmarried daughters, Mary and Constance.[17] The McCurry sisters finally received title to the land in October 1927, when it was surrendered by the Toronto General Trust Corporation, executor of the will. The Corporation of the Town of Parry Sound seized portions of the land for unpaid taxes in 1930, 1938 and 1939. The bulk of this property is still owned by the municipality and, although surveyed in 1873, it is still undeveloped.

4

The Beatty Covenant and
the Fight Against Booze

IN ONTARIO TODAY there are literally tens of thousands of bars, beer stores and LCBO outlets. It is hard to imagine the province as it was more than a century ago. In 1864, the government of Upper Canada legislated the Duncan Act, which introduced the concept of local option to municipalities. The prohibitionist spirit was much stronger then and the residents of many villages voted in referendums to keep their areas "dry." As late as 1875 there were only 4,794 tavern licenses in the whole province. The Canada Temperance Act, or Scott Act, extended the local option concept to cities and counties across the country in 1878.

From the time that William Beatty Jr. acquired complete control of the Parry Sound townsite from his father and brother in 1872, Beatty had very definite ideas about the type of person that would be allowed to reside there. As he controlled the granting of land in the developing community, he could essentially limit access to those he felt would enhance or perpetuate the society that he envisioned. He had witnessed the ravages of alcohol in other lumbering centres and was determined that Parry Sound would be a respectable, permanent town, and this entailed making it a model temperance community. He remained steadfastly opposed to liquor throughout his lifetime.

Under Beatty's watchful eye, the residents of McDougall Township voted in 1872 to accept the Duncan Act, and the village of

Parry Sound remained dry under its provisions. Beatty wrote to his future wife shortly after the vote:

> I have no doubt you will be glad to learn that we passed the Duncan Temperance Bill by a unanimous vote of the electors a few days ago. We have always prevented the sale of intoxicating liquors here, but this will give additional strength to our efforts to make this a temperance place....[1]

Beatty could not be entirely sure, however, that residents would always continue to support temperance and he, therefore, set out to make the people legally obligated to follow his wishes. In consultation with a Toronto lawyer, Beatty, already a law school graduate himself, drew up the "Beatty Covenant" in 1873. The covenant was included in the deed for every parcel of land purchased from Beatty within the townsite. It was an agreement entered into between Beatty and the purchaser that the land would be granted only on the condition that the buyer did not sell, barter or exchange intoxicating liquors on the premises. The covenant was to be enforced during the lifetime of Queen Victoria's grandchildren living when the property was bought and for 21 years thereafter. By its terms, Beatty or his descendants could repossess the land of violators.

The stipulations of the Beatty Covenant governed all real estate transactions in the 24 township lots in the southeast corner of McDougall Township, purchased from the Crown by the Beatty family in May 1867. Not until March 1950 did the Private Bills Committee of the Ontario Legislature vote, almost unanimously, that the covenant be stricken from the deeds to these properties.[2]

An editorial shows the *North Star* was dead against repeal:

> As we mentioned before, the majority of property owners want the covenant. As for being outmoded, we think it is 90 years ahead of its time, and in the future something of this nature will have to be done by individuals to curb the yearly rising trouble caused by excessive drinking. Obviously the province will not do anything. They derive too much revenue from the sale of booze.

Scan the papers: Ontario sold more liquor last year than in any year in the history of this province. Prominent mayor kills best friend: cause, drink. Father shoots son in beverage room because he will not drink with him. Mental institutions crowded with alcoholics and many, many other instances.

No, the Beatty Covenant is not outmoded, or contrary to public opinion at least not to those who have their homes and interests in Parry Sound.

It is more desirous today than it was in 1867.[3]

Much to Beatty's disdain, a sister village, Carrington (later Parry Harbour), developed in the mid-1870s on the opposite side of the Seguin River. Whereas the Beatty grant occupied the southeastern corner of McDougall Township, Parry Harbour was situated on lots 149 and 150 on Concession A of Foley Township. This fringe development was unaffected by the prohibitive terms of the covenant.

In the fall of 1872, a petition circulated in Foley requesting that alcohol be prohibited in that township under the Duncan Act. The first of the 34 male signatures was that of Joseph Hunt, owner of the land that became Parry Harbour. At the council meeting of December 4, 1872, the petition was presented, but the politicians chose to ignore it and instead passed Bylaw 4 allowing for a maximum of two licensed taverns.[4]

Joseph Hunt sold his 179-acre homestead to the partnership of Patrick McCurry and Robert Pauncefort Carrington for $2,000 on Christmas Eve in 1872. Shortly after the sale, Foley council repealed Bylaw 4. In its place, Bylaw 5 prohibited the sale of alcohol throughout the township and called for a referendum of the voters to take place at the school house at 10 a.m. on February 19, 1873.[5] Advertisements were placed in the *Northern Advocate* at Bracebridge.

A majority of ratepayers must have been in favour of a wet township for council repealed Bylaw 5 and immediately issued a liquor licence to Charles Hodges for his Enterprise Hotel.[6] Although the location of this establishment is unclear today, Hodges gave his occupation as engineer at the time of the 1871 census. In January

Dr. Thomas Smith Walton acquired the Thomson House and numerous
other east ward properties for $619 at an October 1892 sheriff's auction.
By the time Dr. Walton sold the hotel to Sarah and Charles Alonzo Phillips
in October 1900, the licensed hotel had been renamed the Canada Atlantic
Hotel. *Taken from the Parry Sound Directory, 1898–99.*

1875, he was appointed auditor of Foley and he became the township tax collector in September 1879.

Taverns, by law, had to contain a minimum of four bedrooms
with suitable bedding, beyond that required for the comfort of
the tavern keeper and his family, and stabling facilities for at least
six horses. There was to be both a dining room and a sufficiently
stocked barroom to meet the needs of travellers. There was, however, not to be any card playing or gambling of any kind and
drinking was forbidden from 7 p.m. on Saturday night until 8 a.m.
on Monday. It was also unlawful for the tavern keeper to sell or
furnish intoxicating liquors to any persons addicted to drinking
to excess, after being forbidden to do so by another resident.[7]

The penalty for a tavern keeper failing to abide by these rules was
a fine of not less than $20 and not more than $50 for first-time offend-
ers, while a second conviction was punishable by a jail sentence not
exceeding three months. Subsequent convictions warranted jail sen-
tences of not less than one month and not more than three months.

To obtain a tavern licence at that time, under the statutes of Ontario, the applicant had to petition the elected officials of his area and council would send an inspector to look over the premises. The inspector would then advise the police commissioner or municipal clerk as to whether the facilities were adequate. Upon the presentation of a certificate of approval signed by the mayor, reeve or clerk to the local issuer of licences, a stamped licence was granted, upon payment of the fee. The issuer of licences retained six per cent of all money received by him as his stipend.[8]

Foley council granted a second liquor licence to James Duncan for the Globe Hotel on November 19, 1874.[9] This particular establishment flourished under a succession of owners, renovations and name changes. In its last incarnation it was the Queen's Hotel run by Charles and John Monteith. Located on the Parry Sound Road property recently occupied by National Grocers, it was destroyed by fire on February 4, 1918. A third licensed premises in Parry Harbour was the Thomson House, owned by Robert Thomson and opened for business during the summer of 1880.[10] This was the first tavern on the site of the former Kipling Hotel, which burned on November 30, 1986.

The wet Parry Harbour and the dry Parry Sound coexisted on opposite banks of the Seguin River until April 1887, when they were united to form an incorporated municipality. This presented a problem, however, because under the bylaws of Foley Township, Parry Harbour possessed licensed taverns. Incorporation meant that Parry Harbour, now Parry Sound's east ward, fell under the jurisdiction of a new set of bylaws formulated by a new Parry Sound town council. This council was dominated at the outset by temperance-minded elites originating from the Beatty townsite.

Four months after the incorporation, council unanimously passed a resolution that the sum of $25 be placed at the disposal of Mayor John McClelland to assist the licence inspector enforce the Canada Temperance Act. Furthermore, in addition to the sum allowed by the provincial government, the sum of five dollars was to be paid by the town treasurer to the informant in each case where the prosecution resulted in a conviction.[11] On February 28, 1888, the town reimbursed *North Star* editor William Ireland

After 1900, the Canada Atlantic Hotel underwent extensive renovations that included the addition of towers and verandas. *Courtesy of the Parry Sound Public Library Historical Collection, VF II Hotels 12.*

$20 for hiring detectives to secure convictions against three men and a woman who had violated the Canada Temperance Act.[12]

A June 26, 1888, council resolution authorized town solicitor and clerk Walter Lockwood Haight and chief constable Samuel Lawson Boyd to prosecute any persons selling intoxicating liquors in the town regardless of whether they had a licence. The resolution passed without resistance and a copy of the resolution was sent to the liquor licensing board for the district.[13] This passage meant Parry Harbour tavern keepers became susceptible to prosecution despite possessing valid licenses to sell liquor.

William Beatty Jr. appeared before council on November 25, 1890, with a petition signed by 163 residents requesting that council pass a bylaw prohibiting the sale of intoxicating liquor in Parry Sound. Two months later delegates of various temperance organizations came to council urging passage of the bylaw without delay.[14]

There were signs of trouble when clerk Haight brought to a council meeting a copy of the *North Star* with an article announcing residents of the east ward planned to make an application to the Ontario legislature to secede from the town over the proposed bylaw. Still, council went ahead and passed Bylaw 70 after a 66-vote majority in a referendum of voters held on March 9, 1891.[15]

On December 28, 1897, council passed a bylaw to repeal a previous one after a 95-vote majority in a December 24 referendum. Frank Montgomery and Dr. Thomas Smith Walton obtained tavern licences for the Montgomery House and the Canada Atlantic Hotel in January 1898.[16] According to the repealing bylaw, the lack of tavern licences in Parry Sound had failed to prevent the sale of liquor, but it did unfairly curtail the business of east ward hotel owners:

> Whereas a large number of ratepayers of the town of Parry Sound, have by their petition in that behalf represented that it would be to the advantage and interest of the said town to have good hotels and good accommodation for the travelling public and that said Bylaw 70 operates against the successful carrying on of the same, and that the object sought for by said bylaw, namely, the restriction of the liquor traffic, is not affected thereby, and have therefore prayed that said bylaw be repealed.[17]

However, council found that one way to limit liquor licenses was to make the them prohibitively expensive. In January 1905, ratepayers in Parry Sound voted in a plebiscite at a rate of nearly four-to-one to hike the fee for a liquor licence, which at $470 was already the highest in the province according to the *North Star*, to $800. The new fee, of which $730 went to the town and $70 to the province, became the highest per annum in any community in Canada.[18]

On March 22, 1916, the Conservative government of Premier William Hearst announced plans for the Ontario Temperance Act and the imposition of prohibition to become effective in September. Prohibition effectively closed all bars in the province until 1934, when the government of Premier Mitch Hepburn initiated legislation for the sale of beer and wine by the glass in areas where it passed the local option test. Legislation passed March 10, 1927, had established the Liquor Control Board of Ontario, but this permitted only government liquor stores, not licensed taverns.

In June 1918, *North Star* editor John Schofield Dick lamented

Top: Albert Gentles and his brother Charles acquired the hotel from Charles Alonzo Phillips in a card game in May 1904 and renamed it the Kipling in honour of Rudyard Kipling. A guest, Storey Phillips, died in a fire that destroyed the hotel on March 25, 1915. *Courtesy of the Parry Sound Public Library Historical Collection. Bottom*: A routine investigation by John McKenzie of the Ontario Fire Marshall's office in Bracebridge could not determine the cause of the Nov. 30, 1986 blaze that destroyed the Kipling. It was the last surviving tavern on the east side of the Seguin River. *Courtesy of Adrian Hayes.*

that the institution of prohibition had inadvertently caused a decline of the splendid hotels of Parry Sound:

> We are minded to again call attention to the deplorable hotel accommodations that Parry Sound has to offer to the travelling public. The conditions that exist both in their inadequacy and their inferior quality are a standing advertisement of our lack of enterprise and our lack of regard for the good name of our town.... No one is probably regretting the passing of the bar, but it cannot be denied that when we had the bar in Parry Sound, we had infinitely better hotel accommodations than we have today....[19]

The movement to repeal the Beatty Covenant as a consideration in land transfers in Parry Sound was not directly related to the question of liquor licences, as one might expect. In November 1940, lawyer Charles W. Cragg addressed council and stated he represented clients who intended to ask for legislation to break this clause as they considered it detrimental to progress of the town.[20] The objection had nothing to do with the liquor aspect. It was a fact, he said, that no loan companies would lend money on property in the town while this clause remained in the deed. The companies felt that the owner was merely a tenant on the property as, according to the deed, ownership is liable to revert to the original owners following a conviction for the sale or disposal of intoxicating beverages.

Mayor Charles Carlisle Johnson remarked that the question was too important to give any decision at present. The whole matter, he said, was explosive and had to receive a very careful consideration before the council would pass any resolution.

In the fall of 1945, Johnson chaired a citizens' committee opposed to applications for liquor licences made to the Liquor Authority Control Board by the owners of the Brunswick Hotel and the Kitchener Hotel. William S. Beatty acted as secretary.[21] The board refused to grant the licences after an acrimonious meeting at the Barrie courthouse on November 1, where the committee presented petitions with the signatures of 1,087 Parry Sound residents opposed to the licences. There were also written objections from the Parry Sound Public Library, St. James' United Church and Fellowship Baptist Church. Donald McLaren, lawyer for the Beatty Lands and Timber Company, explained to the board that the Beatty covenant would militate against the applicants in the disposition of beer and wine on the properties.

Top: The Queen's Hotel, run by Charles and John Monteith, was destroyed by fire on February 4, 1918. *Bottom:* Inside the Queen's Hotel bar. *Both photographs courtesy of AO/David L. Thomas Collection, C253 Tray 5-2.*

The issue of repealing the Beatty Covenant resurfaced four years later, after the election of Abe Adams as mayor. In a December 5, 1949, referendum, the ratepayers of Parry Sound voted 822 to 544 in favour of council asking MPP Allister Johnston to introduce a private bill in the Ontario legislature to release property owners from the restrictions of the covenant.[22]

In 1950, when the covenant was finally repealed, the Kipling Hotel was the only licensed establishment on the east side of the river, although a liquor store and a beer store were also located there. The Belvidere Hotel, which was only open five months of the year, was also licensed through a legal error. During the Depression, lawyers had advised the William Beatty Lands and Timber Company that a tax sale of the hotel properties had destroyed the binding character of the liquor restriction contained in previous deeds. In 1945, when it was discovered that the legal opinion had been incorrect, the Beattys brought legal action against the hotel owners to enforce the restrictions. After considerable time and expense, the Beattys discontinued the case after being counselled that there were too many legal difficulties to obtain a ruling in their favour.

5

Prohibition and the Press

A DECADE AFTER THE ONTARIO LEGISLATURE passed the original Free Grant and Homestead Act, opening many ownships within the Districts of Parry Sound and Muskoka to settlement, H.R. Page of Chicago, one of several publishers of county atlases, set out to prepare the *Guide Book & Atlas of Muskoka and Parry Sound Districts*. Throughout 1878 and the first half of 1879, John Rogers and Seymour Richard George Penson travelled the region preparing maps of the townships on a sufficiently large scale to show each settler's name and the position of his house on his lot. Roads, schools and sawmills were also marked. In addition to the maps, there were portraits and pictures of farms and villages. Prior to the atlas, potential settlers looked to Thomas J. McMurray, one of the most ardent supporters of the colonization process, who offered advice and guidance on the pages of the *North Star* and its predecessor, the *Northern Advocate*.

Thomas J. McMurray was born May 7, 1831, at Paisley, Scotland, the son of a weaver from County Armagh in Northern Ireland and Jane Baxter from Alloa, Scotland.[1] He followed his father's occupation briefly, commencing work as a draw-boy at the age of seven and at eleven became a weaver. Not satisfied with his trade, he served a three-year apprenticeship to a butter and egg merchant and obtained a limited education by attending night school. At age 15, he became a sailor, but abandoned ship in New York on his first voyage and sought employment with the New York and Erie Railroad.

McMurray returned to Scotland in 1848 and worked as a salesman in Glasgow for a time. Following his marriage to his second cousin Elizabeth on June 10, 1850, he settled at Paisley, where he commenced a mercantile business of his own. In 1852 the couple moved to Belfast, where McMurray accepted employment as a commercial traveller.

The urban destiny of McMurray's life was radically changed in May 1861, as a result of the decision by the government of the United Canadas to dispatch J.A. Donaldson to Great Britain and Ireland to promote immigration to the provinces of Canada West and Canada East.[2] Advertisements in the Belfast newspapers stated that Donaldson would be at the Plough Hotel for a time and those interested in immigrating to a new life could obtain information from him. Whatever Donaldson told McMurray about the wilderness north of Toronto, he had obviously been enticed. On May 10, 1861, the McMurray family set sail from Londonderry and arrived at Quebec City after a ten-day voyage.

McMurray made his way to Toronto with his family and rented a house for them while he set out to locate a homestead in what later became the District of Muskoka. He travelled north to Orillia and met with Richard Jose Oliver, who had been appointed in 1859 as the Crown land agent for settlement along the Muskoka Colonization Road. Upon hearing of McMurray's plans, several people in Orillia tried to persuade him to abandon his foolish notions of settling in the north. One man apparently went so far as to say "if you go up there you will die, and there will be no one to bury you."[3]

Undaunted, McMurray proceeded north. Although the first contracts for the Muskoka Colonization Road from Washago had been distributed in 1858, by the spring of 1861 the road had only reached as far as the south branch of the Muskoka River in Draper Township, where it intersected with the Peterson Road. It was anticipated that this site, at the junction of two colonization roads and with a cascading 175-foot waterfall, would become the leading community of the Muskoka District. With this in mind, McMurray selected 400 acres of land about two miles east of Muskoka Falls. He also struck an agreement with Richard Hanna, a contractor working on the Peterson Road, to halt his road construction work for one month and redirect his men to clear ten acres and erect a log house on the property.

Thomas McMurray left for his family in Toronto and duly returned one month later to Muskoka Falls fully expecting his house to be finished. While the frame had been erected in his absence, the dwelling lacked a roof and floors. The family, weary from the trip northward, decided to make the best of the situation and retired for the night. Several years later McMurray looked back on his first night as a homesteader:

> On retiring to rest all was pleasant, but at midnight the clouds began to gather, the lightning played, the thunder rolled, and the rain descended in torrents. There we were out in the wild woods, miles from human habitation. Moments of eternal duration passed away, at last morning came, when we got changes from our chests, and a fire started. This was our introduction to backwoods life.[4]

Others soon joined the McMurray family at Muskoka Falls and took up homesteads until the population had risen sufficiently that the townships of Draper, Macaulay, Stephenson and Ryde successfully incorporated into a united municipality in 1869. The residents elected McMurray as the first reeve.

During the years spent as a settler in Draper Township, McMurray had become convinced of the viability of agriculture in the Georgian Bay region. Consequently, he found it highly gratifying when the Ontario legislature passed the Free Grant and Homestead Act giving free land to settlers who had proven themselves capable at clearing and farming a homestead.

It remains unclear how McMurray initially became friendly with William Beatty Jr., the founder of Parry Sound, but the two men clearly shared a belief in the future of the north. Beatty encouraged him to relocate to Parry Sound and establish the first newspaper serving homesteaders in the free grant lands of Ontario. The first issue of the *Northern Advocate* rolled off the press on September 14, 1869.[5]

McMurray left Parry Sound to move to Bracebridge in September 1870 and there he re-established the *Northern Advocate*. As settlers arriving from southern Ontario passed through Bracebridge on their way north, this community seemed better suited to his goal of promoting the north. T. J. McMurray prospered greatly at Bracebridge, opening a general store and real estate business, and he erected a large residence known as The Grove.

He took an active role in encouraging the Northern Railway to extend a line through the Muskoka District and his persistent efforts were rewarded when the Toronto, Simcoe and Muskoka Junction Railway finally reached Gravenhurst on November 13, 1875. He also promoted the improvement of roads and bridges, as well as the building of churches and schools.

Thomas McMurray, founder of the *North Star* newspaper in Parry Sound. This illustration is taken from McMurray's book, *The Free Grant Lands of Canada*, 1871.

In 1871, McMurray published his first book, entitled *The Free Grant Lands of Canada from practical experience of bush farming in the Free Grant Districts of Muskoka and Parry Sound*, intended to serve as a useful guide to settlers. McMurray was concerned about the suffering of the poor in the British Isles as well as in Canadian towns and cities, and he strongly believed that the fertile and suitable climate of the free grant lands offered a solution. He wrote in his book:

> Here we enjoy the utmost liberty, and can boast of a freedom beyond even that of the mother country. Our magnificent forests are free, and you can roam where you will without running the risk of aristocratic vengeance, while our beautiful streams abounding with fish, may, in their season, be enjoyed by all without molestation. I believe in the sentiment 'all men are created equal.' Here men are measured, not by their gold, nor the extent of their domains, but by their moral worth. Hence all stand upon a grand equality, so that the honest poor man is as much respected as the millionaire.[6]

While Thomas McMurray acquired a sizable estate, he had also overextended himself in numerous ventures, which made him vulnerable to the depression which began in the fall of 1872. By July 1874, he was forced into bankruptcy. Faced with a dim future, he was once again offered an opportunity by William Beatty Jr.

McMurray shared Beatty's belief in total prohibition and from the time that the first *North Star* rolled off the press on October 6, 1874, it served to promote the temperance cause. He had become first connected to the temperance movement at the age of 14, in Paisley, when he joined a total abstinence society, and became involved with the Irish Temperance League in Belfast in 1858. In that first *North Star*, McMurray wrote:

> Believing that intemperance is our national curse, and that nothing short of the total suppression of the liquor traffic will remove the evil, and politically this important reform shall engage a large morally, religiously and politically, this important reform shall engage a large share of our space, as we take for our motto, "Total Abstinence for the Individual, and Prohibition for the State."[7]

On March 17, 1875, T.J. McMurray was appointed Crown land agent at Parry Sound, replacing John David Beatty who had vacated the post to assume the management of other family interests at Sarnia. Perhaps no other agent at Parry Sound was better suited to the position as McMurray for he could offer advice based upon his own experiences as a settler.

In March 1879, McMurray sold the *North Star* to Baptist Noel Fisher and resigned his position as Crown land agent as of June 30. He moved to Parkdale, now part of Toronto, in July with the intention of further pursuing his temperance work. At that time the Canada Temperance Act included a local option to every province and this offered encouragement to temperance societies and church groups to push harder for total prohibition.[8]

As early as January 1870, the *Northern Advocate* reported that McMurray had been appointed one of the travelling agents of the Canada Temperance Union and would shortly make a tour eastward. In September 1879, the *Christian Guardian* stated that he was working as an agent of the Ontario Branch of the Dominion Alliances for the suppression of the liquor traffic, under the direction of the executive committee, and holding a series of temperance meetings in Grenville County. In the following month the same newspaper gave an account of a lecture tour in eastern Ontario saying "his style is forcible and earnest, though ever logical and kind, his arguments and are convincing and happy."[9]

McMurray eventually rose to the important position of provincial deputy grand worthy of the Sons of Temperance, but he still enjoyed speaking tours. The *Christian Guardian* reported in April 1883 that he had personally organized five new divisions at Port Perry, Altons, the Gore of Toronto, Stouffville and Brampton during the previous month.[10]

Thomas J. McMurray's last-known lecture tour was conducted in the eastern townships of Quebec for the Grand Division of Quebec of the Sons of Temperance, and was documented in the *Christian Guardian* in February 1884. The *North Star* reported McMurray's death in August 1900.[11]

6

Dirty Politics 1887

B ETWEEN 1868 AND 1880, many of the 46 townships comprising the District of Parry Sound were opened to settlement under the Free Grant and Homestead Act. Working simultaneously during the colonization period, however, were the lumbermen who were trying to harvest trees from their licensed berths before homesteaders could obtain patents. While it may appear there would have been great conflict between these two groups, lumbermen became an essential part of the homesteading process and contributed significantly to the development of the area. It was the lumbermen who became the social, cultural and political leaders in this new frontier and, while they undeniably used their power to protect their business interests, they were also highly protective of settlers, whom they viewed as important allies.

Early in 1875, William Beatty Jr. supported John Clauson Miller, the manager and secretary-treasurer of the Parry Sound Lumber Company, in his bid to defeat James Long of Bracebridge and become MPP for Muskoka-Parry Sound. Long spoke at a campaign meeting held in Parry Sound in January and proclaimed that he was best suited to represent the constituency because the voters were primarily agrarian and he was himself a farmer. He insinuated that Miller, being a lumberman, was not interested in the needs of settlers. Beatty stood up on behalf of the local candidate, amid cheers from the audience, and said although it was true that Miller was a lumberman, he was anxious to promote the interests and welfare of homesteaders.

Mr. Long cried for reform because timber holders were monop-
olizers; but he (Mr. Beatty) affirmed that improvement and
development of the settlements could be attributed to the lumbering interests. There was no hostility manifested by
lumbermen in these parts towards the settler.... He held that
the lumberman was dependent upon the farmer and the farmer
upon the lumberman.[1]

Beatty's statement was greeted with more cheering and J.C. Miller
easily won the February 2, 1875, election by 839 to 592.

The lumbermen of Parry Sound and Parry Harbour were behind
the merger of the twin villages into an incorporated municipality. In 1886, when Beatty's warehouse and the storehouse of the
Parry Sound Lumber Company were both destroyed by fire, the
top representatives of the three big lumber companies in the two
villages became concerned about the lack of fire protection. If the
villages were to become a single incorporated entity, they rea
soned, fire fighting equipment could be purchased.[2]

A committee consisting of Beatty, Patrick McCurry, Joseph William
Fitzgerald, John McClelland and Dr. Thomas Smith Walton was
formed to inquire into the procedures for incorporation. On April
23, 1887, an Ontario statute incorporated the villages into a single
municipality, autonomous from Foley and McDougall townships.[3]

On May 12, 1887, the ratepayers of the new town of Parry
Sound met at the courthouse to nominate contestants in the election for a mayor and six councillors, to be held exactly seven days
later. This meeting and the subsequent election results show how
much the residents of Parry Sound viewed the lumbermen as their
natural leaders and spokesmen.

John McClelland and Dr. Walton accepted nominations to contest the office of mayor and Fitzgerald was one of the five candidates
chosen to run for the east ward, formerly Parry Harbour. Even
before the actual passage of the act, the *North Star* reported that
many residents were campaigning to have Beatty acclaimed as the
town's first mayor, but he declined.

The first of the mayoral candidates to speak at the nomination
meeting was McClelland. His speech was rather lacklustre, but he

John McClelland was mayor of Parry Sound in 1887–89, and a councillor in 1894–95, 1900 and 1902–03. He passed away in Toronto on December 8, 1922, at the age of 74 years and was interred at Hillcrest Cemetery in Parry Sound. *Taken from the Parry Sound Directory, 1898–99.*

was in favour of the immediate establishment of a fire department and a bylaw to regulate stovepipes and chimneys.

Born in Ireland in 1847, John McClelland was Beatty's first cousin, as their mothers were sisters (Rose Esther Hughes McClelland and Frances Hughes Beatty). He replaced Nathaniel Parker Wakefield as the village postmaster as of January 1, 1870, and, a short time later, became the issuer of marriage licences following a personal recommendation from Beatty to Prime Minister John A. Macdonald.[4] McClelland later worked as a bookkeeper for the Parry Sound Lumber Company and, when William E. Dodge withdrew from the business and John Clauson Miller assumed the presidency, McClelland became secretary-treasurer. He was the first reeve of McDougall in 1872 and a councillor for the years 1875–79.

Dr. Thomas S. Walton was born at Sheffield, England, in 1838 and graduated from the Royal College of Surgeons in Edinburgh at the age of 20. He had established his medical practice in Parry Sound in 1874 after first settling in Humphrey Township with the intention of becoming a gentleman farmer. He also became Indian agent for the Parry Sound area in April 1884.[5]

As expected, Dr. Walton echoed the promises made by his opponent, but he then launched into an attack on McClelland's suitability for public office. He charged that the lumber business was not a "straight-forward descent business" and that McClelland would represent the interests of the Parry Sound Lumber Company before those of the taxpayers. He was also vehemently opposed to McClelland possibly being on a council with Fitzgerald, the manager of the Midland and North Shore Lumber Company. Dr. Walton claimed: "Either of these gentlemen alone would be all right, but together they would be invincible, and if both were on a council board there would be the devil to pay."[6]

Fitzgerald, who was born at Millbrook, Ontario, in 1847, went to public school at Fenelon Falls and attended McGill University in Montreal. He worked at a law office in Montreal for a time before volunteering to fight for the Union Army in the U.S. Civil War. He saw combat under General George H. Thomas at Missionary Ridge, Larch Mountain and Franklin before being wounded. After his discharge, Fitzgerald ran his father's business at Fenelon Falls and then opened his own pharmacy. He was appointed Crown land agent for the District of Haliburton in

Joseph William Fitzgerald served as a councillor for Parry Sound for the years 1887–92, 1896 and 1898, and mayor in 1897. He ran as the Liberal candidate in Muskoka/Parry Sound in the March 1892 federal election, but was defeated by 141 votes by Col. William Edward O'Brien of Shanty Bay. Fitzgerald passed away in Parry Sound on June 20, 1908, at the age of 61 and was interred in Hillcrest Cemetery. *Taken from the Parry Sound Directory, 1898–99.*

1874, with his office at Minden, before becoming manager of the Midland and North Shore Lumber Company sawmill in Parry Harbour in 1883. His father-in-law, Dalton Ullyot of Peterborough, was a major stockholder in the company.[7]

The *North Star* wrote that there could be no question as to who would be the new mayor and cited McClelland's "superior fitness and ability." The paper advised readers:

The ratepayers will do well to give the doctor an opportunity of staying home and attending to his onerous duties of physician and Indian agent, which by the way should be sufficient to occupy all of his time without the necessity of his dabbling into municipal affairs.[8]

The election took place on May 19 with McClelland and Fitzgerald both emerging winners. The *North Star* proclaimed, "The defeat of Dr. Walton shows that our estimate of the electors was right and they were above being influenced by the demagogic appeals made to prejudice them against their employers and fellow citizens...."[9]

Both John McClelland and Dr. Thomas S. Walton enjoyed long careers in municipal politics. McClelland was mayor for the years 1887–89 and 1896, and councillor in 1894–95, 1900 and 1902–03. Dr. Walton was mayor in 1890, 1894–95 and a councillor in 1901. Apparently, the animosity of the 1887 election was quickly forgotten. McClelland was a pallbearer at Dr. Walton's funeral in January 1902. As a member of council, McClelland put forth a motion that all members attend the funeral of so esteemed a citizen. The resolution passed unanimously.[10]

7

Running Water, Fire Bells
and a Lawsuit

T HE NEWLY INCORPORATED TOWN of Parry Sound may
        have been a prosperous community, but a traveller would
        not have confused it with Toronto. There were no sanitary
sewers, but rather outhouses and night soil buckets. There was
no running water and the population relied on wells. Fire protection was something the 1,600 residents could still only dream
about. But Mayor John Galna's council of 1891 was determined
to change all that and procure the amenities of civilization, even if
the fledgling municipality could not yet afford them. But bad business decisions, shoddy workmanship and a lawsuit were to make
matters much worse.

During September 1893, *North Star* editor William Ireland was
alarmed that taxes for the coming year had been set at 38 mills
on the dollar, the highest rate in any community in the province.
He wrote in a late September issue:

> How in the name of common sense our town fathers have man-
> aged during the current year to spend such a large sum as to
> call for such an extraordinary levy is beyond our comprehen-
> sion.... Let something be done at once before the town becomes
> bankrupt.[1]

Although council passed a bylaw in April 1888 for the preven-
tion of fires, which set out specific rules regarding chimneys,

renovations and the destruction of refuse through burning, no steps had been taken to deal with fires once they had started. Both candidates for mayor in the 1887 election—John McClelland and Dr. Thomas Smith Walton—promised fire protection, but it was to be years before council took any firm action and then only after ratepayers had voiced their support for the idea at a series of public meetings.

At a November 15, 1889, public meeting residents favoured accepting an offer from the Waterous Engine Works Company to supply a steam fire engine, which the company guaranteed would throw water within seven minutes after the coal was ignited in the firebox. The company shipped the engine on November 29 subject to council passing a bylaw to close the deal.[2]

At the December 17 council meeting, Mayor McClelland stated that while payments would extend over a period of not less than ten years, the entire cost to the town including interest, wages of a caretaker, and wear and tear of hose would not exceed $700 per year. Council passed Bylaw 45 approving the purchase by a margin of four to three, but not before Councillor William Joseph Fitzgerald stated that it was his intention to seek a court order quashing the bylaw. From his perspective, the town could not afford such a cost and a referendum had not been held on the issue, thus making the purchase illegal. Councillor John Galna and Mayor McClelland pointed out that residents had already voted in favour at public meetings.[3] A new council headed by Mayor Walton repealed the bylaw on January 21, 1890.[4]

On March 6, 1890, three children under the age of 16 died when their home on Wakefield Street went up in flames. Council voted to give $25 compensation to the grieving parents, William and Margaret Robinson.[5] Later in that same month, council established a committee composed of Mayor Walton, past mayor McClelland, councillors Galna and Fitzgerald, stipendiary magistrate Patrick McCurry, future councillors Donald W. Ross and William Rabb Beatty, and town treasurer Walter Read Foot, to investigate the cost of equipment such as a steam engine, water tanks, ladder, fire hall and fire bell.[6]

Councillors Fitzgerald and Joseph Calverly proposed the purchase of a used fire engine from the town of Waterloo and the construction of a fire hall in April 1890, but a month later ratepayers rejected a bylaw to finance the $5,000 acquisitions through debentures.[7] In June, council passed Bylaw 55 to lease the Waterous steam engine after receiving a petition from William Beatty and 64 others in favour of renting.[8]

Council asked the volunteers who had been operating the Waterous steam pump to organize themselves into a permanent volunteer fire brigade and to practise their firefighting skills regularly. In July, at the recommendation of the firefighters, council spent $50 to erect landings or platforms in the east ward and on both sides of Seguin Street for the operation of this steam pump.[9] Coal boxes were also put at convenient locations. But by the end of 1890, council had overspent its budget and could not afford to give the firefighters any more money. Alex Logan appeared before council on behalf of the fire brigade in December and begged the town to buy 1,000 feet of hose, claiming that the supply on hand was inadequate and as a result a house had burned unnecessarily.[10]

During the four years since the incorporation of the town there had been frequent outcries from ratepayers for a well-equipped fire department and periodic promises from the politicians to comply, usually in the aftermath of a fire. In recapping this early period of the town's history, the *North Star* wrote:

> If there is any crime which can be laid at our doors it is not the crime of undue haste. The scare is over and some other o' the wisp topic blooms out in the papers, our zephyr thoughts are caught on another breeze and the need of a [fire] brigade is relegated to the future until another fire breaks out to cause us to gasp again. As a community we are like Mark Twain's jumping frog that swallowed the belly full of buckshot. We made a move to jump and for a little [while] it looks like something were going to happen, but it ends in a convulsive heave and a lapse back to the old spot.[11]

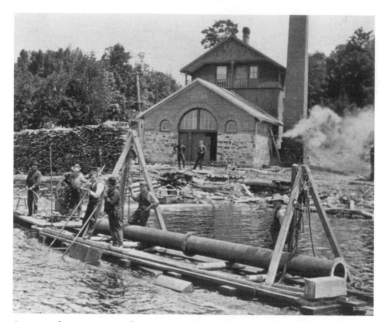

Laying the water intake pipe at the Parry Sound pumphouse,
1892. *Courtesy of AO/David L. Thomas Collection, C253 Tray 4-8.*

In January 1891, the voters elected John Galna as mayor. A four-
term councillor, he had consistently been in favour of greater fire
protection. Among the four new councillors was undertaker and
contractor Alexander Logan, a member of the fire brigade, who
not only had first-hand knowledge of fighting fires but had built a
large number of buildings around the town. In April, council
approved the $250 purchase of a hook and ladder truck after receiv-
ing a petition from former mayor John McClelland and 22 others.[12]

Councillor John Moffat told council in July 1891 that the fire protection system then in use was unsatisfactory and it was his intention
to introduce a bylaw to erect a waterworks so the town could have
water mains and hydrants. In December, council passed Bylaw 81
to raise $28,300 for a waterworks through debentures to be issued
in denominations of not less than $100, with interest redeemable
annually at five per cent.[13] The ratepayers had approved the bylaw
by a majority of 19 in a referendum held a month earlier.

In May 1892, council accepted a $25,393 tender from John H.
Armstrong, a Toronto consulting and contracting engineer, to build
the waterworks system designed for the town by civil engineer

The first Parry Sound water tower was built by the local contracting firm of Logan & McAllister in 1892. The house, now at 10 Ashwood Drive, was constructed for Canada Express agent George Moore during the summer of 1900. *Courtesy of the Parry Sound Public Library Historical Collection, Maurice Brais Collection #113.*

John Galt.[14] This was the lowest of six bids the town received on the project, but only a few hundred dollars less than that of local builders, Logan & McAllister.

Armstrong subcontracted the construction of the brick water tower on Belvidere Hill in July to Logan & McAllister, as well as the masonry and woodwork on the pump house. By then pipes had been laid to Gibson Street and along Church and James streets, and council passed a resolution in August to pay Armstrong $6,000 after Galt inspected his work and found everything satisfactory.[15]

Workers began laying pipe in the east ward in October, but by now Armstrong was already in default of his contract, which called for all work to be completed on the waterworks system on or before September 7. Councillor Frederick C. King would later remark this was because the contractor had puttered along with too few men to save wages, and lost money and time by doing so.[16]

That winter it became obvious all was not as it should be with even that portion of the waterworks system that had been completed. Waterworks engineer John R. Campbell thawed 18 frozen hydrants during a sudden cold snap and then covered them with barrels packed with manure to prevent a recurrence. Constable George Townsley would later spend his days thawing water mains, frozen because they were not buried deep enough.[17]

In January 1893, a new council headed by Mayor Solomon Byron Purvis decided not to pay Armstrong any more money until he had completed the entire project. Within days council received a letter from the Toronto law firm of Blake, Lash & Cassels threatening the town with a lawsuit.

Town clerk and solicitor Walter L. Haight responded on January 30:

> The council of this town after mature deliberation decided that Mr. J.H. Armstrong was not entitled to any further sum under the terms of his contract with the Corporation than that already advanced to him and this decision was duly conveyed by me to John Galt some days ago.
>
> While it is impossible to offer any hope of compliance with your demands on behalf of the contractor, I desire to disabuse your minds of the idea that your client has been badly treated by the municipality, and to disclaim on their account any intention of treating him otherwise than in a fair, just and reasonable spirit.
>
> By the contract referred to the waterworks system was to have been completed on or before the 7th September last under a penalty of $25 for every day thereafter the system remained unfinished but as yet it has neither been completed, tested nor accepted.... Mr. Armstrong therefore stands in the position of a man who has been dealt with strictly according to the letter of his engagement....[18]

Alex Logan complained to council that Armstrong had not paid the $650 owing on the subcontract work completed by Logan & McAllister on the water tower and pumphouse. Logan told council that he had threatened Armstrong with a lawsuit and Armstrong had written back telling him to get his money from the town. Council decided it could not pay Logan, having already refused

The Parry Sound pumphouse, built by Logan
& McAllister in 1892. *Courtesy of the Parry
Sound Public Library Historical Collection,
Album IV #26.*

to pay anything more to Armstrong until the contract was completed and the work inspected.[19]

When John R. Campbell complained that he had not been paid
his salary as waterworks engineer for December 1892, council
bickered about who hired him and whether he was employed by
Armstrong or the municipality. Finally, council decided to pay
Campbell and charge his salary to Armstrong's account.[20]

Council engaged Britton Bath Osler, QC, of the Toronto law firm
of McCarthy, Osler, Hoskin and Creelman to defend the town against
Armstrong's suit. Osler was a well-connected litigation star who
had served as one of the prosecutors of Louis Riel in 1885 and was
defence counsel in many of Ontario's prominent murder trials.

Already faced with an uncompleted waterworks system and a
potentially costly lawsuit, mayor Purvis presented plans and spec-
ifications to council in early May for a fire hall and hose tower.

The firm of S.L. White & Son won the contract with a bid of $994.[21] Council then agreed to pay $300 to the Bell Telephone Company of Canada for the installation of a magneto fire alarm system with four-inch bells in the home of each firefighter.[22] A visit to town by a representative of Blake, Lash & Cassels to conduct an examination for discovery in the Armstrong lawsuit and take evidence from mayor Purvis, former mayor John Galna and town clerk Haight apparently did not cause council to pause even momentarily to rethink their decisions.

A.E. Edkins, a representative for the Boiler Inspection and Insurance Company of Canada, conducted a thorough assessment of the waterworks system on June 1 with Armstrong, the mayor and council, and the fire brigade in attendance.[23] The first test involved running the steam pump to a pressure of 140 psi and discharging water from one of the mains for five minutes. A gauge at the corner of Seguin and James streets showed the pressure there to be 110 psi.

The second test, which involved running the pump for 30 minutes at 125 psi while discharging water through a hose, showed the average pressure through the system to be 80 psi. For the third test, the pump had to run at 100 psi, 53 double strokes to the minute, and discharge 750 gallons of water per minute for one hour. During this final test the pump showed it possessed more than the requisite capacity by reaching the required number of strokes at only 80 psi while continuously throwing two 1 3/4 inch streams of water. "Such a volume of water was discharged that had it not been thrown back into the lake there would have been danger of a flood," commented the North Star.

A test that evening on the east side of the Seguin River proved less successful. The water pressure on River Street was 62 psi, but fell to 10 psi within 20 minutes, showing there was a considerable leak, probably where the pipe crossed the Seguin River. "When the leaks are repaired, the intake pipe made watertight and the pipes covered at the proper depths, the system will be a splendid one," the North Star stated optimistically. Just days after the tests, council received a telegram from Blake, Lash & Cassels proposing a settlement in the lawsuit. Council refused to accept.[24]

Civil engineer Alan Macdougall presented council with a report in early July on the work required to complete the waterworks system.[25] In many places on the west side of the Seguin River, he wrote, there was rough and unfinished work and evidence of unfinished trenching and filling. The average soil covering the water pipes was only four feet, four inches deep and, on Seguin Street in particular, the pipes needed to be down another 15 inches. To raise the pipes and excavate to the proper depth would cost nearly three times the original cost per yard. On the east side of the river the trenches were also not down to the required depth and improperly filled.

Later that month a diver discovered the pipe crossing the river to be unsupported, apart from angle joints at the riverbanks. From the strain of the weight of the pipe and water, the rivets in several places had been torn out and there were numerous bad leaks. Workers placed boxes filled with gravel under the pipe and recaulked the pipe where necessary.[26] Yet another consulting engineer hired by the town, W. J. Jennings, discovered that the quantity of pipe laid by Armstrong was from 1,500 to 2,000 feet less than called for in the plans and estimates.[27]

S.L. White & Son completed the Mary Street fire hall in September, as set out in the contract, but council then paid $164.75

Parry Sound fire brigade at the fire hall, 1907. *Courtesy of the Parry Sound Public Library Historical Collection, VF IV.*

In April 1919, council authorized the purchase of Parry Sound's first
motorized fire truck for a cost not to exceed $750. With the truck are,
bottom sitting: George Murray; *second row*: Chief Andrew C. Logan, driver
Bill Tough, Fred Spencer, Herb Childerhose; *third row*: Ross Miller, Bob
Morrish, Bert Morrish, Reuben Thompson, Dave Campbell and Tan
"David" Geddes. The photo was probably taken in 1919 after the Parry
Sound Fire Brigade won the banner at the tournament of the Northern
Volunteer Firemen's Association, held at Penetang over the August 7 Civic
holiday. The association consisted of the fire brigades in Barrie, Burk's
Falls, Gravenhurst, Huntsville, Bracebridge, Orillia, Midland, Parry Sound
and Penetang. *Courtesy of the Parry Sound Public Library Historical Collection,
Album IV #21.*

for extras after construction. When it was discovered that heat
had been overlooked, council paid J.E. Begg $10 for installing a
chimney and a stove was purchased for $15.[28]

By December, the *North Star* clearly felt that the present council had mismanaged the whole waterworks affair. Legal costs in
the lawsuit were already over $1,000, while the town had spent
less than $500 on road maintenance during the year. The news-
paper's anonymous editorial writer, known by the pen name of

"M. Dash," called on voters to think wisely when casting their ballots in the approaching municipal election:

> The present condition of the town is sufficiently serious to call for the most careful consideration of the ratepayers. We need in the council next year the very best businessmen in the place and they must be pledged to a policy of retrenchment in every possible direction. The enormous salary roll must be reduced, officers must be required to perform their duties faithfully and in some cases officers can be dispensed with and the duties performed by those permanently employed. For example, the offices of lamp lighter and sanitary inspector cost $160 and we have a chief constable at a sufficient salary, with little or nothing to do; give him work enough to keep him from idling around with his hands in his pockets and his pipe in his mouth.
>
> I commend the action of council in making the constable do the collecting of the taxes; there is no reason why he and the waterworks engineer, between them, should not do the bulk of the work of the corporation. This is done in other places and at salaries no larger than we pay, and in some cases not so large.[29]

Clearly, Parry Sound residents were no more content than the *North Star* about how municipal business had been handled. Only one of the politicians on the 1893 council was returned for the following year, Jacob Josiah Jolliffe. The *North Star* claimed this happened "simply through the retiring of some persons in the centre ward put up to oppose him who withdrew at the last moment."[30] Dr. Thomas Smith Walton was elected mayor by a 24-vote margin. Purvis, who was already suffering from liver disease, would die in June 1897 at age 55, without ever again being a candidate in municipal politics.[31]

Dr. Walton wrote to McCarthy, Osler, Hoskin and Creelman in January 1894 and offered directions for settling the lawsuit, feeling things had dragged on long enough. Council accepted a proposition that Armstrong be paid a $4,000 settlement with both the plaintiff and the town responsible for their own legal costs.[32]

The report on the municipality's finances for 1894 by auditors John Henry Knifton and A.C. Neff was also highly critical of the practices of town treasurer Walter Read Foot. A local pharmacist and owner of Foot's Drug Store, he was paid $75 per year for maintaining the municipality's accounting ledgers.[33] The auditors reported the municipality's bank account was short $2,886 as of January 1, 1895, and yearly shortages could be traced back four years. As reported by previous auditors, they wrote, the books were not kept to readily show throughout the year the cash balance which should be on hand. Town and school board funds were also kept together in one bank account instead of separate accounts, as they should be and as ordered by council.

8

Arthur Starkey: Adventurer or Remittance Man

JUST WHAT WOULD MOTIVATE the son of an English squire to forsake life among the gentry and join the hordes of 19th-century immigrants sailing to Canada to start over as homesteaders? Was Arthur Starkey an adventurer or a classic remittance man, living in backwoods Ontario on funds sent by his family in England to ensure that he would not return home and become a source of embarrassment? It's an intriguing mystery.

Arthur Starkey was born in India in 1847 as the eldest son of Henrietta Suft and Major Samuel Cross Starkey, who was on service with the British army.[1] On April 4, 1855, John Cross Starkey passed away and his son and heir, Major Starkey, inherited his properties. The family sailed back to England to take up residence at Wrenbury Hall in Cheshire.

The small chapelry of Wrenbury had been originally bestowed upon Richard de Wrenbury during the final years of the reign of King Henry III. Young Arthur Starkey grew up at Wrenbury Hall and knew that he would eventually inherit it, and yet, Starkey opted to sail from Liverpool for New York aboard the passenger steamer *Persia* in May 1866. The death of his mother, the remarriage of his father and the births of numerous step-siblings may have played a part.

Starkey joined the wave of settlers lured to the District of Parry Sound by the Free Grant and Homestead Act of 1868 and selected two 100-acre properties in Carling Township for his free grant.

Arthur Starkey's cabin in Carling Township, as pho-
tographed by Duncan Fraser Macdonald in 1870.
*Courtesy of the Parry Sound Public Library Historical
Collection/John Bellamy Miller #242.*

He erected a small wooden cabin on the second of these properties and set to work clearing the land. By the time of the 1871
census, he had eight acres ready for cultivation and that year har-
vested 25 bushels of oats, three bushels of corn, 125 bushels of
potatoes, 60 bushels of turnips, and 1.5 tons of hay, and processed
30 pounds of maple sugar. He had also trapped eight muskrats and
one mink for furs which he sold.[2]

One of Starkey's earliest and closest friends in his new homeland
was Duncan Fraser Macdonald, a wood ranger and Crown timber
agent for the Department of Crown Lands, who had resided in or
around the village of Parry Sound since 1867. Macdonald was born
in the township of West Flamborough in Wentworth County on
August 3, 1842. He would spend over 50 years in the Parry Sound
area, apart from a brief period in 1870 when he served as a pho-
tographer with the Wolseley Expedition to squash the Métis uprising
at Red River.[3] It was Macdonald who took the only known photograph of Starkey's cabin in Carling Township and frequently wrote
of him in a pocket diary that he kept between 1872 and 1919.

Every five or six years Starkey made the hazardous transatlantic crossing to visit his family in Cheshire. Invariably he would call upon Macdonald to say farewell before departing. Starkey made his first trip back to Cheshire in May 1876.

There was little doubt that Starkey would return to Carling Township as on April 29, 1876, he had received the patent to his Free Grant claim. That same day, he also purchased a further 74 acres from the Department of Crown Lands at 50 cents per acre.[4] However, on the night of December 22, 1876, shortly after returning from England, Starkey's days as a homesteader in Carling ended when a fire destroyed his log cabin. The structure was insured for $300, so he received partial compensation, but nothing was saved from inside the cabin.[5]

Starkey chose not to rebuild and instead he moved into the village of Parry Sound, although it is still unclear what employment he held during the next four years, if any. In January 1877, he entered into a partnership with five of Parry Sound's leading citizens in the Parry Sound Brick Manufacturing Company, an enterprise located in Parry Harbour.[6] Starkey's partners were Dr. Walton, baker Frank Dowell, miller Joseph Farrer, hotel keeper Henry Jukes and clerk John Galna.

Starkey was an accomplished sailor, as indicated by his frequent wins in the yachting regattas held at Parry Sound and, in November 1880, he was appointed purser of the Parry Sound Lumber Company's steam barge *Lothair*. At the time of the 1881 census, he was a resident of Robert Kirkman's Seguin House Temperance Hotel, located on the site of the present Canadian Imperial Bank of Commerce.[7]

By the early 1880s William Beatty Jr. still owned almost all of the 2,198 acre parcel at the mouth of the Seguin River granted to his family in 1867. The village of Parry Sound, with a population of 800, composed a portion of this acreage, but most was unsettled wilderness. Waubeek Street, for example, stretched to the northwest into dense brush and ended abruptly, where it presently joins with Prospect Street. There were no houses along the street as Beatty had not yet sold any property in the area. It was presumably in this undeveloped neighbourhood that Starkey intended

Arthur Starkey's boathouse as it appeared in May 1884
when photographed by Parry Sound Lumber Company
president John Bellamy Miller. *Courtesy of the Parry Sound
Public Library Historical Collection / John Bellamy Miller #221.*

to live and, on February 22, 1882, he purchased a two-acre rec-
tangular parcel on the west side of Waubeek Street from Beatty for
$100.[8] The southern boundary ran parallel to the one-chain shore
allowance for three chains[9] and the property was six-chains deep.

In August 1882, Starkey paid Macdonald another of his charac-
teristic visits before departing for England. Apparently, Starkey
was uncertain about his future in Parry Sound. Macdonald wrote:
"Poor fellow felt lonely and broke up."[10]

In the fall of 1883, Starkey approached McDougall Township council about purchasing the shore allowance separating his property
from the water. The council passed Bylaw 25 on November 5, 1883,
authorizing Starkey's acquisition of the property, and, on October
6, 1884, passed a resolution to allow Reeve John Farrer to sign a
deed. Starkey apparently did not pay cash for the land as council
minutes indicate that he had previously bartered the deed for a right
of way through The Cedars.[11]

There is no evidence that Starkey ever built a residence on The
Cedars, but he did construct a large boathouse and extensive docks,
which appear in a photograph taken by John Bellamy Miller in May
1884. The boathouse was home to Starkey's steam yacht *Ida* and

he very much enjoyed taking friends on cruises around the bay as well as on picnics on the islands which dot its surface. The boathouse and dock remained unchanged until the publication of the Underwriter's Insurance Plan of Parry Sound in October 1908. It was destroyed in the fire that razed the neighbouring sawmill operated by George Niebergall & Son on September 11, 1912.[12]

Although seemingly a gentle and mild-mannered man, Arthur Starkey could at times display a temper. In his diaries, Macdonald recorded an incident which occurred in December 1884. Starkey and Macdonald walked to the courthouse together and there was heated discussion in the office of Patrick McCurry. "The judge called Starkey a liar and Starkey in return struck the judge," Macdonald wrote. "I held Starkey back and it ended in some more talk."[13]

Apparently the congenial Starkey had a good many friends in the area and at the nomination meeting of December 28, 1885, Dr. Walton suggested he be a candidate for reeve of McDougall Township. Although Samuel Oldfield seconded the motion, Starkey declined to accept.[14] As far as can be determined, Starkey never ran for any elected municipal position while in Parry Sound and was never really involved in politics, but he had been a member of the committee to elect Parry Sound Lumber Company president John Clauson Miller as MPP for Muskoka-Parry Sound in the election of February 2, 1875.

Aubrey White, assistant commissioner of Crown Lands, was a close friend of Duncan Fraser Macdonald and there are frequent references in the dairies to the two "bumming around" Parry Sound together with nothing better to do. White frequently passed on wide-ranging assignments in the District of Parry Sound to Macdonald, and the latter even named a son Aubrey White Macdonald. Macdonald may have pulled strings to get Starkey appointed as registrar of deeds for the District of Parry Sound on July 19, 1883.[15]

The appointment was not universally welcomed, however. As a result of a petition to the Ontario government, Starkey found himself in a Toronto courtroom in November 1886, facing eight charges that questioned his fitness to occupy the position, the manner in which he obtained the appointment, and that included alleged breaches of official duty. The province appointed Hamilton lawyer and politician Æmilius Irving, QC, to act as commissioner of the inquiry, while Starkey was represented by Walter Barwick of the Toronto firm of Moss, Falconbridge & Barwick.[16] While Irving's report appears not to have survived and the *North Star* remained silent on the outcome, Starkey continued as registrar for another three years.

Mayor Samuel Cross Starkey passed away in 1889 and his eldest son, Arthur, inherited both Wrenbury Hall and the title. He left Canada to live as an English squire at Wrenbury, but missed the life he had created for himself in the village of Parry Sound. In February 1893, he returned for an extended visit via the transatlantic steamer *Germanic*. In the fall of 1898, he made another visit to Parry Sound, and, on his way back to the port of New York, he stopped at Buffalo to visit Reverend G. Herbert Gaviller, who had been the minister of Trinity Anglican Church from 1886 to 1892. While there, word reached him that his old friend William Beatty Jr. had passed away, and he travelled back to Parry Sound to act as a pallbearer at the funeral.[17]

Starkey kept up correspondence with the Beatty family and in December 1899 he wrote to Beatty's daughter, Frances Margaret:

> You may hardly believe me, but I still have very serious thoughts of returning to Canada. You know that I have a pretty old home in England, but the climate does not suit me half as well as Canada, so damp, and I find myself getting very rheumatic.... I cannot give anything like the same amount of pleasure to my friends in England, that I used to succeed in doing in Parry Sound, for the simple reason that they are all so much richer than I am here....[18]

Two of Beatty's daughters, Anna Georgina (Bobelle) and Adelaide (Addie), visited Wrenbury Hall during a European tour in October 1905. Starkey was genuinely touched that young people remembered him. He still missed Parry Sound very much, but he

Arthur Starkey with Mrs. J.C. Miller during a
visit to Wrenbury Hall in March 1910. *Courtesy
of the Parry Sound Public Library Historical Collection / John Bellamy Miller, 1910 / 1912 Album.*

also realized that the village he remembered no longer existed,
as progress and industry had radically altered it.

In a January 1910 letter to Rosetta (Rose) Beatty, Starkey wrote:

> I think it so sweet that you remember an old man like I am,
> when you have so many to think of, and to write to. However,
> you may be assured of one thing, and that is that old people
> appreciate little acts of kind thoughtfulness quite as much, if
> not more than those who are much younger....
>
> I hardly knew the old place the last time I was there, which was
> in 1903, but I am now told that if I thought the place changed
> then, I shall not know it the next time I come. I quite believe it
> myself, for certainly I cannot imagine how the cars can go from
> Parry Harbour over the great Belvedere rocks, and away down
> the North West Road and I see by the *North Star* (that also arrived
> this morning) that more large industries are being put up. Well if
> all goes well, I shall hope to be in Parry Sound just once more....[19]

Top: Wrenbury Hall as it looked in March 1910. *Courtesy of the Parry Sound Public Library Historical Collection/John Bellamy Miller #641. Bottom*: Wrenbury Hall as it looks today. A fire around 1914 damaged the building and parts were rebuilt. This accounts for Wrenbury Hall appearing quite different in the previous photograph taken in 1910. *Courtesy of Adrian Hayes*.

Arthur Starkey passed away at Wrenbury Hall on October 9, 1912, having never been married and leaving no children. Following the probate of his estate, his nephew, Kenneth Vere Starkey, inherited The Cedars. A deed dated January 14, 1914, transferred the title to the property, which at that time had an assessed value of $5,000 for municipal taxation purposes.[20]

Up to the time of Starkey's death, taxes on The Cedars were relatively low, being just $22 in 1904 and rising gradually to $55 in 1912. But, in 1914, the taxes jumped dramatically to $125 and kept increasing.[21] As an absent landowner, Kenneth Vere Starkey probably would have been prudent to sell such a piece of property in a distant country, which had no sentimental value to him. Instead, he held on to it, but balked at paying the taxes.

Parry Sound lawyer, John Roland Hett, on Starkey's behalf, negotiated a settlement with the 1930 court of revision that a receipt for three years taxes be granted on payment of the taxes for two years. Council, however, refused to accept the compromise as the town solicitor advised that the court of revision lacked the authority to make such arrangements. The Corporation of the Town of Parry Sound seized The Cedars for $5,223.37 in unpaid taxes and became the legal owner of the property in November 1930.[22]

J.R. Hett addressed the Parry Sound council at a February 1931 meeting to state that the value of the property was very small and that the assessments had not been reduced. The compromise, he felt, would have been a good way of granting an adjustment to his client. Hett disputed the town solicitor's legal opinion regarding the powers of a court of revision. He wanted to arbitrate the matter before a judge, at the expense of his client, stating that he and the town solicitor differed on the subject and that judges were supposed to know more than lawyers.[23]

Councillor Solomon Shamess objected vehemently to the proposal, stating that the Starkeys were entitled to no different treatment than local citizens, and, that if such a procedure were followed in this instance, other delinquents would be entitled to the same consideration.

Council was once again confronted with a property issue involving the Starkeys in the early 1960s when the federal Department of Transport contemplated an expansion of the Coast Guard base. It became apparent that Arthur Starkey's heirs still owned Starkey's Point and a water lot, but as the properties did not appear on the town assessment roll, no tax bills had ever been sent to the family. Clerk-treasurer, John Cranston Campbell, faced the dilemma—the town could not legally seize the land for non-payment of taxes unless it could be proven that notices had been sent and the taxes had gone unpaid for three consecutive years.

Novice councillor Joe Brunatti later discovered that Campbell had commenced sending tax bills to the Starkey heirs, but their cheques were not being cashed. On February 19, 1963, council passed a resolution, moved by Brunatti, that:

> The Corporation of the Town of Parry Sound relinquish any claims they might have on Starkey's Point and water lot and the clerk-treasurer is directed to accept the draft from Bellyse & Eric Smith, solicitors for the Starkey Estate in payment of arrears of taxes. And that a letter is forwarded to the Department of Transport hoping that this resolution will put the corporation and the Department of Transport on good relations that we have enjoyed in the past. And that a letter be sent to the Starkey Estate solicitors advising that cheque has been deposited.[24]

Wrenbury Hall still stands today, but it is no longer in the Starkey family as Kenneth Vere Starkey sold the Hall and about 164 acres of land to Cheshire County Council in 1920. The structure served as a training centre run by the British Red Cross and the Order of St. John of Jerusalem for tuberculosis sufferers. In the 1950s, it became a Cheshire Area Health Authority training centre for ambulance personnel. The Hall has been a private residence since 1982, when it was purchased by the present owners.

9

Dr. Walton: Scoundrel or Victim
of Political Patronage

WHILE PATRONAGE APPOINTMENTS to federal and provincial governments are still often made to reward loyal party followers, the practice was even more accepted and widespread during the 19th century. The defeat of the party holding power usually resulted in the mass termination of employees whose political leanings were not compatible with those of the cabinet ministers heading the various government departments. Almost a century ago, Dr. Thomas Smith Walton, the Indian superintendent at Parry Sound, found himself in just such a situation.

Dr. Walton was born February 12, 1838, at Sheffield, England, and began working in the surgery of Dr. J.M. Scott in 1852, when still a boy. He received a diploma in midwifery in 1855 and then graduated as a physician from the Royal College of Surgeons in Edinburgh in 1858. For several years after receiving his medical degree, Dr. Walton served as a doctor aboard the Allan Brothers & Co. ship the *Nova Scotian* on voyages between Liverpool and Canada. He was later employed by the African Steam Ship Company on such vessels as the *McGregor Laird* sailing between Liverpool and South Africa.[1]

Although Dr. Walton married Elizabeth Hannah Moffatt on September 16, 1861, and they started a family, he did not have much opportunity to see his children. The death of a son, James Moffatt Walton, at Liverpool on May 18, 1869, probably caused him to ponder his life and future. Becoming a gentleman farmer in Canada seemed a much better alternative to a life spent at sea.

Dr. Walton, his wife, their young children and Dr. Walton's unmarried sister Ellen settled on 200 acres at the north end of Lake Joseph in Humphrey Township, 15 miles from Parry Sound, in the fall of 1869. Dr. Walton cleared land and attempted to farm, although his land was totally unsuited to agriculture. Advertisements in the *Northern Advocate* indicate, however, that he was still practising as a physician at this location to supplement his income and that he went back to sea during at least one period in 1872.

Although William Beatty Jr. had attracted Dr. Alex Stephens to Parry Sound as early as 1869, he did not stay long. The need for a permanent physician in the growing village persuaded Dr. Walton to abandon his homesteading ideas and establish a practice in Parry Sound. Indeed he had considered abandoning his farm earlier. He wrote in a March 1870 letter to his father, James Walton, who was the collector of inland revenue at Ripon, England:

> The doctor in Parry Sound is talking of leaving (and well he may) and Elizabeth and Ellen are quite full of my going and taking his practice, but somehow I don't feel quite so sanguine about it as they do and yet I do not feel inclined to let the chance slip. Parry Sound will undoubtedly in a short time become the centre of a thickly settled district of country and I might rise to a position of influence and independence.[2]

Dr. Walton purchased a lot on the east side of James Street from William Beatty Jr. in November 1874 and built a large house on the site of the present Wright Clinic. He had a medical office at the front of the house and rooms upstairs for the patients. As the only doctor, Walton was assured of not only a steady income, but also the social prominence and influence he craved. He served as mayor of Parry Sound in the years 1890, 1894 and 1895.

In the fall of 1883, the Indian superintendent at Parry Sound, Captain Charles Skene, retired from the position and Dr. Walton wasted no time in writing to Prime Minister John A. Macdonald asking for the job.[3] At Confederation, control of Indian matters had been given to the federal government and the responsibility was delegated to the Department of the Interior shortly after. Macdonald

Dr. Thomas Smith Walton with sons Frederick *left*,
and Ernest. While Ernest became captain of the
steamer *City of Midland*, Frederick ran a general store
in Parry Sound. Dr. Walton's youngest son, John, was
killed in August 1892 when he was struck by debris
as workers were blasting trenches for the town's first
water mains. *Courtesy of John Macfie.*

served as his own Minister of the Interior and consequently also
held the position of Superintendent-General of Indian Affairs.

As Superintendent-General, Macdonald recommended in a
November 17, 1883, letter that Walton be given the position recently
vacated by Skene. A few days later, an order-in-council appointed
Walton to the position at an annual salary of $900.[4]

Dr. T.S. Walton performed his duties as Indian agent admirably
for the next 13 years, covering a huge area extending all the way
from the Gibson band south of Parry Sound to the Temagami band
to the north. In this role he served as the middleman in relations
between the administrators in Ottawa and the Native Peoples,

visiting the bands to accept grievances and distribute the Robinson Huron Treaty annuities.

In the election of June 1896, the Liberal party under Wilfrid Laurier swept into power with a majority of 33 seats and, thus, an 18-year reign by the Conservatives came to a close. In July, Laurier was sworn in, along with an impressive team of cabinet ministers that included three successful provincial premiers—Sir Oliver Mowat from Ontario, William Stevens Fielding from Nova Scotia and Andrew G. Blair from New Brunswick. Clifford Sifton, the Liberal MP from Brandon, Manitoba, was appointed as Minister of the Interior and, thus, he also became the head of the Department of Indian Affairs.

The replacement of Conservative employees at the Department of Indian Affairs by the Liberals began almost immediately. One of the first to go was Deputy Superintendent-General Hayter Reed, who had only just been appointed in 1893. His successor was James A. Smart, the Liberal deputy minister of the interior. Smart delegated most of his responsibilities, however, to departmental secretary J.D. McLean, chief accountant Duncan Campbell Scott and James Andrew McKenna, Sifton's private secretary.

William Henry Pratt, president of the Conger Lumber Company in Parry Sound, wrote to Sifton early in the spring of 1897 to complain about Dr. Walton's conduct during the recent federal election. Walton was a Conservative and had done all he could to secure the election of George McCormick as MP for the constituency of Parry Sound/Muskoka. Pratt, on the other hand, had been the unsuccessful Liberal candidate and he vehemently attempted to get back at Dr. Walton for his participation in McCormick's election campaign. In a scathing letter, Pratt wrote:

> No more persistent or effectual efforts were made by any man in the Parry Sound riding at the late election to defeat the Liberal candidate than that made by this man Walton. He did all he could to compass my defeat and being an influential man he contributed a good deal toward that result.

He is not only a bitter partisan, but he never fails to let it be known. I hope that the Department of which he is still an acting agent may find it consistent with its duties to dispense with his further services....[5]

While the top policy executors at Indian Affairs frequently disregarded complaints about Indian agents from the Natives under their charge, Dr. Walton now found himself in the unenviable position of being a Conservative employee within a Liberal administration. It was not long before the department resuscitated an old complaint against Walton received from Chief Nebenayancquod of the Shawanaga band. The chief had complained that Dr. Walton misused his position to make financial gains during the sale of timber located on the reserve in 1895.[6]

In the spring of 1897, George Lang Chitty, a timber inspector from the Lands and Timber Branch of the Department of Indian Affairs, was dispatched to investigate the allegations made against Dr. Walton and subsequently submitted a report that condemned him. Chitty, also a Conservative, had reason to fear for his own job.

Conger Lumber Company president William Henry Pratt ran unsuccessfully as a Liberal in the riding of Muskoka/Parry Sound in the June 1896 federal election. *Courtesy of Doreen Nowak.*

The report recounted that roughly 400 acres of timber on the Shawanaga River had sustained fire damage during the spring of 1895 and Walton had reported this to the department in August.

He had advised that unless the damaged timber was surrendered and sold, a greater loss would result for the Indians through decay. The administration consequently authorized him to obtain a surrender from the band for all timber on the reserve. If the Natives were not amenable to this, however, he was to seek a surrender of the burnt timber only.[7]

The Native Peoples refused to agree to a surrender and expressed a desire to cut and sell the timber themselves, a fact that Dr. Walton passed on to his superiors. While the department agreed to this, Walton urged that such a plan would be hazardous and endeavoured to have a white man employ the local Natives to do the work. The Department of Indian Affairs, however, did not want nonnatives invading the reserve and clearly told this to Dr. Walton. He was instructed to call for tenders for the timber to be cut by Natives with the consent of the band.

Dr. Walton subsequently informed his superiors that the lateness of the season demanded immediate action before winter set in. As a result, the Department of Indian Affairs in Ottawa gave Dr. Walton permission to accept the most advantageous bid on his own. On December 4, 1895, Walton notified the Department of Indian Affairs that he had accepted an offer from the contracting firm of Johnson and Beveridge for $7.25 per 1,000 board feet for logs delivered to Georgian Bay and $115 per 1,000 cubic feet of square timber. He also stated that the Shawanaga band council had passed a resolution to issue a cutting permit to Chief Adam Pawis, with the profits going to the workers and the elderly members of the band.

Dr. Walton subsequently obtained a power of attorney from Chief Pawis, a move of which the Department of Indian Affairs strongly disapproved. In written instructions, he was again told that only Natives were to be employed in the harvesting of the timber and cutting was to be confined to the burnt area only.

After receiving the Chitty report, Clifford Sifton wrote to the Governor General in Council on April 15, 1897, and reiterated the serious charges made against Dr. Walton.[8] He stated that Dr. Walton had coerced the Natives into selecting Pawis as foreman and manager and, after obtaining the contentious power of attorney, he

Dr. Walton with his family, circa 1901. The two children are Marjorie Beatrice, *left*, and Winnifred Glen, the daughters of Dr. Walton's son Frederick. *Courtesy of the Parry Sound Public Library Historical Collection, VF I People.*

entirely ignored the chief and his band in the harvesting of the timber. Also, while the department had confined the cutting operations to the burnt area, Dr. Walton had not read his instructions and actually advised the Indians to permit Johnson and Beveridge to cut green timber.

While Dr. Walton had also been instructed to allow only Native labour to cut the timber, he had apparently allowed white men onto the reserve to cut the square timber. White labour was also utilized to haul the logs at a rate of $3 per 1,000 board feet. On the other hand, Native workers had been used to construct the sleigh roads, but proper agreements and records had not been kept and, consequently, they were not adequately compensated for their labour. While Pawis and the Native Peoples had done some work hauling the logs, the absence of paylists made remuneration impossible.

The final condemnation was that Dr. Walton had compelled the Indians to purchase nearly all of their supplies from his son and daughter, Elizabeth and Frederick, proprietors of a general store in Parry Sound. Sifton wrote:

> It was inconceivable that an agent so experienced as Dr. Walton could have so erred or misunderstood the plainly expressed wishes of the Department; that there was no doubt that the best wishes of the Indians had not been served by the arrangements made by him in connection with the sale of timber....[9]

Clifford Sifton's letter to the Governor General in Council with its recommendation that Dr. Walton be dismissed was approved on April 20, 1897. By a subsequent letter of June 2, Walton was advised that he was being replaced. The same letter told him that his successor was to be William Brown McLean, who incidentally was a Toronto resident and Pratt's son-in-law.[10]

While an order-in-council of May 28, 1897, had appointed Maclean as the new agent, he was not able to carry out his duties for the entire summer.[11] Dr. Walton refused to surrender the records of the superintendency and repeatedly wrote to Ottawa protesting his innocence. On August 31, 1897, he wrote deputy superintendent-general James A. Smart that he had not suggested Pawis, but rather the Shawanaga band council had consented to allow Pawis to cut the timber and consequently he was the only one who applied for a permit. He also denied that he had ignored the wishes of the Native Peoples after obtaining the power of attorney.

Dr. Walton argued that he would have been unable to carry out his duties:

> [U]nless clothed with the protection of a power of attorney and protection of such a document. Had such a power of attorney not been obtained, disaster and inextricable confusion would most probably have resulted. For instance, how could I or anyone become responsible for supplies if the advances had been paid directly into the hands of Pawis. The probability in such a case would probably have been that a wild saturnalia would have taken place, debts would have remained unpaid and the whole would have come to a sudden and disastrous stop....

I respectfully submit that no proper investigation was held by the timber agent. I believe a private inquiry, from which I was excluded, took place at which the inspector interviewed several Indians, took down somewhat of what they said, apparently believing them and ignored what I subsequently said in rebuttal. Such a secret inquiry cannot be called an investigation. I was never notified that there was to be an investigation in any formal way—or what the charges were—the inspector never furnished me with any report on the matter—I had no opportunity to know what was witnessed against me or of cross-examining the witnesses, nor was I ever called upon to make any explanation or defence....[12]

Throughout the months of September and October, Walton wrote numerous letters to the editor of the *North Star* newspaper protesting his innocence in the matter. Editor William Ireland enjoyed the scandal enormously and kept the controversy alive by printing several anonymous responses. One letter, signed "Inquirer," asked if it was not true that Dr. Walton had made an agreement allowing him to pocket five per cent of all timber sales made on behalf of the Shawanaga Indians. The author alleged Walton had stood to make $13,000 by the transaction with Johnson and Beveridge.[13]

By the spring of 1898, the Conservative MP for Parry Sound-Muskoka, George McCormick, had grown concerned about the controversy and suggested that the House of Commons request the Minister of the Interior make available all copies of letters, telegrams, and correspondence related to Dr. Walton's dismissal.[14] Dr. Walton had been fired without benefit of his superannuation, despite having paid into the retirement fund for 13 years.

Deputy Minister James A. Smart informed J.D. McLean on June 1, 1899, that Minister of the Interior Sifton had decided it wise to reopen the Walton case due to persistent objections to the report submitted by timber inspector Chitty. Reginald Rimmie of the legal branch was dispatched to Parry Sound to check the accuracy of Chitty's report, but Chitty was allowed to accompany him to defend his own findings. Rimmie was given the power to summon witnesses and place them under oath, as one of Dr. Walton's complaints had been the lack of judicial spirit in the original investigation.[15]

Deputy Minister Smart notified McLean on July 21, 1900, that on the basis of Rimmie's report there seemed to be serious doubt about Dr. Walton's guilt. He wrote that the minister felt it would be a great injustice to withhold Dr. Walton's pension of $234 per year, although he did not think it possible to reinstate him as Indian agent.[16]

Sifton wrote to the Governor General in Council on July 24, 1900, that there was no evidence that Dr. Walton had a direct financial interest in the timber transaction and had fully accounted for all money received by him. He recommended that Walton receive his superannuation, based upon the 13 years that he had been employed by the Department of Indian Affairs.[17]

Dr. Thomas Smith Walton never did receive his pension from the Department of Indian Affairs as a report of the Committee of Privy Council recommending that his superannuation be denied was approved by an order-in-council of June 6, 1901.[18] Dr. Thomas Smith Walton passed away in Parry Sound on June 8, 1902, at the age of 64 years. Undoubtedly, the lengthy ordeal of trying to clear his name contributed to his death at a relatively premature age.

10

The Struggle for a Railway

MORE THAN A CENTURY AFTERWARDS, one cannot help but wonder about a meeting held in the Parry Sound council chambers during the spring of 1893 that dramatically changed the destiny of the town. Previous writers have not been kind to the local businessmen in attendance, stopping just short of calling them traitors and scoundrels. In truth, these long since deceased local entrepreneurs were the victims of too much trust in the assurances of an outsider. They accepted the promise of Ottawa Valley lumber king John Rudolphus Booth that he would complete a railway into their town, not expecting him to disregard the carefully prepared survey plans for the final miles.

In November 1884, William Beatty Jr. had turned the thoughts of his fellow citizens in Parry Sound to the possibility of a railway connection between the village and the more populated centres to the south. But, as previous attempts to interest established companies in building a line to Parry Sound had failed, Beatty came up with the novel idea of the citizens themselves incorporating a railway to build a line eastward to link with that line which was slowly moving northward between Bracebridge and North Bay.

Residents showed immense interest in the railway scheme at a meeting held at the Parry Sound courthouse on November 21, 1884. Those present passed a unanimous resolution that Beatty and Patrick McCurry approach the council of McDougall Township for funds with which to acquire a provincial charter. Both men appeared at a McDougall council meeting on behalf of the proposed company and obtained a promissory note for $200. The council of Foley Township also pledged $100 to the project.[1]

The provincial legislature incorporated the Parry Sound Colonization Railway on March 30, 1885, to build a rail line from Parry Sound to a point on the Northern and Pacific Junction Railway at or near Burk's Falls in Armour Township.[2] The company was authorized to sell 2,000 shares of $100 each to achieve a capitalization of $200,000. While many of Parry Sound's citizens invested in the company with their savings, the major stockholders and directors were Beatty and McCurry, as well as lumbermen John Bellamy Miller, Joseph W. Fitzgerald and Samuel Armstrong Jr.

Patrick McCurry was elected president and he lobbied relentlessly for construction subsidies from both the provincial and federal governments. Appearing before the McDougall council once again, he convinced the local politicians to petition both MPP Jacob William Dill of Bracebridge and MP William E. O'Brien of Shanty Bay.[3] When there had still not been any response on the granting of subsidies. McCurry chaired another public meeting at the courthouse on January 17, 1886. Those in attendance unanimously decided that delegates from the various area councils would meet at the provincial legislature in Toronto on February 5 to lobby for a railway subsidy.

The Foley council decided to send a delegation consisting of Reeve David Macfarlane and James S. Miller to the meeting at the legislature. McDougall council agreed to send Reeve John Alexander Johnson, councillors Robert Fawns, John Moffat, John Darlington and William Rabb Beatty, as well as *North Star* editor William Ireland. A railway meeting chaired by McCurry in the village of McKellar on January 19 also resulted in a unanimous decision to send delegates to Toronto.[4]

While the lobbying in Toronto apparently did not have any effect, as a subsidy was denied, William O'Brien's efforts in Ottawa proved more rewarding. A federal statute of June 2, 1886, granted the Parry Sound Colonization Railway a subsidy of $3,200 per mile to construct a line from Parry Sound to the village of Sundridge in Strong Township.[5] This line of 50 miles was to connect with the Northern and Pacific Junction Railway and the total amount was not to exceed $128,000. Construction would have to commence within two years of August 1, 1887, and be completed within four years.

The Parry Sound Colonization Railway remained but a paper dream for four long years after receiving its charter, but the venture received new impetus following the incorporation of Parry Sound. Mayor John McClelland, then secretary-treasurer of the railway, began lobbying for more subsidies from both the federal and provincial governments. In March 1889, petitions bearing the corporate seal of the town were sent to both levels of government through the area's MP and MPP and council authorized the spending of $200 to send a delegation to Ottawa to assist in procuring a railway grant.[6]

In the provincial legislature, MPP Samuel Armstrong Jr. of McKellar, another director of the Parry Sound Colonization Railway, successfully generated the company's first provincial subsidy. A statute of March 23, 1889, granted a subsidy of $3,000 per mile for a line from Parry Sound to Burk's Falls. The efforts of the delegation to Ottawa resulted in a May 2, 1889, statute that renewed the subsidy authorized three years earlier for a line to Sundridge, which was not to exceed $128,000.[7]

On May 29, 1890, the directors of the Parry Sound Colonization Railway entered into a contract with William G. Reid of Montreal to construct and equip a railway line from Scotia Junction to Parry Sound. The project was to be completed by July 1, 1892. The directors received a preliminary survey report from chief engineer S.R. Poulin, dated June 18, 1890, in which he stated that the easiest route from Scotia Junction to Parry Sound would be through the townships of Perry, McMurrich, Monteith, Christie and Foley.[8]

Poulin wrote that the terrain was very rough and the line would run at virtual right angles to the main valleys. He also warned that to navigate the terrain there would be deviations from a straight line which would increase the total length by about 15 per cent. He proposed a series of trestle structures over the valleys that would be filled in gradually over the next decade.

It was generally agreed to commence construction at Scotia Junction and work towards Parry Sound, as this way the completed portion could be used while construction was still pushing forward.

The engineer estimated that the total cost of the first 30 miles west from Scotia Junction to be $446,342 or $14,800 per mile.

With the full knowledge of the staggering costs to be incurred, the directors entered into a subsidy contract with the Ministry of Railways and Canals in July 1890 in which they agreed to have the full line completed by November 1, 1892.[9] On August 6, 1890, president McCurry and vice-president Beatty filed a plan of location of the Parry Sound Colonization Railway with the Surveyor's Branch of the Department of Crown Lands for the first 30 miles westward from Scotia Junction. Work immediately began on the first ten-mile section, which was to include not only the tracks, but also a station, water tank, engine house and a turntable.

Clearly, the company struggled to remain solvent during construction and a May 1891 statute of Ontario amended the Parry Sound Colonization Railway's charter to authorize a possible amalgamation with the Canada Atlantic Railway, the Northern and Pacific Railway, the Grand Trunk Railway, or any two or more of the companies.[10] Under such a merger, the debts, duties and obligations of the Parry Sound Colonization Railway would be assumed by the parent company.

In a desperate move to obtain more operating capital, Parry Sound Colonization Railway secretary-treasurer James Marcus Ansley informed the minister of Railways and Canals that the initial section would be completed and ready for inspection by June 15. In truth, while the track was laid, none of the terminus buildings had been erected and the inspector reported this.[11] The directors were hoping to receive a portion of the subsidy equal to the work which had been completed, but Collingwood Schreiber, the chief engineer for Railways and Canals, would not recommend such a move to the minister.

In June 1892, the Parry Sound Colonization Railway's general manager, William G. Reid, submitted revised survey plans for the second ten-mile section of the railway to the new minister of Railways and Canals, John Haggart. Reid stated that negotiations were being conducted by the directors of the Parry Sound Colonization Railway with the Grand Trunk Railway and the Canada Atlantic Railway regarding a possible takeover of the financially troubled line.[12]

He requested to be released from his commitment to construct the terminal buildings as their location was dependent upon which of the two potential buyers took control. In a similar letter to Prime Minister Sir John Abbott, Reid wrote that he would be showing the completed portion of the line to John Rudolphus Booth, president of the Canada Atlantic Railway, during the following week and that the location Booth had in mind for the terminus was quite different from those of the Grand Trunk directors.[13]

Thomas Ridout of the Department of Railways and Canals inspected the 20 miles already completed of the Parry Sound Colonization Railway westward from Scotia Junction on September 28, 1892, and submitted a report to chief engineer Schreiber on October 5.[14] He reported that while the tracks and roadbed were constructed in accordance with the government contract, with the exception of a single culvert in the second section, the water tank, engine house, turntable and station in the first section had still not been built.

While the total federal subsidy applicable to the two sections was $63,210, he estimated the uncompleted work at $3,990, leaving $59,220 to be paid to the railway company. He also estimated that there was $19,000 worth of rolling stock operating on the line, consisting of two steam locomotives, a first-class passenger car, a baggage car, a mail car, an express car and 23 flat cars. Following Ridout's report, an October 14, 1892, order-in-council approved the extension requested by the directors of the Parry Sound Colonization Railway for completion of the railway.[15]

On April 26, 1893, Ansley submitted the profiles and plans of that section of the Parry Sound Colonization Railway covering the proposed right-of-way between the 20th mile and the town of Parry Sound, to John Haggart, the minister of Railways and Canals.[16] A map covering the route of the last 30 miles was also filed with the Surveyor's Branch of the Ontario Department of Crown Lands on May 4, 1893.

It was at this point in the spring of 1893 that the Parry Sound Colonization Railway came under the direct control of J.R. Booth.[17] From his humble beginnings as a farmer's son, Booth had become the largest timber limit owner in the entire British Empire, with

John Rudolphus Booth of Ottawa betrayed his fellow lumbermen in Parry Sound when he bypassed their town and built the terminus of the Canada Atlantic Railway at Depot Harbour. *Courtesy of LAC, PA-28000.*

4,000 square miles in Ontario and Quebec. By 1902, the largest year of production, Booth's mills cut 125 million board feet of lumber; in 1904 he established a modern pulp mill, turning out 150 tons of newsprint daily.

Booth wielded immense political influence in Ottawa, especially during the years when the Conservatives held power. Prime Minister John A. Macdonald was a close friend who often visited the Booth home on Wellington Street to hold long private discussions with the lumberman. This relationship proved mutually beneficial and, in 1889, Booth obtained financial aid from the federal government for a bridge at Coteau Landing, after successfully engineering the election of Conservative candidate John Ferguson in the riding of Renfrew. Booth, however, always emphatically denied he was the recipient of patronage.

Booth was extremely conservative and often tyrannical in relations with his workers and yet he could also be extremely kind. He contended no man was worth more than $1.25 per day and forbid union activities in his sawmills. When a Royal Commission on capital and labour called upon him to testify in 1886, he freely admitted to ignoring the newly instituted Factory Act, which forbid the employment of children under 12. However, this same man knew many of his workers personally and gave gifts of food and fuel to the families of employees who were sick or injured. Old men who had served faithfully would be assured of jobs as night watchmen in their golden years.

In addition to being the renowned lumber king of the Ottawa Valley, Booth also became a major figure in railroad construction in Ontario, although the two activities were closely connected. Booth dealt heavily with the American market and, by the late 1870s, he was in need of an alternative to the water route because his business had exceeded its capacity.

A consortium of Scottish lumbermen in the delta of the Ottawa and St. Lawrence rivers had incorporated the Montreal and the City of Ottawa Junction Railway Company in 1871 to build a line from Ottawa to Coteau Landing on the Grand Trunk mainline, 33 miles west of Montreal. The project was no sooner underway, however, than there was a depression and decline in investment, resulting in a work stoppage.

Six years later, Booth took control of the failed railway and formed the Canada Atlantic Railway in May 1879. No bonds were issued to finance the venture and, even when the expenditure ran into millions, there was no floating debt. Instead, Booth and his two partners personally provided all capitalization.[18] Construction on the railway resumed in 1880 and the 80 miles between Coteau Landing and Ottawa were quickly completed. Indeed, the first train steamed into the capital in September 1882.

Once the Clarke Island/Lacolle section of the railway was opened for traffic two years later, a ferry transported trains across the St. Lawrence from Coteau Landing to the United States. Traffic grew rapidly with freight increasing eight-fold and passengers three-fold in the first four years of operation. In fact, the traffic became so heavy that in 1889 Booth had to construct a bridge across the river. This substantial project was completed in less than 11 months and opened in February 1890.[19]

Booth had originally intended the Canada Atlantic to transport his timber to the American market, but by the late 1880s it had become a general purpose railway. He turned his eyes to the western part of the province with the same aspirations. To the west of Ottawa there was not only a vast expanse of forest, but also prairie wheat. Booth knew that if he could deliver the wheat by the shortest possible route, the traffic would underwrite the prosperity of the railway.

The Ottawa, Arnprior and Renfrew Railway Company was incorporated in March 1888 to lay the first 55 miles of track between Ottawa and Renfrew. Six weeks later the Ottawa and

In the construction of the Ottawa, Arnprior and Parry Sound Railway,
narrow cuts through the rock terrain were blasted out with dynamite.
The broken rock was then removed by simple winch and horse-drawn
sled. *Courtesy of Algonquin Park Museum Archives / J. W. Ross.*

Parry Sound Railway Company was incorporated to lay the track
between Renfrew and an undetermined point on Georgian Bay.
A federal statute of July 1891 amalgamated these two railways to
form the Ottawa, Arnprior and Parry Sound Railway Company.[20]

The last annual stockholders meeting of the Parry Sound Colonization Railway to be held in Parry Sound took place in the town
council chamber on June 3, 1893. Directors John Christie, Francis McDougall and William Anderson of Ottawa, A.J. Campbell of
Arnprior, and William Beatty Jr. and J.W. Fitzgerald of Parry Sound
were present, but the president of the company, Patrick McCurry,
was absent due to his magistrate duties. William Beatty Jr. took the
chair. A bylaw was passed to move the head office to Ottawa and
Charles Jackson Booth, son of J.R. Booth, was elected president for
the coming year. McCurry became the new vice-president.[21]

Construction resumed on the Parry Sound Colonization Railway
and, in August 1894, Andrew Fleck, secretary-treasurer of the Canada
Atlantic Railway, informed the Department of Railways and Canals
that the third ten-mile section would be completed and ready for
inspection on the 29th. Early in the following month, the department dispatched Thomas Ridout to Scotia Junction and he reported
that he had inspected the first three sections and found them well

built. In accordance with the subsidy contract, the company was
granted the earned subsidy of
$99,000 for the three sections.[22]

Work progressed at a steady rate
and on December 14, 1894, Francis Lynch inspected the fourth
section which ended in Foley
Township, just short of Parry
Sound.[23] Following the inspection, the construction crews were
relocated to work on other parts
of the line while Booth contemplated a serious dilemma.

When he had obtained control
of the company in 1893, Booth
had promised to make Parry
Sound the Georgian Bay terminus
of the Canada Atlantic Railway

Charles Jackson Booth was
elected as president of the Parry
Sound Colonization Railway
Company in June 1893. *Courtesy
of LAC, PA-25739.*

system, a maze of track that extended all the way to Vermont.
Thus, the local directors had eagerly allowed his takeover because
they believed Booth had far better resources behind him to complete the project, and allowing Parry Sound to become the
Georgian Bay transshipment point of his system would bring prosperity to the town.

Instead of keeping his promise to his fellow lumbermen in Parry
Sound, Booth decided to seek a terminus site on Parry Island, a
nearby Indian reserve. Depot Harbour had the reputation of being
the best natural harbour on the Great Lakes and Booth knew he had
enough influence in Ottawa to obtain the necessary right-of-way
across the Indian land. In February 1895, surveyors working under
Booth's direction trespassed upon the reserve and ran lines across
the island from Rose Point Narrows towards Depot Harbour.

The residents of Parry Island became incensed about this illegal
survey and, in a council meeting held in the following month, it
was categorically stated that the band had no intention of allowing
a railway to traverse its land. Hayter Reed, deputy superintendent-

general of the Department of Indian Affairs, notified Dr. Thomas
Smith Walton, the local Indian agent in Parry Sound, to inform the
Indians that the department "would do its utmost to guard their
interests in every way."[24]

The Department of Indian Affairs took a diplomatic stance as
the Parry Island band, under Chief Dan Tabobandung, passed two
resolutions in May and September, but it was now impressed upon
Dr. Walton that the department could not intervene to prevent
the railway from entering the reserve if its presence served the
public interest. An 1887 amendment to the Indian Act had permitted expropriation of reserve land for railway purposes.

It is obvious that, by April 1895, Booth had already used his
influence in Ottawa to obtain unofficial approval for his plans on
the Indian reserve. At the end of that month chief engineer George
A. Mountain of the Ottawa, Arnprior and Parry Sound Railway
called upon the North Star and stated, "it is settled beyond doubt
that the company will make the actual terminus of the road on
Parry Island at Deep Bay."[25]

No documents exist to show that Booth had even approached
Indian Affairs about the matter at this time. Mountain further
claimed that the reason the railway was unable to bring its tracks
into Parry Sound was that the only location found where enough
property could be acquired for its purposes was at the camp
grounds and the best grade that the surveyors could find was an
extremely steep 53 feet to the mile.

In September 1895, the Parry Sound Colonization Railway filed
a revised plan of the right-of-way covering the distance between
the 40th and 48th mile with the Surveyor's Branch of the Department of Crown Lands in Toronto. On the plan, the tracks terminated
at the Rose Point Narrows, the channel separating Parry Island from
the mainland. Later that month, J.R. Booth wrote to T. Mayne Daly,
the superintendent-general of Indian Affairs in Ottawa, to acquire
314.26 acres of land on the Parry Island reserve for his railway.[26]
In October, Indian Affairs dispatched Commissioner James J. Campbell and timber agent George L. Chitty to negotiate a formal
surrender, but if they were unable to do so they were instructed to
inform the band of the government's intention to expropriate.

With single and duplex homes, boarding houses, stores, a school, three churches and a hotel, the railway community of Depot Harbour on Parry Island boasted a population of more than 600 residents by the 1911 census. *Courtesy of AO/David L. Thomas Collection, C253 Tray 5-16.*

Campbell and Chitty, accompanied by Dr. Walton and fortified with five pounds of tobacco, met with the Indians and coerced them into a surrender on October 9. Faced with the knowledge that the government intended to take the land in any case, the Natives voluntarily gave it up for $9 per acre, which was two dollars more than the rate paid to settlers for bush on the mainland. A formal surrender was signed on this day.[27] By January 1896, work on the Ottawa, Arnprior and Parry Sound Railway had reached the Rose Point Narrows and construction commenced across Parry Island in the following month.

Rail traffic from Ottawa to Depot Harbour began with the completion of the line in 1897 and within a year the facilities included a massive one million bushel grain elevator, over 2,000 feet of dock space and extensive freight sheds and warehouses. *The Parry Sound Directory, 1898-99* states that ships were already running from the Ottawa, Arnprior and Parry Sound railhead to Chicago, Milwaukee, Duluth and Port Arthur, and grain carriers from the Upper Great Lakes were visiting the port with increasing frequency.[28] A railway roundhouse capable of housing ten steam locomotives and a railway station were added shortly.

In July 1899, Andrew W. Fleck applied to Indian Affairs on behalf of the Ottawa, Arnprior and Parry Sound Railway for an additional 110.5 acres adjoining the right-of-way on which to construct residences for the railway's employees. Schreiber, chief engineer for the Department of Railways and Canals, advised the government that the land was not necessary for the actual operation and business of the railway, but as Parry Sound was a considerable distance away, it was required for the sake of convenience.

Indian Affairs dispatched Reginald Rimmie, a law clerk with the department, and timber inspector Chitty to Parry Island near the end of July to raise the question of Booth acquiring more land on the reserve at a special meeting of the Indian band. The government representatives once again explained that Indian Affairs, under the Indian Act, had the power to expropriate lands for railway purposes. This did not prevent the band council from sending their local Indian agent a copy of a resolution in August stating that they refused to voluntarily sell any additional land. An August 19, 1899, order-in-council authorized the sale of the 110.5 acre parcel to the Ottawa, Arnprior and Parry Sound Railway for $10 per acre.[29]

Following the acquisition of the additional acreage, Booth commissioned a 12-street plan adjacent to the transshipping facilities and established a townsite. The village of Depot Harbour came to include 69 detached and semi-detached dwellings, a three-storey bunkhouse, the imposing Island Hotel, three churches and various stores. The community also had running water, electricity, sewers and fire protection.

When the Canadian Northern Ontario Railway and the Canadian Pacific Railway were constructed through Parry Sound in the early 20th century, the town was merely one of a series of stops along the respective lines. Neither railway was interested in developing Parry Sound as a transshipment centre because there was no need. Depot Harbour had successfully usurped Parry Sound of this privilege and no amount of effort by the Parry Sound council and the citizens of the town could change this fact.

Mining Fever: Boom and Bust

As neighbouring Depot Harbour prospered during the late 1890s, Parry Sound residents wondered what "might have been" if only the Canada Atlantic Railway had come to their town. The discovery of a seemingly huge copper deposit on the homestead of Thomas McGowan Sr. offered Parry Sound a second chance at that future. Prospectors and speculators poured into the area in search of the elusive mother lode.

William Ireland, editor of the *North Star* and a relentless booster of the community, was determined not to let opportunity slip away. He publicized the activities of the Parry Sound Copper Mining Company, as well as those of the Hattie Belle Gold, Copper and Nickel Company of Parry Sound, the Ontario and Colorado Copper Mining Company and the Consolidated Copper Mining Company in a special mining issue. He also told readers he was studying mining mineralogy and geology, and expected to enrol in a special course at the Kingston School of Practical Science during the coming winter in order to fully qualify himself to keep pace with local mining developments.[1]

In the fall of 1899, Ireland made a bold statement that the *North Star* believed in the future of Parry Sound by building the imposing two-storey stone and brick structure at 67 James Street that even today is home to the newspaper. For the previous quarter-century the newspaper had been located in rented accommodations at various locations around the town.[2] The *North Star* also published *The Parry Sound Directory, 1898–99* to furnish "information, reinforced with maps and engravings that will enable persons contemplating investment of capital or settlement in this district to form a correct opinion."[3] This immense undertaking was not to be repeated by the newspaper during the next 100 years.

> People are beginning to realize the fact that this district is at last being recognized as mining country and that there are mining claims here worth owning.... It will shortly be demonstrated that the Parry Sound mines have no superior of their kind on the continent. We are safe in saying that never has such a body of high grade ore been taken out of any mine for the amount of work done as has already been taken out of the McGowan mine. Already the Parry Sound Copper Mining Company has taken out enough ore to pay for their investment in the mine and as they go down the vein grows wider and the quality is better.[4]

Ireland's mining fever proved contagious among local residents. Judge Patrick McCurry discovered a large vein of gold-bearing quartz near McCurry Lake and announced plans to form a mining company. [5] Charles Alonzo Phillips, proprietor of the Canada Atlantic Hotel, purchased the mineral rights to some 5,000 acres with the intention of selling to a mining company for a tidy profit.

The *North Star* reported in July 1899 that J.F. McLaughlin of Toronto had made a $1 million offer to buy the McGowan mine on behalf of a syndicate of Canadian investors. Parry Sound Copper Mining Company vice-president Robert Forbes "promptly refused the tempting offer saying he believed the mine would shortly prove to be worth many millions."[6] The company received an offer of $3 million from an American syndicate a month later.

Thomas McGowan was born in Glasgow, Scotland, in 1829, and came to Canada in 1844 with his parents and brother William. The family originally settled in Peterborough County and young Thomas married Ellen Mahoney, a recent arrival from Ireland, in 1854. In the following year, McGowan and his bride moved to Thornbury in Grey County, where they resided for the next decade. In 1864, the couple moved to Parry Sound, where McGowan went to work as a foreman for J. & W. Beatty and Company.[7]

William Ireland, *left*, was both the editor and publisher of
the *Parry Sound North Star* from January 1880 until July
1895, when his son-in-law, William Henry Bundy, became
a partner in the business. Prior to his arrival in Parry
Sound, the 28-year-old Ireland spent eight years at the
Aurora Banner, after completing an apprenticeship in
printing at the *Newmarket Era* and the *Sarnia Observer*.
*Courtesy of the Parry Sound Public Library Historical Collec-
tion / John Bellamy Miller #199.*

As the population of Foley Township gradually increased with
the influx of settlers attracted by the provisions of the Free Grant
and Homestead Act, McGowan and his family moved out of Parry
Sound to stake a homestead. In April 1872, he claimed 199 acres
under the Act, receiving the patent just over five years later. A further 130 acres were purchased outright from the Crown in June
1882, as were 18 acres from James Badger in January 1889.[8]
McGowan farmed to some degree, acted as a contractor of work
on the various colonization roads and also drove the mail stage to
Rosseau for a number of years.

Following the incorporation of Foley Township in 1872, McGowan
was elected as the first reeve and served several more terms. He was
the president of the District Liberal Association for many years and,
in the words of the *North Star*, "he and the late Frank Strain may be

said to have been the fathers of the Liberal party in Parry Sound." [9] Numerous times he declined to accept the party nomination to contest elections to represent Parry Sound in the Ontario legislature, but the newspaper felt certain that if only he had had the confidence to accept he would surely win due to his great popularity.

It was during the early spring of 1894 that members of the McGowan family discovered green stains on their property on the shores of Little Duck Lake (lot A, concession B), which proved to be verdigris, indicating the presence of copper in the rock. McGowan, his sons Thomas Jr. and John, and his son-in-law James Calder, the Parry Sound blacksmith, detonated several dynamite charges in the area in attempts to uncover the vein, but could do little more until the snow melted.

The following summer the men engaged the help of former Crown timber agent and local adventurer Duncan Fraser Macdonald and they continued blasting, resulting in the discovery of a gold deposit by John McGowan. Samples sent away for analysis confirmed that the discovery was indeed rich in gold and bornite. The men excavated an open cut or trench westward from the site of this discovery. Although high levels of copper had been evident, the find was treated primarily as a gold deposit. [10]

In a provisional partnership agreement concluded among McGowan, McCurry, and division court clerk David MacFarlane on December 22, 1896, McGowan agreed to the formation of a company to mine the deposit and, in April 1897, the McGowan Gold Mining Company of Parry Sound Limited was incorporated under the Ontario Joint Stock Companies Letters Patent Act of 1874, with an authorized capitalization of $1 million divided into shares of $1 each. [11] McGowan was president, while McCurry was vice-president and MacFarlane secretary. The treasurer was William Rabb Beatty, the mill manager of the Conger Lumber Company, while merchant Donald W. Ross and James Calder were the other directors. McGowan sold the company a total of 59 acres for $15,000 on March 14, 1898. [12]

In 1891, the Province of Ontario had established the Bureau of Mines, which was responsible for supervising the collection and publication of information useful to those actually engaged in the

Work on the inclined shaft at the McGowan mine site began in 1897 and
reached a depth of 160 feet when it was abandoned in 1900. A windlass
hoisted the ore to the surface on a narrow gauge railway. *Top*: An original
North Star photograph from a special mining issue in 1899, intended to
promote the efforts of the companies then operating in the area. *Bottom*:
The waters of Little Duck Lake have so risen over the years that today the
shaft is almost totally submerged and well-camouflaged by the foliage of
the shoreline. *Bottom photograph courtesy of Adrian Hayes.*

mining industry, such as prospectors, miners, and mine owners, as well as promoters and capitalists looking for opportunities. At the time, most mining companies could not afford complex machinery and accessed their claims by pick and shovel surface trenches, as the McGowans initially did. In 1894, the Bureau purchased a diamond drill for use by the government geologists, and to be rented to private developers. In 1897, the new McGowan Gold Mining Company Limited rented the diamond drill and bored three test cores which apparently produced promising results.

Thomas Heys, a consulting chemist employed by the Assay and Analytical Laboratory in Toronto, and Arthur P. Coleman, a professor at the School of Practical Science in Toronto, examined the property at the request of the company directors. On the basis of the core samples and their favourable opinions, two shafts were sunk. The first of these was the inclined shaft on lot A, concession B, and the second was a perpendicular shaft on lot 146, concession B.[13]

Shortly after the incorporation of the McGowan Gold Mining Company of Parry Sound Limited, the directors appointed George Monteith of Rosseau as the official broker of stock in the company, and he was successful in selling small amounts locally. He travelled to England in the fall of 1898 to attract foreign investors to the scheme, but the trip was only marginally profitable. Without capitalization, the company was unable to continue working the properties.

It was during this period of relative despair that several McGowan grandchildren, while swimming, found a large purplish patch on the rock beneath the waters of McGowan Lake (lot 146, concession B), which proved to be bornite and chalcocite. The discovery prompted renewed interest in the McGowan properties and a syndicate of American investors from Minnesota purchased not only the mine site, but also the mineral rights to hundreds of acres around it. On February 1, 1900, the McGowan Gold Mining Company of Parry Sound Limited sold the 59 acres originally purchased from McGowan along with another 103 acres at lot 146, concession A, for the considerable sum of $110,000 in Canadian funds.[14]

The Parry Sound Copper Mining Company Limited was incorporated under provincial letters patent in March 1899 with an authorized capitalization of $5 million divided into shares of $1 each.[15] The directors were: president Frank Johnson and secretary Otto Monson; two capitalists from St. Paul, Minnesota; treasurer William Foulkes, an attorney-at-law from St. Paul; vice-president Robert Forbes, a mining engineer from Duluth; and Simeon Franklin Pierce of St. Paul. While the head office was located in the IOOF building in Parry Sound, a branch office from which the directors operated was situated in the Germanic Life Insurance Building in St. Paul, Minnesota.

The new company began work immediately on a quarry on the shores of McGowan Lake, approximately 800 feet southeast of the incline shaft. They removed 300 tons of first-class ore and 3,000 tons of second-class ore before the blasting caused cracks in the bedrock and the waters of the lake flooded it. The owners also began to work the vertical shaft, midway between the quarry and the incline shaft. It was proposed to continue the shaft to 500 feet and explore in all directions at 100 foot levels. The incline shaft, which had followed the vein down at a 30-degree angle, had been abandoned by the McGowan Gold Mining Company after it ran into barren rock at the 75-foot mark. However, the Parry Sound Copper Mining Company pumped out the shaft and picked up the vein again by shifting the direction of the cut.

Six carloads of ore, weighing 143 tons, were shipped to the Orford Copper Company's refinery in New Jersey in June 1899, and netted the producers $5,399 after deducting the costs of shipping and smelting. This ore came from the open quarry on the shore of McGowan Lake. Another shipment of about 24 tons was made to Orford a month later.[16] More shipments probably followed, but there are no surviving records to support this supposition.

An inspector from the Ontario Bureau of Mines visited the McGowan site and reported on the operation in September 1899. He wrote that hoisting at the incline shaft was accomplished via a narrow-gauge railway and a windlass, while ore was raised from the vertical shaft with a steam engine equipped with a 12-inch drum. He reported that 40 men working on the site were lodged in a suitable boarding house. There was a well-equipped assay office and construction had begun on a concentrator plant on the shore of McGowan Lake.

Workers quarry rock at the McGowan mine site in 1899. *Courtesy of the Parry Sound North Star.*

The concentrator plant was a 10-stamp mill which stood 63 feet square and 60 feet high. The building was erected on a hillside and utilized the slope of the land in its construction. The raw ore was fed in at the top level and two batteries of five stamps, each weighing 850 pounds, fell 100 times per minute from a drop height of eight inches, thus pulverizing it. By shaking the granules, the metal particles gradually worked their way to the lower floor and were extracted, while the worthless rock was jettisoned. In a 24-hour day, the mill could purportedly handle between 20 and 40 tons of raw ore and the *North Star* jubilantly reported that in one period, in February 1900, it had run 144 hours without a single stop, the longest possible run permitted by law.[17]

There can be no doubt that the directors of the Parry Sound Copper Mining Company believed that the ore body they were working was much greater than it actually was. As early as April 1899, a delegation appeared before the Parry Sound town council, led by vice-president Forbes, to request the support of council for the construction of a railway spur line to serve both the mine and the town.[18] While the Ottawa, Arnprior and Parry Sound Railway ran from

Ottawa to Depot Harbour, it was still an arduous trip from the railhead into nearby Parry Sound.

To initiate the railway scheme, Forbes gave a glowing report to the citizens of Parry Sound of the prosperity of the company and of its intentions to erect a smelter and establish a factory within the town to produce copper wire. He predicted that within five years Parry Sound would be a good-sized city and the railway would allow the town to exploit the mineral and forest wealth of the surrounding area more successfully than ever before. In August 1899, William Beatty Jr.'s widow gave the company 40 acres northwest of the Patent Cloth Board Factory on which to construct a smelter.[19]

The Parry Sound Copper Mining Company Limited had other claims in the Parry Sound area at the time that it was carrying on the McGowan excavations. The Wilcox mine on Spider Lake in Cowper Township, discovered by Thomas Wilcox and Henry Harris of Waubamik in 1895, had been purchased by the American company in the summer of 1899. The company also worked another claim in Hardy Township.[20]

Although annual returns were filed with the office of the Provincial Secretary of Ontario until 1905, the company withdrew from the Parry Sound area at least two years before then. Peter Weller appeared on behalf of the Bell Telephone Company at the court of revision in July 1903 and stated that, due to the closure of the Patent Cloth Board Factory, the Kerr and Harcourt Bobbin Factory, as well as the McGowan mine telephone lines, the revenue produced by the company had decreased dramatically and thus its assessment for taxation should be reduced accordingly.[21]

Forbes, Foulkes and Johnson renounced all personal association with the McGowan properties in February 1904, and the Parry Sound Copper Mining Company mortgaged the land to Eleanor R. Elkinton of St. Paul.[22] The land acted as security on notes totalling $5,000 held by Elkington, which were due to be repaid within one year at six per cent interest. In the event of default, she had the power to sell the property to recover her loss, but after the Parry Sound Copper Mining Company went out of business in 1905, she tried unsuccessfully to dispose of it. D.F. Macdonald noted in his diary in May 1906 that an Englishman was in town to look over the mine workings and completed his entry with "poor deluded fellow." Elkington sold the mortgage to William E. Jones, a grain merchant in Ottumwa, Iowa, for $2,795.75 in September 1914.[23]

The end of the mining boom verified that the surveyors and geologists had indeed been correct in their assessment of the lack of mineral potential in the Parry Sound vicinity. The passage of the mining frontier through the area, however, injected many thousands of dollars into the economy and allowed several local men to live above the level which they normally would have as homesteaders. The most enduring relic of the mining era is the large red brick house standing immediately north of the Shaw-Almex plant, which was built in 1900 by James Peake after he sold his mineral rights to the Parry Sound Copper Mining Company Limited.

Thomas McGowan used his windfall to take a trip back to Scotland. While on the trip he became seriously ill and several times it was feared that he would succumb. He recovered enough to return to his homestead, but never entirely regained his health. He passed away in Parry Sound on July 27, 1903, at the age of 74 years.

Railways: Division and Disharmony

AFTER LOSING THE CANADA ATLANTIC RAILWAY to Depot Harbour, the businessmen of Parry Sound contiued their efforts to have a railway access the town, firmly believing that a rail connection would ensure the community's prosperity. But the arrival of the Canadian Northern Ontario Railway and the Canadian Pacific Railway would result not only in great physical changes to the town, but also in acrimony across members of the town council, the railways, and even local residents whose properties were affected.

In January 1898, a delegation consisting of Mayor John Alexander Johnson, councillors Joseph W. Fitzgerald, Donald W. Ross, Edward J. Vincent, John Moffat, George Beaumont and Walter Read Foot, town clerk Walter Lockwood Haight and residents William Beatty Jr., J.F. Mosley, David Beatty and George Goodwin Gladman, travelled to Toronto to support the James Bay Railway in its bid to secure a provincial construction subsidy.[1] William Mackenzie and Donald Mann, builders of the Canadian Northern Railway in western Canada, had incorporated the railway in 1895 to construct a line from Parry Sound to James Bay. The railway was successful in obtaining provincial funding of $3,000 per mile for 90 miles of track from Parry Sound to Sudbury.

For well over a year, Mackenzie and Mann took absolutely no action at all on the James Bay Railway and, in April 1899, a delegation appeared before the Parry Sound council, led by Robert Forbes of the Parry Sound Copper Mining Company, which was working a copper deposit in Foley. The group requested the support of council for the construction of a spur line to serve both the mine and the town.[2] Council agreed to send a delegation consisting of mayor Johnson, councillors Gladman and Ross and clerk-solicitor Haight to Ottawa to meet with the Minister of Railways to obtain aid for the project.

A committee consisting of Mayor Johnson, councillors Foot, Ross and Gladman, clerk-solicitor Haight, as well as former mayor John McClelland and David Beatty was formed to travel to Toronto in June 1899 to negotiate an agreement with the James Bay Railway to build a spur line. Nothing substantial came out of the meeting, and for almost another year the project remained dormant until yet another local committee went to the Ontario legislature to lobby for a provincial subsidy in April 1900. A provincial statute granted funding of $3,000 per mile for a railway extending from Parry Sound for five miles to connect with the Canada Atlantic Railway at what became known as James Bay Junction.[3]

Councillors Gladman and McClelland introduced a bylaw early in July to raise a bonus of $20,000 for the James Bay Railway through the selling of debentures in denominations of not less than $20 and paying interest at four per cent. W.H. Moore and Alexander Mackenzie, son of William Mackenzie, met with council on the evening of August 16 and stated that it was the intention of the James Bay Railway to commence construction as soon as their engineer located a suitable right-of-way. Furthermore, they pledged to have a line to the east side of the Seguin River completed by January 1 of the coming year and to the water's edge within 12 months. Council passed a bylaw approved by the ratepayers in an August 6, 1900, referendum.[4]

It was not until June 5, 1901, that Moore and Mackenzie met with council to go over a proposed contract between the town and the railway, clause by clause. The town attempted to include a stipulation whereby Parry Sound would become a divisional point on the railway when finally completed northward, but the railway representatives flatly refused and it was struck out. Another meeting on August 29 reopened the whole matter once again when the town insisted that it would pay only $15,500, a portion of the bonus, after the inspection of the line to the Seguin

The first railway to access Parry Sound was the James Bay Railway in 1902. This short five-mile spur from the main Ottawa, Arnprior and Parry Sound Railway linked to Depot Harbour, offered service of one coach per day. *Courtesy of AO/David L. Thomas Collection, C253 Tray 7-1.*

River, and the rest upon the completion of the line to the water's edge.[5] Finally, on November 6, 1901, Moore presented a copy of the agreement and once again the signing procedure was repeated. Construction of the James Bay Railway spur line into Parry Sound began early in 1902, and a provincial statute granted an additional subsidy of $1,000 per mile to the railway for the five-mile spur line and also for the 90 miles to be constructed to Sudbury. The town eventually paid $15,500 of the bonus to the James Bay Railway in February 1903, but the service to the railway's Dufferin Street station consisted of only one coach and a locomotive once per day.[6]

Representatives of the Canadian Pacific Railway (CPR) met in the council chamber with the Parry Sound Board of Trade in July 1904 to discuss the company's plans for construction of a rail link between Sudbury and Toronto. An engineer stated that the railway had awarded contracts worth $2 million for clearing brush, grading and laying track from Romford Junction, seven miles south of Sudbury, to Byng Inlet. Close to 600 men were already at work and this number was expected to increase to 1,500. The CPR representatives made it clear that the railway wanted access to the waterfront in Parry Sound and sufficient frontage for docks and elevators. The railway did not intend to ask the town for a bonus such as the James Bay Railway had received, but it wanted the right to cross town streets "and they desired the co-operation of the town so that no obstacles might be thrown in their way in getting into or out of the town."[7]

Within days of the meeting between the Board of Trade and the CPR officials, the *North Star* reported that the James Bay Railway had awarded contracts for construction of a line between Toronto and Parry Sound and expected to name the contractors for the work between Parry Sound and Sudbury in the coming weeks. In August 1904, workers began cutting out the right-of-way south from James Bay Junction towards Toronto, and although Moore and Mackenzie had not agreed to Parry Sound being a divisional point, the railway did construct an eight-stall roundhouse and repair ships at the north end of River Street.[8]

In May 1905, the *North Star*'s anonymous editorial writer of the 1890s, known by the pen name "M. Dash," complained about the railway:

> An ugly railway cut crosses what is left of the beginning of Avenue Road—while the rest of the "avenue" is swallowed up in a maze of brush, rubbish, stumps, mullin stalks, burdocks and thistles. Everywhere the ruthless axe has laid low the beautiful trees the late Governor Beatty took such pride in.... Last week I started out to find Strain's Lake and after wandering around some hours over brush heaps, around wood piles through a scene of devastation and destruction, I finally stumbled across the lake, surrounded with wood piles, on the side of which was a hideous tract of burnt land and on the other rockcuts and rockfills for a railway track....[9]

The first Canadian Northern Ontario train arrived in Parry Sound on November 19, 1906, at the new station, which was located on the Great North Road, just south of the Seguin Street bridge. The band of the local militia unit, the 23rd Northern Pioneers, was at the station to greet the train along with many cheering citizens. That evening a great celebration took place at the Kipling Hotel. As the track was not completed any further than Parry Sound by that time, the train turned and headed back to Toronto, but with the editor of the *North Star* on board to chronicle the trip:

> From the croakers and kickers we had formed the impression that the new line was in a state of unpreparedness, but the luxuriously upholstered carriages ran along smoothly and nicely, like a train on an old road bed, and there is an absence of the sharp curves and angles the aforesaid croakers have been talk ing about ever since the line was constructed. Otter Lake, Falding were soon passed, and from that point we swung along parallel to the old canoe route between Parry Sound and Lake Joseph crossing Lake Robinson…at the Narrows. Three minutes ahead of time we pulled into the pretty station at Barnsdale…only 37 minutes being consumed in making a trip which by fast canoe travel formerly took us 10 hours of hard paddling and carrying over portages.[10]

Although CPR representatives made it clear to the Board of Trade in July 1904 that the railway intended to build a line linking Toronto and Sudbury through Parry Sound, planning was put on hold when the James Bay Railway made an application to the Dominion Railway Commission to prevent construction of the branch. The James Bay Railway held that construction was not authorized under the CPR's charter and, if the original charter did include the power to construct this branch line, that right had elapsed by time and failure of the CPR to build it sooner. After hearing arguments from both sides, the Dominion Railway Commission referred the matter to the Supreme Court of Canada, which decided in April 1905 that the CPR did indeed have the right under its charter and amendments.[11]

Immediately after the Supreme Court of Canada decision, the CPR awarded contracts for clearing brush, grading, constructing bridges and laying track between Toronto and Byng Inlet. In May, Mayor Johnson, four councillors, clerk Errol E. Armstrong and MPP John Galna met with CPR superintendent of construction J. W. Leonard in Toronto and learned there was little hope of Parry Sound becoming a divisional point as it was too far from Toronto.

Leonard further stated that a line through town would be very expensive and the railway was surveying a line east of Mill Lake.[12]

The CPR informed the town in August 1905 that it would, in fact, be building through the community and council tentatively approved the plan, but it was not until April 1906 that two railway representatives attended a council meeting to present a detailed map of the route and to request the closure of numerous streets to be crossed by the tracks. Pressured by the railway representatives to act immediately so that the CPR could commence work in town, council passed two resolutions calling for the closing of several unspecified streets.[13]

Property owners reacted swiftly. Within days the municipality received a letter from lawyer Walter L. Haight on behalf of Canada Express agent George Moore, druggist and former town treasurer Walter Read Foot and Foot's widowed sister, Ethel Letitia Muntz, vehemently objecting to the closure of Church Street at the intersection with Seguin Street.[14] Church Street, at that time, continued past St. Andrew's Presbyterian Church and the water tower almost to Belvedere Avenue. Judge Patrick McCurry forbade the closure of James Street in the east ward as this was private property. Entrepreneur Charles Alonzo Phillips, a councillor and former owner of the Canada Atlantic Hotel, stated the closure of Railway Avenue would adversely affect the value of a number of lots he owned in the area and that he would seek compensation from the town if council proceeded. Likewise, the heirs of William Beatty Jr. complained that the closures of all streets between Armstrong and Cascade also would affect the value of properties.[15]

The CPR hired former Parry Sound mayor George G. Gladman to represent the railway in negotiations with local property owners whose land was required. The route of the CPR, unlike that of the Canadian Northern Ontario, passed through the centre of town necessitating the purchase of numerous properties.

In September 1906, council approved a plan for a CPR spur line leaving the main line in the vicinity of Strain's Lake and running along the waterfront from the waterworks pumping station to the Conger Lumber Company yard and across the Seguin River to the Peter Estate sawmill, providing the railway compensated the private property owners.[16] But the issue of the street closures was still unresolved. Construction of the 1,800-foot steel viaduct spanning the Seguin River 120 feet above the water had also not begun, even though the project was expected to take 1.5 years to complete.

Local lawyer Edwin Pirie, representing the CPR, asked council in October to set December 4 as the date that it would consider passing bylaws to close the streets. The *North Star* reported it understood council proposed to sell the streets to the railway for nominal amounts and expected the railway to pay the damage claims made by property owners.[17] By December, however, it was apparent that the CPR did not plan to pay compensation to property owners affected by the street closures, but rather expected the town to assume responsibility. Town solicitor Francis Ronan Powell advised council that it could not legally pass bylaws to close streets knowing that the town would be liable for damages without obtaining the consent of the ratepayers, as the paying of claims for damages would be in the nature of a bonus to the CPR.[18]

Hiram Erskine Stone, Pirie's partner at the law firm of Pirie & Stone, told council they had full authority under the Municipal Act to pass the bylaws and even pay damages without seeking the consent of the ratepayers. He further stated that even if the town did not have sufficient funds in the current year's budget, the deficit could be handed over to the next year's council as an overdraft. Council passed a resolution stating that while it was in favour of closing the streets, it could not do so unless the railway was willing to compensate property owners affected by the closures.

A week later, Stone and Gladman presented council with a telegram from the CPR's chief engineer stating that the railway would locate the freight yards at the north end of town and construct its station in the east ward unless the local politicians immediately changed their position. The threatening tone of the telegram alarmed the politicians, who had already expressed their willingness to close the streets.[19]

It was clear to town solicitor F.R. Powell that council was going to give in to the railway's demands and go against his advice. Powell, who had come to Parry Sound in August 1899 after practising in Toronto for 15 years, resigned and was replaced by John Pearson

Weeks, the only local lawyer not already representing anyone on railway matters. Weeks had been practising in Parry Sound since 1903.

On the first two days of February, town clerk Errol Everard Armstrong posted notices in neighbourhoods to be affected by the proposed street closures. Judge McCurry addressed council twice in March to reiterate his view that council had no power to close James Street in the east ward and, if the CPR wished to obtain clear title to a section of the street, it was a matter between him and the railway. W.L. Haight also objected and F.R. Powell, no longer a town employee, repeated his opinion that if closing municipal streets obligated the town to pay compensation, then council could not legally pass the bylaws without first receiving assent from the ratepayers in a referendum.[20]

Weeks advised council that the closures of streets was restricted to instances where they were clearly in the public interest and in this case it was arguable. If closing the streets benefited only the CPR, then clearly council did not have the power to close them. Furthermore, if council could not pay compensation out of current funds and had to borrow money, then the bylaws would have to be submitted to the ratepayers for approval. Despite opinions from three lawyers and a judge that what they were doing was wrong, council passed three bylaws on March 13, 1907, closing sections of 12 streets and avenues, including Church Street and James Street in the east ward.[21]

Council should have known better than to agitate the district judge. In September 1898, McCurry had the publishers of the *Burk's Falls Beacon* arrested for criminal libel over an editorial criticizing one of his court decisions.[22] Before long, McCurry hired his son James, of the North Bay legal firm of McGaughey & McCurry, to initiate legal action against the Town of Parry Sound.

Council appointed Gladman and dry goods merchant Harry Freer McQuire to meet with residents affected by the street closures and negotiate compensation arrangements on behalf of the town. This was a clear conflict of interest for Gladman, who was already representing the railway's interests.

Through Gladman, the CPR purchased everything on the west side of Church Street, from lot 8 on the original town plan north

Top: Looking north at the Canadian Pacific Railway yards in Parry Sound.
Bottom: Looking south at the Canadian Pacific Railway station in Parry
Sound. *Both photographs courtesy of the Parry Sound Public Library Historical
Collection,* top, *Album III #57,* bottom, *Album III #59.*

to Armstrong Street, including the five-acre Minnewawa Grove,
home of William Beatty Jr.'s widow, Isabella. C.A. Phillips purchased the buildings on these properties from the railway, including
the Beatty house, and moved them closer to the road during the
summer and fall of 1907 to make room for the station, water tower,
freight sheds and sidings. Construction also began on the 1,800-
foot steel viaduct and, in August, the town executed a ten-year
agreement with the CPR to provide the railway with water from
the town system for the steam locomotives, not to exceed 100,000
gallons per day.[23]

Council signed an agreement with the CPR on October 17, 1907, promising to create a new street—Park Lane—to overcome the objections of residents to the closure of Church Street. The agreement included passing a bylaw selling the railway the portions of the streets closed by bylaws 307 and 308 in exchange for $1,700. Council also agreed to pay compensation to property owners affected by the street closures.[24]

The first CPR train from Toronto to Winnipeg arrived at the Parry Sound station on Monday June 14, 1908, and two days later council passed Bylaw 329 authorizing the mayor to sign a deed conveying to the railway the closed portions of the streets. The railway purchased the property initially covered in Bylaw 306 directly from owner Patrick McCurry although the municipality eventually paid legal fees of $54.77 to McGaughey & McCurry with regards to McCurry's abandoned lawsuit against the town.[25]

Restoring tranquility came at a substantial cost to the municipal coffers. The creation of Park Lane in 1908 necessitated the purchase of property by the municipality, and the total compensation paid out to residents adversely affected by the street closures exceeded the $1,700 paid by the CPR. On July 14, 1908, concerned residents—including *North Star* publisher William Ireland, undertaker Alexander Logan and hardware merchant William Smith McKinley—petitioned the provincial municipal auditor requesting an investigation of the town's financial affairs.[26] Toronto chartered accountant Oscar Hudson spent several weeks in Parry Sound going through the ledgers kept by town treasurer John Henry Knifton before determining that there was a shortage of almost $4,000. Knifton made restitution and resigned in October 1908, but the special audit cost the municipality almost $1,200.

The arrival of the CPR not only created disharmony among residents, but it divided the municipality physically through the street closures. Although Mayor J.A. Johnson first spoke about the construction of two subways under the CPR tracks at Armstrong Street and Marion Avenue in his January 1907 inaugural address, council did not pass Bylaw 594 authorizing debentures for the Armstrong Street subway until May 18, 1926. Council expressed a willingness in September 1907 to spend $4,500 to build a subway at

Marion Avenue, but this was never done. As recently as October 19, 1997, 12-year-old Jesse Rachar was killed by a train while attempting to cross the CPR tracks between Marion Avenue and Station Street.[27]

13

Violence and Murder

LOCAL CITIZENS BELIEVED the extension of the railways of southern Ontario into the western District of Parry Sound would at last bring them the amenities of civilization. However, the construction of the railways through the area also brought a wave of violent crime that residents had not experienced—not even when the rowdy lumbermen hit town in the early spring to celebrate the end of a log drive. As the James Bay Railway and the Canadian Pacific Railway wound their way through the rugged terrain, there were numerous incidents of violence among the workmen. Crude knives forged in the railway blacksmith shops were the favourite weapons and stab wounds became the predominant injury.

Parry Sound's first murder was that of east ward resident Sarah Ann Anderson, who was shot in the back and forehead by her husband, Henry, in a fit of jealousy on the night of August 22, 1906.[1] He then committed suicide by shooting himself in his chest and head. But residents throughout the district were horrified when a 70-year-old farmer was brutally murdered and robbed in his own hotel room.

Michael James Davis, a highly respected citizen of Loring, came to town late in February 1910 to negotiate a bank loan of $300, a sizable fortune in those days, as well as conduct some other business. Why he took a room in the east ward rather than going to one of the hotels frequented by businessmen is uncertain. After all, the Bank of Ottawa was across the river at the town's main intersection.

The east ward was a magnet for transients and, about noon on February 28, 21-year-old Louis Young of Philadelphia, Pennsylvania, hit town accompanied by James Donaldson. They had first met in Lockport, New York, several weeks earlier and had been travelling companions ever since. Their mode of travel was a combination of stealing rides on freight trains and walking. On Monday morning they reached Rose Point via the Grand Trunk freight train and then walked into the east ward.

Michael James Davis, a highly respected citizen of Loring, murdered for just 65 cents. *Courtesy of the Parry Sound North Star.*

Young already had a criminal record in the United States for petty crimes and was known by police there under the alias Louis Peterson. Later, when in custody at the Parry Sound jail, he stated that he had been born in Atlantic City, New Jersey, and had no living relatives. His father, mother, brothers and sisters were all dead, he claimed. When he chose to work, his occupation was a steam driller.[2]

Young met Davis on the street Monday afternoon and unrolled a pathetic tale of hardship and starvation. Davis, a man with a big and generous heart, invited Young to his room at the hotel where he would give him some food. At the head of the stairs they were met by Joseph E. Rawson, manager of the Montgomery House, who asked Young where he was going, as he was not a registered guest. Davis replied that Young was a friend and was going to his room for some biscuits. Davis was described as a talkative old man and, no doubt, told the stranger more than he should have about himself, especially about the $300 loan he was to receive that day.

Nothing more was seen of either man until 11 p.m. At that time, Davis was observed walking up the Parry Sound Road towards the Montgomery House, which he entered and went to his room at once. Donaldson entered shortly after and asked the night porter, Chris Dixon, for Young. As Young was not known to Dixon, Donaldson offered a description and suggested he might be in Davis's room.

The Montgomery House on Parry Sound Road, where Louis Young brutally murdered and robbed Michael James Davis in February 1910. While
Young escaped the hangman's noose, Arthur Richard Cassan wasn't so
lucky. In February 1916, Cassan became the first prisoner executed at the
Parry Sound jail. He had been convicted of killing James Degeorge over a
horse, harness and buggy worth $160. *From* The Parry Sound Directory,
1898–99.

Dixon went up to Davis's room and tried the door, which was
locked, and, not hearing any sounds within, returned to Donaldson, saying that there must be some mistake and that he would
look at the register. While Dixon was examining the register, Young
came down the stairs and went into the washroom.

Donaldson noticed blood on Young's hands and told Dixon. The
two men rushed to Davis's room, the same one Dixon had been at
just a few moments before, and there they found the old man murdered. Davis was lying across the bed with his clothes on and his face
down. His head and face were terribly smashed and lacerated and
the pockets of his clothes were bloodstained and turned inside-out.

While Dixon and Donaldson were in Davis's room, Young escaped
from the hotel, but was soon pursued down the Parry Sound Road by

Rawson and several others. He was captured near the store of Milton Pearce, less than 200 yards from the scene of the crime. Young offered very little resistance and, after being thoroughly secured, he was marched back to the hotel. They summoned chief constable Harry Forder, who charged Young with Davis's murder and took him to the jail.[3] Ironically, when searched at the jail there was only 65 cents in Young's pockets.

The Supreme Court assizes at the Parry Sound courthouse always attracted considerable attention from area residents, especially when it was anticipated that the accused would receive a death sentence. On a spring day three years earlier, a packed

Louis Young, of Philadelphia, was sentenced to life in the Kingston Penitentiary. *Courtesy of the Parry Sound North Star.*

courtroom had witnessed Justice James Teetzel sentence railway labourer Frank Capelle to hang on August 1, 1907, for the fatal Christmas day stabbing of William Dow in Burpee Township. Residents of the town had been disappointed when Capelle won a reprieve until November 1 and then the Governor General commuted his sentence to life imprisonment at Kingston.[4]

On April 24, 1910, Young appeared before Chief Justice William Falconbridge and several dozen anxious spectators to stand trial for the cold-blooded murder of Michael Davis. However, due to the sudden disappearance of Donaldson, the main Crown witness, the case could not proceed.[5] Falconbridge issued a bench warrant for Donaldson's arrest at the request of Crown attorney Walter Lockwood Haight.

Young remained incarcerated in the district jail for another six months. On the morning of October 17, he was once more led into the Parry Sound courthouse, this time to stand trial before Justice Roger C. Clute. But, because Donaldson had still not been apprehended, Clute ordered the case adjourned until the following morning or until such time as the absent witness could be produced. It was not in the interests of justice to proceed without this witness, he told the court.

The case took an unexpected turn two days later. Young's lawyer, Francis Ronan Powell, KC, rose and changed his client's plea from "not guilty of murder" to "guilty of manslaughter." Powell then made an eloquent address to the court asking for a lenient sentence.[6] Justice Clute thanked Powell for his words, but stated that since the prisoner had pleaded guilty, the law must take its course. He then sentenced Young to the Kingston Penitentiary for life.

Early the next morning Louis Young was taken to Kingston in chains by deputy sheriff James E. Armstrong and Matthew Fisher, turnkey at the district jail. Also on his way to a 20-year-sentence at Kingston was Joseph Arthur Roy of Depot Harbour, convicted of raping a 13-year-old girl in McDougall.

14

The Northern Pioneers in
the First World War

AFTER RECORDING THE EVENTS OF JANUARY 19, 1904, in his pocket journal, Duncan Fraser Macdonald went on to speculate: "I wonder if the Pioneers will ever pull trigger in defence of the land of the Maple Leaf, the home of the beaver, rock, lake and river, and when."[1]

The 23rd Northern Pioneers were the local regiment of Canada's pre-war militia and had only recently been organized. In March 1903, the Department of Militia and Defence authorized the formation of a unit in the District of Parry Sound to fill the geographical gap between the company of the 35th Simcoe Foresters at Huntsville and the headquarters company of the 97th Algonquin Rifles at Sudbury.

The Northern Pioneers were activated as of September 1, 1903, with companies spread throughout the District at Parry Sound: Kearney, Sundridge, Powassan, Callander, Loring and North Bay.[2] Commanding the regiment was Lieutenant-Colonel John Henry Knifton, treasurer for the Town of Parry Sound. He had 24 years of militia experience with the Queen's Own Rifles of Canada and another nine years with the 36th Peel Regiment.

On September 15, 1909, John Bellamy Miller, president of the Parry Sound Lumber Company, was appointed commanding officer of the Northern Pioneers with the rank of lieutenant-colonel. For many years, Miller had been a captain in the Queen's Own Rifles of Canada and had transferred his commission to the Northern

Francis Pegahmagabow enlisted in the 23rd Northern Pioneers on August 13, 1914, just days after Britain and her colonies, including Canada, declared war on Germany. As a scout and a sniper, he would be awarded the Military Medal three times during his First World War service with the 1st Battalion. He served as chief of the Parry Island band council from 1921 to 1925 and 1942 to 1945. *Courtesy of Duncan Pegahmagabow.*

Pioneers, obtaining an immediate promotion to major.[3] He stepped down as commanding officer on June 26, 1920, to be replaced by Lieutenant-Colonel Reginald Heber James.

While the regiments in urban centres drilled in armories throughout the year, the scattered companies of the Northern Pioneers usually came together for two-week training camps. These were held during the summer months at regular army bases such as Niagara-on-the-Lake. Over time, the companies often moved from one village to another, often depending on the place of residence of the company commander. By 1914, the North Bay company had relocated to McKellar, while those in Callander and Sundridge had moved to Utterson and Bracebridge respectively.

When war was declared on Germany on August 4, 1914, the Canadian mobilization plan called for the six divisions of the militia to be converted to an active fighting force. In Parry Sound a tent camp was quickly erected on the agricultural grounds as a rallying point for members of the Northern Pioneers. However, barely 100 of the several hundred men on the regimental rolls showed up. Among the officers, Lieutenant Aubrey White Calquhoun Macdonald, the youngest son of diarist D.F. Macdonald, was determined to immediately go overseas with the men.

The activation of the Northern Pioneers was likely no slower than that of other militia units across the country. Perhaps, because of this situation, Colonel Sam Hughes, the minister of Militia and Defence, scrapped the entire Canadian mobilization plan and decided instead to raise new battalions that were to be known by number and thus did not perpetuate the traditional names of the militia regiments. Volunteers were to be concentrated at Valcartier, outside Quebec City, where no camp yet existed.

The Northern Pioneers boarded a Canadian Pacific Railway train at Parry Sound bound for Valcartier on August 20. "May they prove themselves to be soldiers, men and Canadians worthy of their names and blood," Macdonald wrote to conclude that day's journal entry.[4]

At the new camp the contingent was amalgamated with several hundred volunteers from Windsor, London, Sarnia, Stratford and Galt to form the 1st Battalion, otherwise known as the Western Ontario Regiment. The unit was placed under the command of 48 year-old Lieutenant-Colonel Frederic William Hill, a lawyer and former mayor of Niagara Falls, who, up until then, had been a major in the 44th Lincoln and Welland Regiment.

The Northern Pioneers who passed physical inspection received basic training in musketry and marching at Valcartier and sailed from Quebec City with the rest of the 31,000 men in the Canadian Expeditionary Force on September 25, 1914.[5] The Canadians were equipped and exercised on the Salisbury Plain during the wettest winter in living memory. Formed into the Canadian Division under Lieutenant-General Edwin A.H. Alderson, they were deemed ready for France at the end of January 1915.

By the time the Canadians arrived in Europe, the quick advances of the war's early months had bogged down. A continuous front extended between the opposing armies from the North Sea to neutral Switzerland. The Northern Pioneers in the 1st Battalion saw their first combat at the Ypres Salient, the last Belgian soil still in Allied hands. The battalion suffered 404 casualties in a counterattack against the German lines in front of the village of Pilckem early in the morning of April 23, 1915.[6]

Throughout the war, the 1st Battalion was involved in every major offensive including Givenchy in June 1915, Mount Sorrel in June

After serving 18 months in the 23rd Northern Pioneers, 19-year-old Andrew Chisholm Logan travelled to Toronto and enlisted in the 92nd Battalion, recruited largely by the 48th Highlanders of Canada, on August 20, 1915. While on leave from the 15th Battalion he probably visited relatives in Scotland and met Christine Chisholm Campbell Morton, whom he married in Montreal on June 30, 1921. *Courtesy of Dora Taylor Logan.*

1916, Courcelette in September 1916, Vimy Ridge in April 1917 and Amiens in August 1918. In all, the battalion was awarded 24 separate battle honours.

During the first year or so following the outbreak of the war, many young men left Parry Sound to join battalions being recruited in southern Ontario. The number of death notices in the *North Star* began to increase as these units reached the front lines. Not a week went by when a family wasn't mourning the violent death of one of its sons.

Lieutenant Aubrey Macdonald, who had been rejected at Valcartier and sent back to Parry Sound, tried again and went overseas as a lieutenant in the 58th Battalion, recruited in the area of Niagara-on-the-Lake. Reaching France in February 1916, he spent four and a half months in the trenches and took part in two general engagements.

"Sherman was right when he said 'war is hell.' That describes this place to a T," Macdonald wrote home in April 1916. "I for one will not be sorry when it is over. The sooner the better as one has to have nerves of steel to stand the wear and tear of it all."[7] Following the assault on Mount Sorrel in June, Macdonald was invalided to England suffering from shell shock. He was granted leave to Canada and was back in Parry Sound by September 1916.[8]

D.F. Macdonald's eldest son, Alexander Fraser, joined the Calgary-based 89th Battalion as a lieutenant on June 2, 1916. Another son,

William Ross Wilkinson, enlisted as a private on March 30, 1916, in the 94th Battalion, recruited in the Port Arthur area. Ross would die at Brandon, Manitoba, in June 1925, from injuries he received in France.[9]

About a year and a half into the war Prime Minister Robert Borden announced that Canada's armed forces would be doubled in size to half a million men. Three divisions of volunteers were already wallowing in the European mud by the end of 1915, but the plan called for another two. In order to increase rural enlistment, each district or county became a battalion recruiting area. The idea was that friends and neighbours would enlist together, knowing that they would be going overseas as a group. To heighten the feelings of camaraderie, prominent local citizens were appointed as officers.

An order of December 22, 1915, authorized the formation of the 162nd Battalion to recruit in the District of Parry Sound, and MP James Arthurs was appointed commanding officer with the rank of lieutenant-colonel.[10] Likewise, the 122nd Battalion would recruit in the District of Muskoka. Both units were intended to serve as part of the 5th Canadian Division.

From the start of 1916 local men joined the 162nd Battalion at recruiting offices scattered throughout the district. During the winter and spring the volunteers drilled in the streets of Parry Sound, leaving in May for yet more training at a temporary camp just outside Sundridge. The response of Parry Sounders to the war effort had always been fairly high, but the kinship offered by the 162nd Battalion attracted unlikely volunteers. One of these was Crown attorney Walter Lockwood Haight, a longtime officer in the Northern Pioneers.

Born into a staunch Loyalist family at Picton, Ontario, Haight received his education at Upper Canada College and Osgoode Hall Law School, from which he graduated at the Easter 1884 convocation. Haight became the first lawyer in Parry Sound and then served as the new municipality's first clerk for a number of years. In 1898, when Parry Sound became a separate judicial district with its own federally appointed judge, Haight became the first Crown attorney.

Haight resigned his appointment as paymaster of the Northern Pioneers in August 1916 and became supernumerary lieutenant to the 162nd Battalion.[11] When the unit moved to Niagara-on-

Left: In the fall of 1916, Parry Sound Crown attorney Walter Lockwood Haight purchased tickets and secured lodgings for his wife to spend the winter away from Parry Sound, and turned his law practice over to an administrator in preparation for sailing to England as a captain in the 162nd Battalion. Shortly before the battalion sailed from Halifax on October 31, the battalion's officers decided the 56-year-old Haight should stay at home as he was near the age limit for the rank he held. *Courtesy of Lockwood Haight.*

the-Lake for more advance training, the 56-year-old Crown attorney went along. The *North Star* reported in late September that Haight had qualified as a captain in the regular army.[12]

Haight purchased tickets and secured lodgings for his wife to spend the winter away from Parry Sound and turned his law practice over to an administrator in preparation of his own trip into the trenches.[13] When the 162nd Battalion sailed from Halifax for England aboard the *Caronia* on October 31, however, Haight was not among the 30 officers and 766 men. At the last moment it had been decided that he was too old and he was forced to return to Parry Sound, disappointed at missing his chance to fight.

"This is a mistake in our opinion as Captain Haight was largely responsible for getting up and recruiting the 162nd Battalion," lamented *North Star* editor William Ireland, who was a major in the 23rd Northern Pioneers. "We should suggest, if our suggestions count for anything with the military authorities, that as soon as the 162nd is sent overseas, authority be given to raise another battalion in these districts and that Captain Haight be given the temporary rank of lieutenant-colonel with authority to raise another battalion."[14]

Ireland was also disappointed that there had been 93 desertions from the battalion before it left Niagara-on-the-Lake for Halifax, although he pointed out that none of them were Parry Sound boys. Always a hardline patriot, he wrote:

> People who will hide or harbor a coward are no better than the cowards who in the face of danger sneak away, and the punishment for aiding these men to avoid arrest is severe. It has been the practice of the courts to send deserters to the penitentiary, but these fellows would rather go to jail than fight as it is and instead they should be sent right into the forefront of the battle lines. If the cowards knew that desertion meant death or fighting in the trenches at once there would be fewer desertions.[15]

The men of the 162nd Battalion were to engage in more training in England before deployment to the battlefields of western Europe, where Canada already had four divisions in combat. Instead, Brigadier-General Arthur Currie, commander of the Canadian Corps, decided to disband the 5th Division. He augmented each of the 48 battalions already serving in the field with men drawn from the battalions newly arrived from Canada.

The 162nd Battalion ceased to exist as of January 4, 1917, and the men were transferred to the 4th Reserve Battalion, which provided reinforcements to the 1st, 18th and 47th Battalions. A number of the men ended up in the 1st Battalion with the survivors of the Northern Pioneers.

Recruiting in Parry Sound continued as other battalions set up tents in the town to draw men for overseas service. The 230th Battalion from Hull, Quebec, sought French-Canadian volunteers in September 1916. The *North Star* advised: "If you are French-Canadian go and enlist. If you are not, go and visit the boys of the 230th and encourage them by your presence and friendship."[16]

The 227th and 228th both made recruiting drives in town in December 1916. Captain G. Macdonald, chaplain of the 228th, spoke at Trinity Anglican Church in the morning service and St.

Andrew's Presbyterian Church in the evening. Likewise, Captain Irvine, chaplain of the 228th, preached in St. James' Methodist church in the morning and the Fellowship Baptist Church that evening. Later that night, prominent local citizens spoke at the Princess Theatre before a packed house. Lieutenant-Colonel Knifton and Judge Francis Ronan Powell urged all able-bodied young men of the town to enlist at once.[17]

Parry Sounders continued to enlist and the *North Star* continued to run the names of those killed and wounded in the fighting. By the end of 1918, the four-year conflict had bled Canada dry by claiming 60,000 dead and leaving over 70,000 disabled veterans.

At 11 a.m. on November 11, 1918, the battlefields fell silent as the armistice came into effect. Owing to the difference in time zones, celebrations began in Parry Sound at 5:30 a.m. with a huge bonfire at the intersection of Seguin and James streets. The power-house whistle blew continuously until 8 a.m. and the *North Star* recorded that the fire bell rang intermittently during the whole day "until one thought there was something wrong when it had stopped for the supper hour."[18]

A parade through town began at the fire hall, using every vehicle "to be had or stolen." All the town's bands led the parade followed by 50 wounded veterans who had been released from service. The *North Star* commented that the parade was so long the bands passed under the CPR bridge on the Great North Road even before the tail had left the fire hall.

One by one Parry Sound soldiers returned home during the spring of 1919. In February 1919, council passed a resolution that all returned soldiers disembarking from trains at Parry Sound for rural communities be met by the night constable and accommodated with bed and breakfast at the town's expense.[19]

The Northern Pioneers remained active in the district until December 14, 1936, when the regiment's nine companies amalgamated with companies B, C and D of the existing Algonquin Regiment. On July 22, 1940, the Algonquin Regiment received orders to mobilize for active service in the Second World War and later served overseas with the 4th Canadian Armoured Division.

15

The Day the Dam Burst

IN JUNE 1919, Parry Sound residents endorsed, by a margin of 315 to 57, a bylaw to raise $150,000 for the construction of a new hydro-generating plant in the town. Little did they know the constant bickering in council and the endless additional costs that their decision would bring. Beginning with the inaugural meeting of the new council in January 1920, Mayor Richard Reece Hall was in constant conflict with the chairman of the light and power committee, Councillor Harry Freer McQuire, who wanted to construct numerous concrete storage dams along the Seguin River watershed to hold back water for the power plant. Hall constantly protested that the town not only couldn't afford the lavish projects, but it also wouldn't be able to pay the heavy damages for drowned land claims from property owners.

By the end of the year Hall decided to leave municipal politics and not seek another term as mayor, but he spoke publicly about McQuire at the December 1920 meeting to nominate council candidates. Most taxpayers seemed to side with the mayor, who was also the sitting MPP for Parry Sound:

> Mr. McQuire stated that he had not run the council this year, that the council for 1920 was one of the best we have ever had. This did not appear to be the impression held by a number at the meeting who hooted and hissed Mr. McQuire and for a few minutes refused to allow him to go on, telling him to "sit down." Mr. McQuire stated that the mayor had been the troublemaker

in the council and that his actions did not allow of due respect being given to him by some of the councillors.... [1]

While the voters did return two members of the council of 1920 who sought re-election, McQuire received only 99 votes and lost his seat.[2]

Just over two months later, on March 21, 1921, a 30-foot section of the west-wing wall of the power dam gave way under the pressure of flood waters from heavy rains during the previous week. Several men were in the powerhouse as the raging torrent swept through, submerging the generators and all the machinery under ten feet of water. While chief operator W.J. Lockhart jumped through a window and escaped to safety, waterworks superintendent George Murray clung to a window frame until rescued from the top of the building by rope. The cost of repairing the dam and putting the power plant back in order would amount to some $30,000.[3] There was also an additional $1,600 expense to purchase the home of Joseph Farrer's widow, which had been seriously undermined by the flooding.[4]

In December 1921, voters approved a bylaw for the creation of a public utilities commission, consisting of the mayor and two elected commissioners, to manage the waterworks and the power plant.[5] Mayor William James Bowes Beatty saw to it that there would be no more squabbling in council involving these two revenue-producing departments. The bylaw stated that the commissioner elected with the largest number of votes in the January 1922 municipal election would sit for a two-year term, while the other commissioner would be in office for one year. Subsequent elections held every two years would always result in one new commissioner to serve a two-year term.

Parry Sound had access to electricity since July 1894, when local businessmen William Henry Pratt, Samuel Armstrong Jr., John Galna and William Beatty Jr. converted the former Beatty gristmill, on the Seguin River at Cascade Street, into a steam-driven electric generating station with the installation of two boilers and a two-cycle generator capable of 150 horsepower. The new Parry Sound Electric Light Company strung miles of transmission lines through town, wired several businesses and obtained, in January 1896, a contract to provide the town with electric street lighting, originally for $17 per lamp per annum.[6] New electric street lamps replaced the coal oil lamps which had been in use in the downtown since 1888.

The Corporation of the Town of Parry Sound acquired the assets of the Parry Sound Electric Light Company in May 1901, after ratepayers approved (118 to six in a referendum) a bylaw to issue debentures to raise the $24,000. The old gristmill was torn down in July 1906 and a new generating facility built that used the Seguin River to drive water wheels and dynamos.[7]

Richard Reece Hall, MPP for Parry Sound. *Courtesy of AO, RG15 54-1 AO 1297.*

When Hall was elected mayor in January 1919, he had definite ideas. He felt that in order for Parry Sound to grow, it needed to attract industry and modern industries required electricity, and lots of it. No stranger to municipal politics, Hall had been a councillor in 1914 and 1915. He lost the 1918 mayoralty race by a slim margin to Henry Milton Purvis.

Richard Reece Hall was born in 1857 at Macclesfield, England, and in Manchester he took up silk manufacturing, designing and card cutting, and also the study of textile machinery—especially weaving and looms. Although married in 1878, Hall emigrated to Canada alone in 1882 and was followed by his wife, Annis, with their two small children almost two years later. The Halls settled at the north end of Parry Sound, where they farmed cattle, pigs, chickens, ducks and geese, and raised a family of three boys and two girls. *The Parry Sound Directory, 1898–99* lists Hall's occupation as a music teacher.[8]

Around 1906, Hall opened the granite gneiss quarry on Mill Lake. It is still operated today by grandson Wilfred (also a former mayor) and has provided employment to five generations of the family at one time or another. He also manufactured concrete block and worked as a contractor on several local construction projects. During construction of the CPR bridge, he had 24 teams of horses hauling gravel from Mill Lake to the site for the concrete piers.

In February 1919, council decided to rebuild Mill Lake dam, install a new power plant sufficient to supply 1,400 horsepower and raise the power dam to the height necessary to generate the required head of water. Council requested the Hydro Electric Power Commission of Ontario send an engineer to prepare a proposal, but also asked the Toronto consulting engineers Mitchell and Mitchell to do likewise.[9]

Mayor Hall had a good deal of faith in the firm of Mitchell and Mitchell. In March he wrote a letter to the *North Star* defending the reputation of the firm. Brigadier-General Charles Hamilton Mitchell was dean of the Faculty of Applied Science and Engineering at the University of Toronto, from which he had graduated in 1892.[10] He had worked as municipal engineer in Niagara Falls, New York, and Niagara Falls, Ontario, during which time he developed expertise in hydraulic and hydroelectric power engineering. Since 1906 he had been in a consulting engineering practice in Toronto, in partnership with his brother, Percival H. Mitchell. The firm was engaged primarily in the design and construction of power plants throughout Ontario and the Canadian West. A proviso to his agreement to take on the deanship, following overseas service during the First World War, was that he would do so only if permitted to devote one-third of his time to his private practice during the teaching session and a portion of the summer holidays, as well.[11]

By April 1919, council had accepted a $139,450 proposal from Mitchell and Mitchell and rejected that from the Hydro Electric Power Commission for $262,540. The Mitchell proposal envisioned using the old plant's generator, capable of 450 kilowatts or 600 horsepower, and a new generator, which together would produce the required 1,400 horsepower. The two proposals were radically different. Whereas the Hydro proposal utilized a vertical type of turbine, which called for a more massive and costly installation of concrete, that of Mitchell and Mitchell had a horizontal type of

Construction of the Mitchell and Mitchell-designed generating facility by W.M. Fletcher & Co. began in 1919. The old plant built in 1906 stands to the right. *Courtesy of the Parry Sound Public Library Historical Collection, VF IV community services.*

turbine that required less elaborate headworks.[12]

Having the support of local voters to raise $150,000 through the sale of debentures for construction of expanded hydro-generating facilities in a referendum, council awarded the contracts on the project. Canadian Westinghouse Company received a $21,060 contract for electrical work, while council accepted a $19,270 tender from the Boving Hydraulic and Engineering Company for hydraulic equipment. Council awarded a $64,700 contract to W.M. Fletcher & Company for all the general construction.[13]

Work on the dam and power plant continued for more than a year. Early in construction there were accusations that the construction was substandard, but the *North Star* tried to put the rumours to rest:

> In speaking to two of the contractor's representatives we were informed that tests of cement and gravel were regularly made by the engineers and no complaint had been made as to quality of any material used.
>
> One of the officials said: "We hear all this foolish talk and on several occasions have endeavored to find out who made the accusation regarding bad gravel or bad cement, but our informant either won't say who said so or can't remember and as these kinds of stories are always rife in municipal works, we never bother about them. We don't want to have every Tom, Dick and Harry hanging

around but if any intelligent ratepayer cares to call on us or the
engineer we have no doubt he will find the latter gentleman ready
to show him all the tests on material that will satisfy anyone that
we know our business and are paying attention to it."[14]

In the January 1920 municipal election, R.R. Hall won a second
term as mayor, defeating two other candidates by a wide margin.
Some two months earlier he had also run in the provincial general election as the liberal candidate for the Parry Sound
constituency, soundly defeating the Conservative incumbent,
Joseph Edgar of Sundridge.[15] Across the province, the Liberals
won 27 seats, becoming the official opposition to the minority
government of the United Farmers of Ontario.

In Hall's inaugural address to the new municipal council, he
expressed concern that the town's light and power department
would require $12,000, or more, than in the previous year to meet
the interest on the debentures. He added that in 1906, when the
town built the previous power plant, three men were employed
while there were now seven men on the payroll who were each
being paid three times as much.[16]

At this first meeting, Councillor McQuire caused immediate fric-
tion with Hall by effectively usurping the mayor's privilege of naming
the members of the various council committees. When Mayor Hall
presented his proposal for the composition of the committees,
McQuire had his own resolution ready. While the mayor wanted the
light and power committee chaired by Councillor John Perks, council passed McQuire's resolution which appointed him chairman.[17]

McQuire had arrived in Parry Sound in June 1898, when he
took over two vacant stores in the Ansley Block on James Street
and opened a dry goods store. The father of four boys and a daughter, he had previously been a merchant in Webbwood, Ontario.[18]
He ran unsuccessfully in municipal politics several times before
being elected mayor for the year 1917, during which he advocated
the construction of a new power plant. Defeated in the mayoralty
races in both 1918 and 1919, he won a seat as a councillor in 1920.

From that inaugural meeting, Mayor Hall found himself at odds
with McQuire. While Hall believed there was an ample supply of

water to run the new plant, McQuire was convinced the town had to build storage dams to meet any sudden demand for power to the extent of the full capacity of both generators. McQuire introduced a motion in February that civil engineer Alexander Dick prepare plans for storage dams at Horn Lake and Isabella Lake, but Hall convinced council to defeat it. McQuire wrote to the *North Star* to explain his reasoning:

> In order to build such dams under the most favorable conditions and thereby save money to the town it is necessary that whoever has the contract, he will have to draw in material during the dry season. Provided any such dams were built during the summer of 1920 they would not be of any use as storage until the summer of 1921. Having these facts into consideration I moved a motion on February 2 to that effect; this was ruled out of order by the mayor and a notice of motion demanded. On February 16 I again moved that Mr. Dick prepare estimates and plans of Horn and Isabella Lakes. This motion was voted down. The mover and seconder of this motion have therefore done their duty.[19]

Mayor Hall vigorously protested a motion put forth by McQuire in March 1920 proposing the electric light committee be allowed to tell the owners of property neighbouring Lorimer Lake that the committee intended to close the dam at Tait's Rapids to hold and store water for the power plant. Council passed the resolution, despite Hall's objections that the town would be inundated with damage claims from the owners whose properties had been flooded.

Seven months later council would pass a resolution to allow the Hydro Electric Power Commission of Ontario arbitrate the claims on behalf of the municipality, which would issue debentures to cover the costs.[20] Mayor Hall expressed concern that the town was having trouble selling the debentures it had already issued. He also wanted to know where the money would come from to pay the interest.

The Corporation of the Town of Parry Sound did have the legal authority to build dams far beyond the boundaries of the municipality. A January 1914 bylaw authorized the council to acquire the property and capital stock of the Parry Sound River Improvement

Looking west at the Parry Sound generating facilities and the power dam. The log chute runs from the top of the dam. *Courtesy of the Parry Sound Public Library Historical Collection, Album II #8.*

Company, originally incorporated in May 1884 to construct and maintain dams, booms and slides and all other works necessary to facilitate the movement of timber down various rivers, including the Seguin River and its tributaries. For $4,500, the town acquired these rights and properties for the purpose of generating electric power.[21]

McQuire infuriated Hall in May by advising that the electric light committee felt that electrical superintendent Gibson Groves should be dismissed. The committee felt Groves, an electrician, would be incapable of overseeing the new plant as he did not have the expertise to regulate the flow of water through the dams north of Mill Lake.

McQuire wanted Groves replaced with Harry Roland Reed, a 28-year-old veteran of the First World War, who claimed to have about three years experience working for the Hydro Electric Power Commission of Ontario. Although Reed did graduate from the University of Toronto in June 1920 with a Bachelor of Applied Science degree, he had benefited greatly from the special concessions granted to soldiers returning from overseas.[22] Reed wanted $200 per month to take the job, while Groves was earning just $15 a month more than the $120 paid to night constable Albert Griffith.

Hall stated that Mr. Groves had held our electric light plant together for some 18 years. In one year previous to Mr. Groves assuming control, we had four superintendents. Mr. Groves made the plant a paying proposition and had kept it running all these years excepting in cases of lack of water. We have had as high a surplus as $11,000 under his management and now when he had a chance to operate an up-to-date plant he is, without a complaint, asked for his resignation. He is to be rewarded by being fired. About the only men who want his resignation are the electric light committee. Instead of giving a superannuation for his long service, we kick him out.[23]

Despite Mayor Hall's protests and a council chamber packed with concerned citizens, five members of council voted to hire Reed. Only Hall and Councillor John Perks voted against the resolution. When Hall complained that he had not been invited to attend meetings of the electric light committee, Councillor William Went stated that it was impossible for him to attend due to his always being in Toronto. "Apparently the committee made up their minds to push this matter through and did not desire to and would not give an explanation," Perks said. "The whole thing was cut and dried some time ago."[24]

A short time after the council hired Reed, residents of the town were astonished to learn that Groves also had to be kept on the municipal payroll because Reed was not a qualified electrician. They were also alarmed that costs for the general construction by W.M. Fletcher & Company had nearly doubled over the terms of the original tender accepted by council. Residents demanded answers at a public meeting held at the Regent Theatre, at which Mayor Hall shared his views:

Mr. Hall again spoke and said we were now going to have a man in the power house who would command $200 a month, and also a man as superintendent at the same salary, whereas Mr. Groves had been dismissed as being incompetent. He was competent to run the plant, and we were being put to a great expense and getting nothing for it. The [electric light] committee said Mr. Groves was not superintendent until they found he was the only man who could connect up, and then they said he was superintendent.[25]

A 30-foot section of the west-wing wall of the power dam gave way on
March 21, 1921, under the pressure of flood waters from heavy rains during
the previous week. *Courtesy of the Parry Sound Public Library Historical Collection.*

In September, the firm of W.M. Fletcher & Company filed a lawsuit against the town for payment, and council hired Toronto lawyer
Robert Mackay to file a defence.[26] As early as February 1920, the
firm had threatened to sue over work completed on the Beveridge
Creek dam, but for which they had not been paid.[27]

By December consulting engineers Mitchell and Mitchell had still
not issued a final certificate on the concrete work on the dam and
power house, but rumours began circulating once again that it was
substandard. In November, the plant had to be shut down when
two planks slipped through the trash gates and damaged the blades
on one of the turbines. Inspection of the concrete flume showed at
least 20 wheelbarrows of gravel and sand had worn off the floor of
the conduit since it went into operation some five months earlier.[28]
In October, Reed had advised the town not to accept the work completed by W.M. Fletcher & Company on the Beveridge Creek dam
because the old portion had been left standing on gravel.[29]

On March 1, 1921, three weeks before the dam gave way, council passed a resolution offering to pay W.M Fletcher & Company

the sum of $10,000 as payment in full for all outstanding claims.[30] Faced with a court battle and mounting legal fees, council felt this was the best solution. Mayor Beatty, who was returned to office unopposed, explained the decision to voters in December 1921:

> There was a disaster at the electric plant. He did not know who was to blame, perhaps the construction and design, but he thought mostly the design. The town had made a settlement with the contractors at $10,500 which our solicitor, Mr. Ludwig, considered to be a very favourable one for us. The sum the contractors claimed was $17,000. The law stated that the final estimate was the basis of payment, and the engineers gave the latter sum as the final settlement. We were informed that there had never been a case where an action against an engineer was successful. There is apparently no way to reach the engineers. The town had to pay.[31]

During 1921, Harry McQuire and his son James Callaghan McQuire became involved in a uranium mine in Conger Township, with connections to the Standard Chemical Company of Pittsburgh and the Radium Company of Colorado.[32] Whether McQuire became rich through the venture is unclear, but he soon moved away from Parry Sound to reside in the Forest Hill neighbourhood of Toronto. Harry Roland Reed resigned his position in May 1921 and returned to Toronto, where he became a teacher at Riverdale Technical School and later Danforth Technical School.[33] In August 1921, council appointed W. J. Lockhart as the electrical superintendent at an annual salary of $2,100. Lockhart, who had first come to Parry Sound as a Canadian Westinghouse Company employee to install the generators in the new power plant, would hold the position of electrical superintendent for almost three decades, until his retirement in November 1959.[34]

16

A Train Robbery, Gunplay and the Inevitable Murder

O N THE MORNING OF SATURDAY, AUGUST 18, 1928, the 3,500 residents of Parry Sound awoke to find the town flooded with Toronto reporters covering a series of events tailor-made for the circulation war raging between the daily newspapers in the city. Correspondents from *The Daily Star*, *The Daily Mail and Empire* and *The Evening Telegram* came for the details of a story that included all the elements necessary to tantalize readers, including a train robbery, gunplay, a villain, local heroes, a car chase and the inevitable murder.

The melodrama began shortly after midnight when two masked and armed men climbed aboard an eastbound transcontinental of the Canadian Pacific Railway. During a mail exchange at Romford Junction, some seven miles south of Sudbury, the men entered the mail car and confronted the three clerks working there.

After ordering the clerks to stand in the corner with their backs to the interior of the car, the two bandits proceeded to tear open registered letters and stuffed those containing money and other valuables into their pockets. The two remained on the train when it made a stop at Byng Inlet for water and coal. As the train pulled into Parry Sound, the two bandits ceased their looting and vanished into the darkness as quickly as they had come.[1]

Shortly after 3:00 a.m. the stillness of the night around the Laird home on Gibson Street was interrupted by attempts to start the vehicle in the driveway. As the car roared away, a sleepy Haughton Laird awoke his elder brother Walter to inform him the blue Buick coupe belonging to their visiting brother-in-law, Lee Lyman, had been stolen from the driveway. The two brothers quickly persuaded Harold Joseph Rolland, a boarder employed at their older brother Frank's jewellery store, to pursue the stolen Buick using his own vehicle.

When the Laird brothers and Rolland finally climbed into the chase car, they must have been at least 15 minutes behind the stolen automobile. The men were successful, however, in tracing the tire tracks of the heavy coupe through the rain-moistened gravel roads of Parry Sound and onto the old Northern Colonization Road.

Ten miles outside of Parry Sound, the road (now Highway 124) curved sharply before it crossed Harris Creek at Waubamik. Here, the pursuers found the Buick with the headlights turned off, seemingly abandoned in a ditch. The driver, unfamiliar with the road, had apparently failed to round the curve and the vehicle crossed the opposing lane to rest on the far side of the road. The pursuers passed beyond the stolen Buick for about 75 yards before turning around and parking across the narrow bridge so as to block any northward escape by the car thief.

At this point, a car occupied by two men and a woman, also travelling northward on the road towards Bolger, came out of the darkness. Upon explaining the situation, the driver, Henry Fraser, a Toronto accountant, joined them on the short walk back to the stolen car. By this time, Rolland, Haughton and Walter Laird had armed themselves respectively with a jack handle, a wrench and a large spring, in anticipation of a possible confrontation with the car thief.[2]

The pursuers returned to the stolen car to discover a scene they had not anticipated. The stuck vehicle's headlights were now on and, in the glaring brightness, local farmer Claude Jackson was struggling to pull the car free with a horse. His father, Thomas, was pushing the vehicle from behind, while a third man was behind the steering wheel gunning the engine.

While Walter Laird walked towards the senior Jackson and explained that the car had been stolen from his brother-in-law, Rolland and Haughton Laird approached the driver of the vehicle, inquiring if he needed help. The man, however, obviously

Inspectors Albert H. Ward and William H. Stringer inspect the crime scene following the removal of the Lyman vehicle. The photograph was taken looking west towards Parry Sound with the Jackson farm visible in the background. The Lyman car is parked between the house and the barn. *Courtesy of AO, RG 23-35 William H. Stringer scrapbook #5, page 85, box 8.*

overheard the conversation between Walter Laird and the farmer and made a sudden movement of his hand inside his jacket.

In a bluff, Rolland shouted to Haughton to "put the gun on him, quick" and the youth pointed the wrench. In the darkness, the car thief could not see that the two men were actually armed with makeshift weapons and slowly he got out the driver's door with his hands raised in the air.

"Don't shoot," he muttered. "I'm coming out."

Once free of the confines of the car, however, the thief made a sudden dash to the rear of the vehicle and a moment later the calm of the night air was pierced by a rapid burst of gunfire.

Walter Laird heard three shots fired as quickly as the gunman could pull the trigger. Furiously angry, and forgetting any risk to himself, he lunged for the gun. There was another shot and Laird felt a searing pain in the left side of his chest. Then the force of his rush knocked the car thief to the ground and Walter Laird fell on top of him, still struggling for the gun.[3]

Another shot echoed in the stillness of the night, but this time the bullet harmlessly hit the mud. Walter Laird heard several clicks as the trigger was pulled again and again, but the weapon had jammed, rendering it useless to the man who was still trying to break free. At that moment, Haughton Laird, recovering from his surprise, ran over and hit the gunman on the head with his wrench.

Panting and reeling from his brush with death, Walter Laird stood up and steadied himself against the Buick as Haughton sat on the unconscious prisoner. It was only then that Haughton saw 62-year-old Thomas Jackson stumbling up the road towards his farm with his hands over his face. After a few steps, he collapsed just inside the gateway leading to the house.

By Saturday afternoon news of the tragedy at the Jackson farm had spread throughout the surrounding area. Curious people gathered at the crime scene to gaze at the Lyman car, which was still in the ditch, and to speculate about the events of that morning. Tourists even brought their cameras and took snapshots, to return home with unusual, if somewhat ghoulish, mementos of their summer vacation.

The captured man told police that his name was John Burowski and he had been born in Poland, although he had been in Canada for almost 15 years. About a week earlier, he said, he had left Toronto to work as a carpenter at Bala. He had been in Parry Sound for about two days and was walking towards North Bay when two men, a mustachioed Swede and a clean-shaven Italian, picked him up in a car.[4]

The Swede was driving too fast and he ditched the car. This man sent him to the farmhouse to get help and gave him the gun and four ammunition clips in case he ran into trouble. The prisoner said the $1,805 in cash and the other items in his pockets, which police later linked to the train robbery, had been on the front seat when he returned to the vehicle with the farmer and his son.

More than a dozen provincial constables, drawn from as far away as Sudbury, were ordered to the Jackson farm when it was realized that the train robbery and the shooting were connected. The constables scoured the bush with citizen volunteers and maintained roadblocks on all roads out of the area. *The Evening Telegram* reported one motorist who refused to stop for police at Waubamik had his gasoline tank punctured by gunfire.[5]

Offering rides to strangers quickly became a thing of the past for motorists travelling the lonely bush roads. Tourists, particularly, were not keen to drive slowly or halt for conversations with strangers, even in daylight. Belief was widespread that the second bandit's only chance of escaping would be to hold up a driver of a car and take the vehicle.

By Sunday night the 22 cells of the Parry Sound jail were filled with drifters who had been arrested on charges of vagrancy and trespassing. All were interrogated about the train robbery. It became so crowded that cots were placed in the corridors, but police were reluctant to release any of the men, fearing they would immediately return to the railway tracks and thus hinder the search.[6]

On Monday evening, Haughton Laird and Harold Rolland, as well as Claude Jackson, told a coroner's inquest what they knew about the circumstances of Thomas Jackson's death. Dr. Charles Scholfield Appelbe stated that Jackson had sustained a puncture wound in the neck from a bullet and died from suffocation induced by blood in his trachea. OPP inspector Ernest Charles Gurnett testified that Jackson had been shot by a fragment of a .45 calibre bullet, which had apparently struck the steel frame of the Buick's rear window and richochetted. Constable Robert George Beatty said Burowski was already restrained with ropes when he arrived at the Jackson farm and the Colt .45, wrestled away from him by Walter Laird, lay on the table along with four fully-loaded ammunition magazines.

Dr. Milton Henry Limbert, the district coroner, said that he did not find it necessary to wait for Walter Laird to appear before the inquest. He was a patient at St. Joseph's Hospital, where he was recovering from the gunshot wound in his chest. As allowed under statute when agreement was reached between the coroner and the Crown attorney, a jury had not been empanelled, and Dr. Limbert immediately gave his verdict that Jackson had come to his death from a wound inflicted as a result of a bullet fired from a pistol in the hands of John Burowski.[7]

At the preliminary hearing on Friday, August 25, the witnesses who had appeared at the coroner's inquest were recalled once again with no real change in their stories. An additional witness was 24-year-old Walter Laird, who had just been released from hospital and had trouble getting to the witness box. He told essentially the same story as his brother and Rolland. Claude Jackson, constable Beatty and inspector Gurnett all repeated their earlier testimony. The three mail-car clerks stated that Burowski had been one of the two men who robbed their train on the morning of August 18. After hearing the evidence, police magistrate James Dean Broughton concluded there was enough evidence for Burowski to stand trial at the fall assize of the Supreme Court in Parry Sound.[8]

The trial of John Burowski opened in the Parry Sound courthouse on the morning of Tuesday, September 25, with a request from his lawyer, John Roland Hett of the local law firm of Weeks & Hett. He petitioned for an adjournment of at least a month or the relocation of the proceedings to another assize, in the event that the Crown was unwilling to postpone the trial. He outlined several reasons for his request, beginning with the fact that his client had been moved to Toronto's Don Jail after the preliminary hearing.

As Burowski had limited funds, the distance impeded lawyer-client consultations and also prevented Hett from taking to several witnesses to Toronto in order to identify Burowski as a man they had seen in Parry Sound on a number of occasions, the last instance of which had been just prior to the mail-car robbery at Romford Junction on August 18. Hett also insisted that despite repeated requests to do so, the Department of the Attorney General had returned the accused to Parry Sound less than 24 hours before the start of the trial, leaving inadequate time to prepare a proper defence.[9]

Crown attorney Walter Lockwood Haight maintained that none of Hett's arguments for an adjournment were worth considering, with the possible exception of that concerning the witnesses. Even this point he refuted as irrelevant because the issue at hand was whether Burowski was guilty of the murder of Thomas Jackson and not whether he was involved in the mail-car robbery. Justice William Henry Wright agreed with Haight that there was no valid reason for either postponing the trial or allowing a change of venue.

Burowski was ushered into the courtroom. Standing in the dock, he stoically entered a plea of "not guilty" to the charge of murder.

Hett protested once again that the trial could not proceed because he needed time to secure the witnesses essential to his defence. Justice Wright granted a continuance until 9:30 on the following morning, and Haight assured Hett that subpoenas would be issued immediately for those witnesses whose testimony he required. *The Daily Star* reported that the defence planned to call 11 witnesses.[10]

The trial resumed Wednesday as scheduled and continued until eight that night. Although most of the testimony and evidence had already been presented at the preliminary hearing in August, the day was punctuated by eloquent pleas, counter-pleas and arguments both for and against the accused. While Haight presented a case to prove Burowski guilty of the murder of Thomas Jackson, Hett tried his best to convince the jury otherwise. He tried to persuade the jury that shots fired from the bushes after Burowski was already subdued may have killed Jackson, but in the event that one of the accused's bullets did hit the farmer, he had not been the intended victim. Burowski had been shooting at the Laird brothers in self-defence, believing they had firearms.

Burowski ended up being the only defence witness and he stuck to the same story he had told since the beginning:

> After I went and got the two Jacksons and the horse the two fellows had disappeared and when I called no one answered. As I got into the car to help get it out of the ditch, I found a roll of money and some jewelry and put them in my pocket.
>
> As they were trying to get the car out, four men came up. One of them asked me if I needed help. I said 'no sir' and then one of them jumped on the running board and said 'hands up.' I put up my hands and got out of the car, on the left side, and saw one of the fellows coming around the front of the car, and then somebody shot and hit me in the finger. Then I fired four shots, the first one by accident. The second I fired towards the man who was coming around the front of the car. The third hit the young boy, and I fired a fourth into the road as I lay on the ground with one of the fellows on top of me. If I had been going

to shoot somebody, I would have shot the fellows were after me, and not the man who was being my friend.[11]

Haight tried to show Burowski to be an unreliable witness and to do this he spent a good deal of time during his cross-examination delving into the prisoner's background, often drawing evasive responses. Haight flashed a poster describing Burowski as a wanted man, but the prisoner refused to admit that the front- and side-view pictures were of him. Fingerprints sent to the United States showed Burowski, alias Stanley Zinwz, alias John Bryda, had served a three-year term for burglary in New York before being released in 1920. He had then been sentenced to five to seven years of imprisonment in Pennsylvania for assault and battery with intent to kill, but escaped in July 1926.

The OPP photographed and repeatedly finger-printed John Burowski. While the RCMP had no record of any convictions in Canada, the OPP received word on September 11, 1928 that he had served time in the United States for assault with intent to kill, as well as burglary. *Courtesy of the OPP.*

Following his cross-examination, Haight called the three mail-car clerks—Harry M. Macdonald, Charles E. Clark and Michael J. Doyle—to refute Burowski's claim that he had been in Parry Sound when the robbery had been carried out. All three men swore that Burowski had appeared in the mail car at Romford Junction and left in Parry Sound about three on the morning of August 18. Haight's intention was to show that Burowski was being untruthful when he said he knew nothing about the train robbery and had only been a passenger in the Buick.

The calling of the three clerks as witnesses against Burowski drew vehement objections from Hett. He argued that his request for an adjournment at the start of the proceedings to permit him time to secure witnesses to testify that Burowski had no part in the mail-car robbery had been denied on the grounds that the trial was concerned only with the Jackson murder.

On the morning of September 27, Haight and Hett both made their summations. "The Crown is trying to prove that instead of watching Laird, who was rushing at him, Burowski turned around and started firing across the back of the car. That is not logical," Hett told the jury. "The shots across the back of the car came from somebody else. You know someone else was shooting. The Crown witnesses have told you that."[12]

The prisoner watched his lawyer with a blank, unchanging expression, occasionally clenching his jaw firmly and blinking. He sat motionless with arms folded. Hett closed his address after one hour by describing the entire Crown case as "resembling a house of cards, reared on inconclusive facts."[13]

The jury retired at 12:30 p.m. and returned to the courtroom just under three hours later. While Burowski had sat stoically through the trial, he showed the first sign of emotion as he stood in the dock and heard the jury foreman read out the verdict of guilty. At the fatal word, Burowski clenched his jaw and a tear rolled down his cheek.

When asked by Justice Wright if he had anything to say, Burowski made several ineffectual attempts to speak. He then said in a low voice, "I believe I have got no justice. I am not guilty of this charge." Justice Wright pronounced that Burowski be executed for his crime on December 7.

Long before the trial, preparations had begun for the residents of Parry Sound to honour Walter Laird, Haughton Laird and Harold J. Rolland for their bravery in capturing the dangerous Burowski without the benefit of firearms. On September 6, Parry Sound clerk-treasurer Harold Polkinghorne wrote to Attorney General William H. Price that the council had recently passed a resolution to officially bring the actions of the three local heroes to his attention, and also to the attention of the postmaster-general of Canada and CPR president Edward Wentworth Beatty. The council, he wrote, intended to make presentations on behalf of the citizens of Parry Sound.[14]

As early as August 25, Crown attorney Haight had written to the deputy attorney general suggesting that the province also pay rewards of $1,000 to Walter and $500 each to Haughton and

Harold.[15] In a similar August 30 letter, the commissioner of the OPP, Major-General V.A.S.Williams, told the attorney general: "I consider this is a case where the government of this province might be generous as it was entirely due to the bravery and initiative of the Laird brothers, assisted by Rolland, that the murderer of Jackson was apprehended, as the robbery and pursuit of the robbers occurred before the police were notified."[16] He did not consider Haight's monetary suggestions as excessive, "as in all probability it would have cost the province considerably more than this sum before this man was apprehended had it not been for the action of the men concerned." A subsequent order-in-council authorized rewards of $500 and $350 to be paid respectively to Walter and Haughton Laird and $200 to Harold Rolland.[17]

At the Parry Sound council meeting held on the evening of Tuesday, November 30, Mayor Charles Carlisle Johnson quickly read the minutes of the previous session and then ordered an adjournment so that the awards could proceed. Local MPP George V. Harcourt presented the reward cheques and letters of appreciation signed by the attorney general to each man.[18] Price had written:

> It is a most important thing that our citizens realize that law and order must be maintained and upheld. One of the outstanding attributes of the British people has always been that they respected the law. Canadians are following faithfully in these footsteps. We must always be prepared to uphold the established institutions of our country, feeling that justice will eventually be meted out in the recognized way. If our citizens fail to uphold the arm of the law then anarchy must ensue. No country can survive anarchy. When every man is a law unto himself the established institutions of our country must fail.[19]

On behalf of the citizens of Parry Sound, Mayor Johnson presented engraved wristwatches to the Lairds and a mantel clock to Rolland. A CPR official gave each an inscribed plate as a token of the CPR's gratitude.

In a five-page brief, Hett appealed to the federal minister of justice in Ottawa for executive clemency, either in the form of a new

At the end of 1965, Walter Alexander Laird retired from his job as a clerk for Canadian National Railways after 40 years service. He died suddenly at Parry Sound District General Hospital on November 15, 1987, age 83. *Courtesy of Jean Laird.*

trial or a commutation of the death sentence, but was unsuccessful.[20] Shortly after 5 p.m. on the afternoon of December 6, Hett delivered an application for a temporary stay of execution to Osgoode Hall with an affidavit from Burowski offering new evidence.[21]

Burowski was scheduled to be hanged at 12:30 a.m. on December 7 and had been given his final meal and last rites when sheriff James E.T. Armstrong received a telegram from the Department of the Attorney General at 12:16 a.m. that Justice John Millar McEvoy had granted a two-week stay of execution. Members of the OPP Criminal Inves- tigation Bureau set out to investigate claims made in the affidavit.[22]

On the evening of Saturday, December 15, deputy attorney general Edward Bayly telephoned Hett to inform him that, as far as his department was concerned, the investigation had been closed. Three days later, Attorney General Price wrote to Hett insisting "there seemed to be very little evidence that would make one believe that the jury erred when they found this man guilty."[23] In an interview published in *The Daily Star* on December 20, Price repeated that as far as the province was concerned, Burowski would hang on the following day: "Nothing has happened as a result of his affidavit and the province is now out of it…. If there is any further action of any kind it will come from Ottawa."[24]

On the morning of December 21, a solemn group assembled in the courtyard of the Parry Sound jail to witness Burowski's execution. Canada's official hangman, Arthur Bartholomew English, alias Arthur Ellis, was on hand to carry out the sentence, which was his 568th hanging since he had assumed the position in 1909. The 62-year-old executioner was dressed appropriately for the somber occasion, wearing a morning coat, grey trousers and a black tie.

The snow fell and the wind blew as the small gathering awaited for Burowski to appear with his escort. After Burowski appeared, it was just a short eight seconds from the time he ascended the stairs of the gallows until he fell through the trap door. The jail surgeon pronounced that death had been instantaneous.[25]

Although there was an attempt in Detroit in 1928 to cash a $100 Canadian war bond stolen in the CPR train robbery, the bulk of the loot was never recovered and no one was ever charged with the crime.[26] Burowski took his secrets with him to his grave. For years afterward, allegations surfaced that this person or that person had been one of the robbers and each time the OPP investigated. The last such accusation, made against a Bear Lake store keeper of Polish ancestry, was investigated and dismissed in December 1950.[27]

17

The Politics of Policing

A T AN APRIL 1938 COUNCIL MEETING, Councillor Anthony Gilchrist Sr. suggested to council that it was time for the town to have a board of police commissioners to oversee the operation of the police department. Apart from a brief period between February 1908 and January 1909 when the town did have such a board, the elected council exercised complete control over the police.[1]

Since 1874, legislation had provided that police boards were optional for towns having a police magistrate, such as Parry Sound, and during this period police magistrates were mandatory for towns with a population of more than 5,000 but optional for other towns.[2] Boards were to be composed of the mayor, the local county or district court judge, and the police magistrate.

The *North Star* reported:

> Coun. Gilchrist rose and remarked that it was time a police commission was appointed in Parry Sound to deal with police matters, outside of council. He said it was the same every year. There was always too much petty stuff in councils. The police were afraid for their jobs from year to year; when municipal elections came around they did not know if they would have a job or not. It is time we got away from this sort of thing, bickering about the police in council every year.[3]

The issue of a police board came up repeatedly over the years. A January 1954 editorial in the *North Star*, of which town councillor and police committee member Agnes Wing was the managing editor, urged the town to study the feasibility of implementing such a board.

> Perhaps a police commission would be the answer to the problem. It has been suggested before and passed up, but time marches on. What was not good yesterday may serve its purpose today and many cities are finding out that a police commission is the answer to their problems....The police commission has complete control of the police activities, such as policy and personnel. Whether this would be acceptable in Parry Sound is controversial, but it certainly is worth some study.[4]

Yet, in March 1958, when Councillor Wing was chairman of the police committee, council turned down a request from the attorney general to establish a board upon the recommendation of her committee.[5]

Ontario Police Commission advisor Robert Russell recommended in December 1986 that the town establish a board, but this suggestion was rejected outright by Councillor John Christie, chairman of the protection committee. Councillor Christie would later remark that "council has to raise the budget (money) and they'd lose control if a board was appointed."[6]

Yet Parry Sound had had a public utilities commission since January 1923, set up to manage the town's electrical and waterworks facilities. Council had eagerly passed a bylaw to surrender control of these departments to a three-man board consisting of the mayor and two elected commissioners. At the time, the *North Star* reported:

> The public utilities commission will relieve the town council of a great deal of routine work and leave them free to devote their time to other matters of town affairs, which the commission having no other municipal matters to attend to will be able to apply themselves wholly to the two revenue-producing departments of the town.[7]

Policing in the town of Parry Sound began when council appointed Samuel Lawson Boyd as constable at a salary of $310 on August 23, 1887, but he was more of a gofer and jack of all trades.[8] Boyd was also the caretaker of the council chambers, located in rented rooms over the Masonic Hall at the corner of Seguin and Miller streets, inspector of bylaws, inspector of streets and sidewalks and the repair crew as well. In his first month of work, council voted funds to buy Boyd a handsaw, hammer, axe, square shovel and wheelbarrow. He was subsequently given the task of blasting rock obstructing the flow of water in front of a Mrs. Graham's house.

Exactly how much of Boyd's time was dedicated to keeping order and preventing crime is unknown. By virtue of the act of incorporation, the notorious Parry Harbour had become the east ward of the town, but apparently crime was not rampant there. As part of his duties, council requested that Boyd make two trips daily into the east ward, once at noon and once during the evening.

Boyd encountered political interference in the performance of his duties in December 1891 when Mayor John Galna advised him not to jail a drunk on Christmas Eve "on account of his family."[9] When Boyd was criticized in a council meeting for not performing his duty, Galna admitted that he had intervened to prevent an arrest.

The early police officers were primarily sawmill labourers looking to better themselves. Most had limited abilities to read and write. The main requirement was above-average body size so drunks could be handled with a minimum of fuss—little else mattered.

The first constable hired from outside town, and who had formal training in police work, was Albert Edward Goodall, son of James M. Goodall, general superintendent of the Toronto Parks Department. In November 1899, the town went all-out to hire Goodall, a respected member of the York County Constabulary. The council offered a salary of $450 per year and free lodgings over the fire hall. Goodall accepted and soon found himself working from 10 a.m. to 11 p.m., seven days a week. His duties, as set out in Bylaw 192, were very similar to those Boyd performed.[10]

Less than a year after Goodall arrived, he was fired by council. An ugly dispute ensued when Goodall accused council of unethical conduct by purchasing supplies for the town from their own businesses, without calling for tenders. Two councillors submitted their resignations over the affair, but the other councillors refused to accept them.[11] Goodall's successor was John Williams, the weigh scales clerk and former inspector of street lights.

While many constables were former sawmill labourers, most felt their wages were less than those of an unskilled workman. Robert Dunlop wrote the town in April 1906 asking for a raise:

> I may say that I put in at least 14 hours a day and many often 18 hours in the streets and comparing my wages with the average working man I find I am getting at least 70 cents a day less than him. Moreover I was promised by the mayor some time ago an increase, but as yet this has not been done.[12]

Although Dunlop got a $5 a month raise, he quit in February 1907 to accept a job as turnkey at the district jail.

In June 1906, council received a petition from Canada Atlantic Hotel owner John Albert Gentles and other east ward merchants requesting an increase in Constable Octave Julien's salary.[13] Julien had been hired in December 1905 to police the east ward after the three liquor dealers requested the appointment of a second constable for that side of town and offered to pay half his salary.

Julien eventually resigned over the issue of low wages, although he was reappointed in April 1907 at a salary of $50 per month. He had written to council:

> I would most respectfully ask for an increase in my wages. I think I am worth at least $50 per month. The present wages I am getting barely affords me a decent living and compared with the ordinary workman I am away below his scale of wages....[14]

Council fired Julien in August 1909, apparently without cause. Julien's lawyer, Francis Ronan Powell, KC, the former clerk of the municipality who would soon become the district court judge, wrote to council:

I desire to say that constable Julien has been an officer of the town for nearly five years and claims that he has at all times faithfully performed, to the best of his ability, the duties required of him, and that in tendering his resignation he should be allowed to answer any charges against him that have been suggested, either before a specific committee of council or before the district judge.

It is not fair and reasonable that constable Julien's resignation should be demanded and accepted in a manner that might leave a cloud upon his reputation and might militate or even prevent him from obtaining employment as constable in any other place....[15]

Harry Forder, a Canadian Pacific Railway constable at North Bay who had served 12 years in the Royal Navy, was hired to replace Julien in September 1909 at a salary of $75 a month, with two uniforms provided each year. Within nine months the *North Star* published a front-page photograph of Forder "who by his clever work is proving himself to be one of the best police officers in Canada."[16]

In February 1914, council passed a bylaw stating Forder was to be on duty as chief of police for 12 hours each day starting at 10 a.m. His salary was set at $900 per year. The bylaw also provided for the town to hire a night constable to be on duty from 8 p.m. until 7 a.m. for $700 per year.[17]

Parry Sound experienced a population surge during the First World War when the explosives plant at Nobel, north of town, expanded for the wartime production of munitions. In June 1916, council promoted Constable Archibald Totman to sergeant and authorized the hiring of a fourth man.[18]

Despite Chief Forder's obvious good work, the imposition of prohibition and its enforcement led to a dispute between council and the chief over who should lay the information in liquor cases, in order that the fines be paid to the town. Councillor David Gillespie made a motion that Chief Forder "be notified that on or about Dec. 15, 1916, his services will be dispensed with."[19] The motion produced considerable discussion, with councillors Albert McCallum, A.T. Granger and Dr. John R. Stone speaking vehemently against it. Chief Forder also addressed council and, as a result, his termination was referred to the fire and police committee for a full report to be presented at the next meeting.

A week later, committee chairman McCallum presented a report exonerating the chief of any wrongdoing. Councillor Harry Freer McQuire strongly objected to adopting a report which would clear the chief without a trial. McQuire moved an amendment, seconded by Gillespie and carried by council, that Forder be suspended from duty until Judge F.R. Powell could investigate.

Councillor Stone took the side of the chief and saw no reason for spending good money investigating charges he claimed were mainly made by foreigners. Frederick Tasker also made a long address in which he favoured a full investigation, but stigmatized the charges as spitework by foreigners whom the chief had prosecuted. He ventured to say no reputable man would come forward with charges.[20]

Mayor James A. Dwyer said he had affidavits in his pockets and, while it was true that the authors were foreigners, many other complaints had reached him and he deemed it best that an investigation be held. The inquiry before Judge Powell began on December 27, with the chief facing a total of six charges.

In January, council passed a resolution that Forder be notified that his services were no longer required and that he be given one month's pay as severance. A month later council passed

Originally from Enfield, England, Archibald Totman emigrated to Canada in June 1911 with his wife and four children. Although he came to Parry Sound to work at the smelter, Totman was hired as the night constable in December 1914 and promoted to sergeant in June 1916. He resigned in April 1917, but was later rehired as night constable in May 1919.
Courtesy of Hannah Christian.

Oliver Josiah Crockford was Parry Sound's police chief from December 1924 to March 1925 and October 1927 to November 1934. Born at Birmingham, England, he came to Parry Sound with his parents in 1889 when he was 22. He worked for the Parry Sound Lumber Company for many years before his appointment as sanitary inspector in March 1916. *Courtesy of Oliver J. Crockford.*

another resolution that the town "take no further action in the matter of the investigation into the conduct of ex-chief Forder."[21] But residents of Parry Sound did not forget Forder and he won election to the municipal council in 1918 and 1919. Even though his service with the town had been terminated, the voters still felt he had the necessary integrity and honesty to represent them.

Parry Sound had three police chiefs between January 1917 and July 1921. To replace Chief Forder, council hired OPP Constable Robert John Markle. Alex Kidd, a sergeant with the Peterborough police, was hired in June 1918 for $1,500 a year. Then Thomas Spencer came from Toronto for $150 per month. By this time, the town's population had declined again and the police department returned to its pre-war size of a chief and night constable.[22]

When Spencer absconded in 1921, council returned to its old ways of hiring local men from within the community. Night constable Albert Griffith became chief at a salary of $125 per month. Upon Griffith's resignation, council promoted night constable William McCullough to chief in March 1925. Likewise, when McCullough quit in October 1927, night constable Oliver Josiah Crockford became chief.[23]

During the Depression, council passed a February 1931 resolution that Chief Crockford and night constable Jackson Heslip be terminated so the town could tender their positions. Chief Crockford spoke in defence of his salary, stating that he received $1,636 as chief and sanitary inspector, as well as $175 from the town as truant officer. He said he had not asked for both the positions of chief and sanitary inspector, but they had been given to him by previous councils.

> Mayor Johnson did not think this resolution was prompted by economies so much as malice and that the chief had given good service to the corporation. Coun. Thompson resented the insinuation of malice and told his worship in no uncertain words that he did not like his insinuations. Coun. Taylor stated he had seconded the motion purely from an economical standpoint and that we could secure the services of the police for less money.[24]

Council later rescinded the terminations and reinstated both Chief Crockford and Heslip after Councillor Solomon Shamess and Mayor Johnson provided evidence that the resolution was illegal.

> Coun. Shamess stated that he had looked up law books in the town office and found that it was illegal to advertise municipal offices without offering a stated salary. Coun. Stanzel doubted his authority and his references, wanting to know how old the book was. Coun. Thompson stated that he had had experience and had studied papers and never heard of such a thing. Mayor Johnson quoted a York Township case. Coun. Thompson then stated that in the list of applicants were many good men at low bids and that the work could be done for less money....[25]

Council again fired Chief Crockford and night constable Jackson Heslip in October 1934. The municipality received over 100 applications for the jobs from across Canada. William Richardson Pringle, who had 28 years experience in police work in Scotland and England, and in Canada with the Canadian Pacific Railway Police and the Ontario Provincial Police, was hired as chief for $1,000 per year. Former RCMP Constable Horace Walter Taylor agreed to come from Regina for $800 per year.[26]

Taylor lasted four years until council fired him in February 1938. Chief Pringle lasted only a few months longer. Allegedly, Pringle insulted police committee chairman James A. Watkinson on the

Parry Sound Police Department, circa 1942. *From left to right*: Const. Donald William Erskine (May 1941–March 1943), Chief Benjamin John Timms (April 1941–November 1944), Const. Robert A. Herbert (December 1941–March 1943), Sgt. Stanley George McDonald (May 1940–August 1944). *Courtesy of Susanne Hughes.*

street and then refused to apologize.[27] To fill the vacancy, council promoted night constable Martin Walter Lang to chief.

The Second World War and the establishment of the Defence Industries Limited (DIL) plant at Nobel, once again, caused the population Parry Sound to balloon. And there was a corresponding increase in the size of the police department to a chief and three constables. In August 1940, Parry Sound purchased its first police car, a two-door Roadking coach, from local businessman Frank Guidotti for $1,068.[28]

In November 1944, council appointed George Wellington Doolittle as chief, to replace Benjamin John Timms, who had resigned because of heart problems. At 54 years old, Doolittle had just retired on pension after 31 years service as a constable with the Toronto police.[29]

Low salaries, which had been a complaint since the early days of the police department, continued to be a problem. In August

1944, Sergeant Stanley George McDonald resigned after council refused to increase his pay to $1,700.[30] Councillor Marcus Nichols, chairman of the police committee, remarked in October 1947 that "good men could not be kept on the present salaries being paid." Constable L.C. McKenna had resigned after two years with the force and Councillor Nichols was "sorry to lose so good a man."[31]

Councillor James. A. Watkinson, chairman of the police committee, requested clerk Harold Barker write to other municipalities of similar size inquiring about their police wages in September 1949. Two months later, Watkinson made a motion that each officer receive a $200 raise. The motion was defeated with only the three members of the police committee approving the increases.[32]

While pay may have been low, the training and education of the police also continued to be deficient. Although the Province of Ontario created the Provincial and Municipal Police Training School in 1935, Parry Sound does not appear to have sent any of its officers away for training before 1948. That year Sergeant Stan Miner attended police school in Sudbury after already being on the job for four years.[33] Arnot Bruce Abbott, hired as a constable in March 1952, did not receive any formal training until he attended the OPP-operated Ontario Police College on Sherbourne Street in Toronto for seven weeks in 1961.

In January 1963, the province opened a new Ontario Police College at Aylmer under the administration and direction of the Ontario Police Commission (OPC). Municipalities could send their officers and the province paid all costs apart from transportation. Two months after the college opened, council passed a resolution, to be forwarded to the OPC, that the province give grants to municipalities equal to police officers' salaries while they're away attending the police college to pay the costs of hiring replacements. That idea didn't get anywhere, but Constable Burton Clarence Brown, a seven-year veteran of the Parry Sound police, and Constable John Kenneth Sheridan graduated from a training course in December. Sergeant Miner attended a supervisory and command course in the fall of 1964.[34]

A 1973, the OPC report on the Parry Sound police found numerous inadequacies in training, discipline and supervision.[35]

Parry Sound Police Department, circa 1950. *From left to right*: Const. Robert John McNabb (March 1946–May 1954), Const. Joseph Arthur Villeneuve (October 1947–April 1952), Chief George Wellington Doolittle (December 1944–April 1965), Sgt. Stanley Elliott Miner (August 1944–July 1971). *Courtesy of Wayne Miner.*

Chief Norman Gordon Graber, hired by Parry Sound council in April 1965, had not received any training since his January 1945 discharge as a corporal from the Canadian Provost Corps. Sergeant Kenneth William Graham Cooke's training went back 17 years to when he was a constable with the Ottawa police.

"When I got here [in June 1975], the average education of the men was Grade 9 and a sergeant on the force had not passed the recruit course at police college," Chief Colin Hayes told the *Globe and Mail* in 1987. "Fifty per cent of the force did not meet the minimum education requirement of the Police Act."[36]

The Parry Sound police were also hampered by a lack of equipment. In 1923, the town had implemented a red-light system for summoning the police. When Bell Telephone converted to direct dialing in 1958, it was no longer possible for their operators to turn on the police red light. The town began paying a dollar per day to the fire hall caretaker to answer police telephone calls and turn on a red light on the water tower if an officer was required.[37] Upon seeing the light, the officer on duty would telephone the fire hall.

In October 1963, Councillor Cahill discussed an accident where a motorcyclist had run into the back of a car at the corner of Church and Cascade streets. Traffic was cleared and the victim had been removed to hospital before the police arrived. His comments were not meant as a criticism of the police, Councillor Cahill said, but a criticism of the methods of communication.[38] The town purchased a Motorola two-way radio for the police cruiser in July 1964.[39]

The 1973 OPC report on the Parry Sound police was highly critical that the police, the town works department and the public utilities commission all used the same radio frequency. Many times the PUC superintendent arrived at accidents before the police and the citizens often overhead information about arrests from a loudspeaker PA system on the works department truck, which rebroadcast all radio transmissions.[40]

Accommodation for the police was also poor. When the town constructed the present municipal building in 1934, the then two-man police force was allocated an office of 144 square feet. As the number of police officers increased, additional space of 108 square feet was acquired in an unheated room separated from the main office by a stairway landing and the council chamber entrance. Not until March 1981, when there was a chief, a sergeant and seven constables, were the police moved into a separate building, and this was only after numerous grand juries and Public Institutions Inspection Panel reports had commented on the shabby quarters.

"The present police accommodation leaves much to be desired, and I believe I can say that it is the worst police office I have seen in my 22 years as a police officer," Chief Hayes wrote in his 1975 annual report.[41]

Chief Hayes tried hard to make the Parry Sound police force better, but he was hampered by a persistent lack of support from council and the protection committee in particular. While he greatly improved the training of the officers, as well as the equipment and accommodation of the force, supervision and discipline problems identified in the 1973 OPC report actually intensified. When one of the two sergeants resigned in November 1975,

successive protection committees refused to fill the position for
11 years. The council also failed to heed a warning in the 1973
report that elected officials were contributing to the morale
problem and undermining the authority of the chief by hearing
verbal complaints from police officers before they had been first
submitted in writing to the chief as specified in Section 3.03 of
Bylaw 76-2679 and Section 3(5) of Bylaw 83-2985, which established the rules and regulations of the police department.

In October 1986, the protection committee asked that a costing proposal be requested for delivering contract policing services
by the OPP instead of the municipal force. In the final report presented to council by the OPP, two policing options were available.
Under the stand-alone option, a staff of one corporal and eight
constables would occupy the current police station at a per capita
cost of $64.63. Under the integrated program, the force would
be stationed with the OPP detachment and would include one
sergeant, one corporal and seven constables. In the integrated
option the cost per capita would be $58.98. The current per capita
cost for the municipal force at that time was $61.46.[42]

In August 1987, council passed a resolution, moved by protection committee chairman Christie, that the OPC authorize the
disbandment of the Parry Sound police, permitting the town to
enter into an agreement with the Ministry of the Solicitor General for the OPP to provide contract policing. The OPC granted
the request in May 1988 after a seven-day hearing to investigate
the operation and administration of the force. Although a full
report of the reasons for the decision was to follow, none was ever
issued as the three inquiry members who heard the evidence—
Wendy Calder, Winfield McKay and David G. Stewart—all left
the OPC shortly afterwards.[43] The OPP took over policing the
town as of 12:01 a.m. on January 8, 1989.

The 1987 annual report for the Parry Sound municipal police force,
the last available, shows it cost $519,937 to operate that year. The
municipality received $125,400 from the Province of Ontario in the
form of a policing grant, representing 24 per cent of its policing
costs. During 1986, the police department cost $486,880 to oper-
ate and the municipality received a provincial grant of $112,5000,

representing 25 per cent. These figures include debentures on the new fire-police building, heat, light and civilian staff.[44]

The cost of OPP policing in Parry Sound has escalated from $595,062 in 1990 to the incredible sum of $1,185,776 for 1998.[45] In part, this increase is due to an amendment to the Police Act to shift the responsibility of courthouse security to the municipalities in which the courts are located. To assist municipalities in adjusting, new policing costs over $90 per household were made eligible provincial compensation from the Community Reinvestment Fund (CRF). CRF assistance represented almost 82 per cent of Parry Sound's total 1998 police costs.[46]

Parry Sound taxpayers are sitting on a tax time bomb as the province is still paying for all the municipality's policing costs in excess of $90 per household. "But that grant money will not be there forever and when we no longer receive it, we will be paying the full amount," Parry Sound Financial Services Director Steven Gilchrist told the *Parry Sound Beacon Star* in December 1999. The gross cost of OPP services for Parry Sound in 2000 was approximately $1.2 million. Parry Sound's 2,811 households paid approximately $253,000 of that total. "I think we are getting a pretty sweet deal," Councillor Jamie McGarvey told the newspaper.[47]

18

There Were Once Three Theatres

AFTER 24 SEASONS OF INTOLERABLE HEAT, uncomfortable seats and intrusive train whistles, the Festival of the Sound relocated from a gymnasium at the Parry Sound High School in July 2003 to a new home at the Charles W. Stockey Centre for the Performing Arts. In addition to the more than 50 events held during the annual three-and-a-half week Festival, the new 480-seat, acoustically sound performance hall has also hosted professional theatre, entertainers like Michelle Wright and Kim Mitchell, and community events such as the Parry Sound High School music department's 2003 Christmas concert.

Festival patrons and local residents alike waited decades for the $12.5 million multi-purpose facility that Mayor Ted Knight predicts will attract people to Parry Sound for years to come.[1] Prior to the Stockey Centre, however, local service clubs and entrepreneurs were largely responsible for the construction of the community's recreation and entertainment facilities.

While council was discussing the construction of the present municipal office in February 1934, the politicians received a petition from taxpayers that the building include an auditorium to accommodate 500 spectators. Residents looked to Huntsville, which had officially opened a new town hall on Dominion Day 1927 that housed an armoury, post office, council chambers, customs office, police department, lock-up, fire hall and an auditorium, as well as a firemen's room and living quarters for the caretaker's family.

"There is no place at present where a concert, play or large public meeting can be held," Judge J.B. Moon told council. "There is a great amount of excellent talent in Parry Sound. Few towns of the same size can boast of better talent among the young people and this should be developed."[2] However, council opted to get Sudbury architect P. J. O'Gorman to design a building (45 × 75 feet) that would include an enlarged public library in the basement, but not an auditorium as this would require the building to be 75 per cent larger.[3] The continuing need for an auditorium came up again in September 1945 when council discussed the construction of a new fire hall and public utilities building on the northwest corner of the Seguin Street and Gibson Street intersection.[4]

Some of the earliest known concerts in Parry Sound took place during the early 1870s in the Orange Lodge's Union Hall on the southwest corner of Seguin and Gibson. Henry Jukes, a baker who carried on business for years in the Albion Hotel on James Street, built the Star Hotel just north of the Union Hall on Gibson Street, which also became the site of numerous concerts. Advertisements for the hotel in the *North Star* boasted assembly rooms and a principal hall measuring 12 feet by 24 feet, suitable for lectures, concerts and socials.[5] Although converted into a garage and car dealership around the time of the First World War, the building was one of oldest in the town when it burned in December 1933.[6]

Edwin Ellis Virgo opened the Granite Skating Rink, close to the Seguin River at the north end of Miller Street, in February 1893. This large structure housed hockey, curling and ice-skating facilities. The main sheet of ice in the middle of the rink was bordered on each side by a sheet of curling ice. For hockey games, boards were erected around the middle sheet and spectators stood around the perimeter, on the ice that was used for curling. During public skating hours, the boards were removed and the entire ice surface was utilized. The rink was demolished in 1919.[7]

Albert John Gentles and his brother Charles, pre-prohibition owners of the Kipling Hotel, opened the Palace Arena at the eastern end of Mary Street in 1915. The arena became the "home ice" when, in 1919, local businessmen agreed to organize and fund an Ontario Hockey Association team in the community for the first time in 12 years. Although the rink burned in January 1927 while

Charles was away with the Parry Sound Shamrocks in Coldwater, the brothers reopened a larger facility 10 months later.[8]

Local curlers played for years on an outdoor rink at the intersection of Church and Seguin streets known as Hagan's Corner, but in 1899 they got together to raise money for a $2,600 building funded through $5 shares in a joint stock company. Local contractor Alexander Logan, himself an avid curler, erected the three-rink, 54 by 150 foot, circular-truss building on the site of the current Bell Telephone office on Gibson Street. "The new rink is a credit to the town and will serve the purpose of a public hall in the summer months," trumpeted the *North Star*.[9] Also used for hockey, ice skating and roller skating, the building was demolished after a new curling rink opened on Johnston Street in 1953.

Around 1904 former speed-skating prodigy John Campbell, then a millwright at the Peter Estate sawmill in the east ward, began recruiting performers of all types for shows at the curling club after the ice had melted. Although travelling vaudeville acts also made frequent appearances at the Union Hall, by 1907 representatives of Spear's Moving Pictures and Professor Green's Moving Pictures were also making stops of two or three nights. Not long after, the Lyric Theatre, managed by John D. Rice, opened in Parry Sound just north of the IOOF building on James Street. A letter in the *North Star* complimented both the manager and the town for the quality entertainment provided there:

> As an occasional visitor to your town, and one who has more or less time on his hands, I wish to say a word about the Lyric motion picture exhibition in your town.... I would like to bear my testimony to the fact that your picture show is among the best I visit in my road of travel and is in the matter and variety, and in its vaudeville attractions, the equal of the best shows of the same class. I trust, Mr. Editor, that you will be able to find space for this little tribute of a traveller who sees shows in all parts of a province and who knows a good thing when he sees it.[10]

The Royal Theatre, built by Thomas Ryder, operated between 1915 and 1944. *Courtesy of the Parry Sound Public Library Historical Collection, Album III #93.*

Other entrepreneurs were not slow to emulate Rice's "good thing." In 1914, Thomas Ryder, a local butcher, opened the Royal Opera House, measuring 30 feet by 80 feet, just north of Rice's establishment (which had been renamed the Odeon Theatre). "Mr. Ryder has spared no pains or money and he is deserving of the highest praise for giving to the town a long-felt want in the shape of a convenient, comfortable and commodious public hall, the seating accommodation being nearly 500," wrote the *North Star*. "Not only in the furnishings and fittings of this cosy theatre has Mr. Ryder worked out the best that can be had, but he has introduced the very latest, right-up-to-the-minute music, having installed a Violiphone... which is alone worth the price of admission."[11] By the end of the year, the Princess Theatre had also opened next to the office of the *Parry Sound Canadian* on Gibson Street. "If the attendance at the picture shows and theatres is any indication of the condition of business in Parry Sound, there must be a prosperous condition and the people have plenty of money to spend," noted the *North Star*.[12]

John Campbell formed a partnership with George "Bud" Spence, the local customs collector, and they brought ever bigger acts to the curling club during the war years, such as the roller-skating bear that entertained in September 1914. "Messrs. Campbell and Spence seem to be making every effort to give their patrons something new all the time and they are exceeding beyond expectations," the *North Star* gushed.[13]

As Parry Sound's population surged to 6,000 residents in 1916, due to the munitions works at Nobel, the variety and quality of entertainment offered by the three theatres improved and the competition intensified, especially after Campbell & Spence took over management of the Royal. It was not uncommon for the Royal and the Princess to purchase half- and full-page advertisements for "photoplays" and live theatre productions. "They have without a doubt the best stock company that has ever visited this town," the *North Star* wrote about the Florence Johnston Co. appearing at the Princess.[14] The Royal's films were promoted with equal fervour: "Such pictures as these which cost a fortune to produce are not secured by nickel picture shows, but only by houses where quality and not quantity counts."[15]

During the war, the town's theatres also served as the venues for recruiting drives and patriotic concerts. Prominent local citizens Lieutenant-Colonel John H. Knifton and Judge F.R. Powell urged able-bodied young men of the town to enlist in a meeting held at the Princess Theatre in December 1916. "The hall was packed to the doors and many turned away," reported the *North Star*.[16] Mayor H.M. Purvis presented the Military Medal won at the Somme by Lieutenant Percy Jackson to the soldier's father, Austin Jackson, at a ceremony held at the Royal Theatre in April 1918.[17] Although Jackson had survived the battle for which he was decorated, he had been killed in action during a later engagement.

The end of the First World War led to the end of prosperity in Parry Sound. The munitions works at Nobel were dismantled and the population plummetted to 3,229 in 1921. The Princess Theatre closed that year and the brick building was acquired by Quinn Motor Sales, a Pontiac and Buick dealership.[18] While the Odeon may have survived only up to 1926, Campbell & Spence's Royal underwent extensive renovations in 1930 that included the installation of speakers and projection equipment for "talkies," as well as a furnace and washrooms. After Spence's sudden death from a

After the First World War, the Princess Theatre building was converted into Quinn Motor Sales, a Pontiac and Buick dealership. It became Groves Motor Sales in March 1929. *Courtesy of AO/David L. Thomas Collection, C253, Tray 18-43.*

heart attack in June 1932, Campbell continued to operate the Royal Theatre, even adding new seats and an air conditioning system. He sold it in February 1939, only three months before his own death in Kentucky.[19]

The new owners of the Royal Theatre, the Theatre Holding Corporation Limited, opened the modern, 644-seat Strand Theatre on Christmas Day in 1940. Parry Sound's population surged once again due to the influx of workers at the Nobel munitions plant, reaching 6,433 in 1942, and the company kept both theatres operating until 1944.[20] The Strand has been the town's only theatre since that time.

The Parry Sound Arena Company Ltd., incorporated in April 1948, attempted to raise the funding required to build a new arena through the sale of $1 shares. The community had gone without a covered hockey arena for seven years after the Palace Arena burned. In October 1948, the local Lions Club took over the raising of money for the new Parry Sound Memorial Community Centre, which opened three months later and served the town until demolished in 1974.[21] Parry Sound service clubs also provided much of the funding for the present Bobby Orr Community Centre.

The Strand Theatre, which opened in 1940, has been
Parry Sound's only theatre since 1944. The theatre was
the scene of two of the town's murders. Mrs. Siama
Borrow, who was in charge of the candy counter, was
brutally beaten to death when she walked in on a
burglary in November 1971. A 17-month-old infant
was also murdered there in February 1979. *Courtesy of
AO, RG 56-11-0-195-1.*

In September 1953, Ronald L. Kerr of Gravenhurst wrote to
the Motion Picture Censorship Board about his plans to construct
a 300-car drive-in theatre on the eastern perimeter of Parry Sound.
A class-D licence was issued eight months later, although an inspector wrote, "by the conditions still present, I believe it opened
several weeks too soon. The tower has no roof and is completely
unfinished inside. The box office is temporary. The land has not
been gravelled and apparently cars are often stuck in the sand the
theatre is built on...."[22] Through the years, there were repeated
problems and the number of cars authorized dropped to 177 by
1961. "Grounds are far from attractive. Lots of grass and weeds,"
commented an inspector in 1966."[23] The last annual licence appears
to have been issued in April 1973, and later that year Councillor

Don Ritchie Sr. reported to council that a building permit had been issued for a $1.4 million shopping plaza on the site, although it failed to materialize.[24]

In the fall of 1962, Dr. Michael Wheatley had an idea for an outdoor theatre which would seat 15,000 people, built into a natural bowl-like depression at Darlington's farm on Mill Lake Road. A local campaign began in January 1963 to generate funds to market the idea across Canada. "This is a job well beyond the power of our limited local resources as the finished theatre will run well into the hundreds of thousands of dollars," campaign chairman Don Ritchie Sr. told the *North Star*. "The money we are raising here is intended to do a local job, that is to set up the organization to raise the large sums necessary to build the theatre.... Before the theatre is built, Eric Handbury, who will be its general manager, will travel the length and breadth of the country in the cause of the national campaign."[25]

Residents of Parry Sound provided more than $20,000 that was spent on salaries for promotion of the scheme, advertising and travel. A press conference held in Toronto in May 1963 generated considerable radio, newspaper and magazine coverage. "This is one of the boldest theatrical ventures anyone has ever tried to pull of," one of Canada's foremost architectural planners told the assembled reporters. "It's even bolder than Stratford."[26] Dr. Wheatley remarked that Parry Sound relied tremendously on tourism dollars but the community desperately needed a unique attraction.

Unfortunately, the *North Star* reported in January 1965 that the dream had died leaving an estate of only $1,304.[27] Despite two years of fundraising efforts, the directors had been unable to attract the large grants and donations necessary to build the theatre. "The people of our community are imaginative, willing to try a long-shot, and those 'hard-headed businessmen,' most of whom contributed knowing this was a very long chance, were willing to back their town," the *North Star* said.

The Festival of the Sound began quite differently in 1979 when renowned pianist Anton Kuerti, who owned a cottage in the Parry Sound area, invited a few friends to present a three-concert series in the local high school gymnasium. In this case, patrons came for the music and the number and variety of the events grew each year, whereas Dr. Wheatley's outdoor theatre committee aspired to build an expensive theatre complex first. At the time that the Festival of the Sound was celebrating its 20th anniversary in 1999, a call was sent out for proposals from architects. The building steering committee chose the Toronto firm of Keith Loffler Architect in partnership with Zawadzki Armin Stevens Architects.

19

HMCS *Parry Sound*

APRIL 18, 1945, was a day that leading stores assistant Joseph Egerton Burnie recalled vividly for the rest of his life. A German U-boat somehow managed to get close enough to the convoy being brought across the Atlantic by the escort group C-7, to torpedo two merchant vessels. Almost immediately, one of the ships sank, while the second, a tanker, burned ferociously and sent clouds of oily black smoke into the air. Burnie's ship, the corvette HMCS *Parry Sound*, broke away from the convoy to chase and pummel the predator with depth charges.[1]

It was the closest Burnie and most of his shipmates ever came to the enemy—and that was just fine with him. The task of corvettes like HMCS *Parry Sound* was to see to the safe and timely arrival of merchant vessels in Britain. They were to route convoys, consisting of 40 to 50 ships, away from danger.

When the Second World War began, the Royal Canadian Navy had only ten destroyers and minesweepers, but Canada's shipyards, which had never built anything over 100 feet long, were soon put to work building warships. On Georgian Bay, the shipyards at Collingwood and Midland began producing flower class corvettes, which were initially 205 feet long with a displacement of 950 tons. HMCS *Collingwood*, commissioned November 9, 1940, was the first product of the Collingwood yards, while HMCS *Midland* was commissioned at the Midland yards on November 8, 1941. Construction of HMCS *Parry Sound*, the sixth corvette to be built at Midland, began June 11, 1943. The hull was launched November 13 and the finished ship commissioned August 30, 1944.[2]

The corvette HMCS *Parry Sound* was commissioned at Midland, Ontario, on August 30, 1944, and made her first crossing of the Atlantic Ocean with a convoy in November. The ship was declared surplus and handed over to the War Assets Corporation, which sold her for scrap in July 1945. *Courtesy of the Department of National Defence, CN3620.*

The naming of a warship for Parry Sound caused considerable excitement in the community. The Georgian Rebekah Lodge organized a corvette committee to solicit gifts for the ship's crew and set a grand example by purchasing an apartment-size piano for $355.[3] So many donations flooded in that the corvette committee put them on display in a vacant store across from the Parry Sound dairy, as well as the store windows of various merchants around town. The contributions came to include a washing machine, musical instruments, a phonograph and records, electric toasters, Thermos bottles, boxing gloves and hundreds of other items.

In June 1944, Parry Sound MP Arthur Graeme Slaght received a written assurance from the Minister of Defence for Naval Services, Angus L. Macdonald, that HMCS *Parry Sound* would not depart the Great Lakes without a stop in the community for which the warship was named.[4] Preparations began for a welcome that the crew would not soon forget.

HMCS *Parry Sound* sailed into the inner harbour at 4 p.m. on Sunday, September 3, piloted by 82-year-old Adam Brown, the almost legendary lighthouse keeper at Red Rock from 1898 to 1937. A large crowd waited on the town's wharf, with the Legion bugle band, the Legion pipe band and the Lions pipe band. Local radio station CHPS broadcast Mayor W.H.C. Jackson's address to the gathering, as well as the dedication by members of the local clergy. That evening the officers and crew attended a banquet at Nobel's Malcolm Club.

On Monday morning and afternoon visitors roamed over the warship, with the officers and crew members explaining the instruments on the bridge, quarterdeck and wheelhouse. Sightseers not satisfied with seeing the upper decks took the trip down to the engine room and the quarters below. "All were loud in their praise of the courtesy displayed by the officers and men," the *North Star* reported. "The only thing that did not appear to be welcome was a camera—in action. Many pictures were taken from the wharf—but while on shipboard—well, it was just not done."[5]

On Monday evening the officers and crew attended a dinner hosted by the Rebekahs at the IOOF building. Mayor Jackson acted as master of ceremonies while MP Slaght was guest speaker. A street dance followed.

The warship departed Parry Sound on Tuesday morning and arrived 24 days later at Halifax, having had additional equipment fitted and ammunition loaded aboard at Montreal and Quebec City. After a training period at Bermuda from October 18 to November 7, she sailed for Londonderry from St. John's, Newfoundland, as one of three escorts to two groups of American-built submarine chasers being delivered to the Russian navy.[6]

In November 1944, HMCS *Parry Sound* joined escort group C-7, operating as part of Western Approaches Command Londonderry. This escort group consisted of the river class frigates HMCS *Lanark* and HMCS *Cap de la Madeleine*, the castle class corvette HMCS *Copper Cliff*, as well as the flower class corvettes *Hawkesbury*, *Owen Sound*, *Merrittonia* and *Parry Sound*.

By this time the Battle of the Atlantic had turned in favour of the Allies. Special support groups—the first hunter-killer groups—had been introduced in April 1943 to intercept attackers before they could reach the close escort screen of convoys. Aircraft carriers equipped with special anti-submarine airplanes

On April 18, 1945 the crew of HMCS *Parry Sound* held a burial service for a young sailor found drifting in the ocean. Seaman Joseph E. Bouchard died a month earlier when the minesweeper HMCS *Guysborough* went down off the coast of France with 51 of her crew. *Courtesy of Joe Burnie*.

helped spread air cover over the entire convoy route. Previously, there had been an immense gap in the mid-Atlantic that even long-range patrol aircraft flying from Newfoundland, Iceland and the United Kingdom simply could not reach. At the same time, British cipher experts had broken the Enigma code used by the U-boats for communication and could determine their location and movements. U-boat losses now reached one or more a day. By 1944 U-boat missions became suicidal with a life expectancy of a single eight-week tour.

The last two convoys escorted by C-7 sailed after VE-Day and, while there was a possibility that U-boats might still be operating, none attacked during this period. The escort group sailed from Londonderry for the last time on May 31, took aboard naval personnel at Glasgow the next day and disbanded on arrival at St. John's on June 7. HMCS *Parry Sound* sailed for Sydney, Nova Scotia, on July 7 for disposal by the War Assets Corporation.[7]

Although sold for scrap to Meyer Brenner & Co. Ltd. of Toronto on October 17, the ship was resold to Transatlantica Financiera

Industrial S.A. of Montevideo, Uruguay. She sailed for Kiel, Germany, to be converted as a whale catcher along with a number of other Canadian and British corvettes, and entered service in 1950 under the Honduran flag as *Olympic Champion*. In 1956, she was sold to Japanese owners and renamed *Otori Maru No. 15*. She was last noted in Lloyd's List for 1962–63.[8]

The bell of HMCS *Parry Sound*, together with a commemorative scroll, was presented to the town on April 10, 1951, and entrusted to the Royal Canadian Legion, Pioneer Branch 117. The Legion branch also has an album of photographs taken surreptitiously by Burnie while serving aboard the warship.

20

A Memorial to the Forest Rangers

THE SUMMER OF 2005 will mark the 30th anniversary of the official opening of the Parry Sound observation tower by the Ministry of Natural Resources. With its magnificent gardens and breathtaking view, the site remains a favourite with visitors to the town, but the setting also has an additional purpose, as Ontario's Minister of Natural Minister Leo Bernier told the assembled crowd during the opening ceremonies in August 1975:

> I think it especially fitting that some memorial such as this should be erected in honor of those forestry pioneers who, long ago, conceived, built and maintained the fire tower network. I refer, of course, to the forest rangers—that breed of man long since gone, who gave Ontario its first fire protection system.[1]

The government of Ontario first assumed responsibility for protecting the province's forest wealth in 1917. The government quickly realized that it was necessary to pinpoint fires in the early stages before they reached unmanageable size. As a result, a network of fire towers was created covering the forested areas of the province.

In 1922, the districts of Parry Sound and Muskoka were designated as the Georgian Bay District under the authority of district forester Peter McEwen, who was based in Parry Sound. He oversaw the erection of the towers in the area under his control and, within five years of his appointment, 40 per cent of the fires in the western half of his district were detected from the six steel towers.

The detection system was simple in principle and worked well in conditions of reasonable visibility. Besides a telephone and binoculars, each tower included a circular map table surrounded by a 360 degree azimuth ring. A long metal instrument with a hair sight, called an alidade, enabled the observer to take compass bearings of a column of smoke on the horizon. The tower's position occupied the central position of the map table and the alidade pivoted on this point. With practice, the tower man could estimate the distance of a suspected fire from his tower and determine its approximate position on his map. An accurate positioning, however, required an intersecting bearing reading from at least one other tower.

In 1925, McEwen sought approval from his superiors for a tower near Parry Sound to fill a gap in the system.[2] The Ontario Forestry Branch purchased a rocky barren site on Westgarth's Hill looking directly over the town, in the following year.

The tower at Parry Sound is believed to have been the only one of its kind ever erected in the province. The district forester wanted a tower specifically designed to fill the dual role of a public observation deck and a fire tower. For this reason, the builder utilized much heavier steel and included a network of stairs and landings inside the outer structural framework rather than just a straight ladder. The tower was also designed to be free-standing, without an array of guide wires that would detract from its aesthetic qualities or ruin the view from the lower levels. Perched on top of the 90-foot tower was an eight-foot octagon, with glass in the upper half, that served to protect the observer and his maps from the elements as he peered at the horizon.

The rangers erected the tower themselves in June 1927.[3] Among those who worked on it were: Peter Touffet, Bill Taylor, Ernie Beaumont, Peter Gregoire, Colin McInnis and Charles Macdonald, who became the first tower man. McEwen himself pitched in to put up the tower.

It appears from the start that McEwen intended that the site should be something more than just the location of a fire tower. He requested and got a tower deliberately designed to attract visitors. He knew that towers that were accessible or visible to the public were normally made as attractive as possible.

In 1927, the Ontario Forestry Branch erected a tower in Parry Sound for the detection of forest fires. Thousands of tourists also climbed the tower to view the scenery of Georgian Bay before it was dismantled in 1973. This Ministry of Natural Resources photo was taken in July 1958. *Courtesy of AO, RG 1-448-1, Box 68.*

Beginning in 1927, McEwen engineered the reforestation of the barren hill on which the tower stood. In all, 15 acres were planted that first year using some 22,000 trees, mostly white, red and jack pine, with some Scotch and a few maples and white birch scattered throughout for colour. In 1930 and 1931, another 18 acres were reforested with mixed conifers and a few hardwoods.

McEwen also had in mind the development of an attractive and charming park, with lawns and gardens that would blend harmoniously with the natural setting. The task, however, was not an easy one. Gravel and topsoil had to be hauled to the site and nearly all of the decorative rock was brought in by scow from islands in Georgian Bay. McEwen was extremely attached to the project and used every available ranger, including clerks and storemen on occasion, whenever he could spare them. There were never any idle men sitting around waiting for fires at the district headquarters.

The fishpond was dug with a scraper and a team of horses and then lined with stone in 1931. Around the same time, McEwen set out to design and build the sundial. In the next year, the rangers extended the parking areas for cars. In 1934, the rock garden around the base of the tower was completed.[4]

While thousands of people ascended the tower each summer, the only known fatality occurred in May 1937 when a local four-year-old slipped while descending the stairs and fell 60 feet to the ground.[5] Margaret Mary Munro died from a fractured skull after being taken unconscious by private automobile to the Parry Sound General Hospital.

The Parry Sound tower occupied a key position in the fire detection system for almost 40 years, but the rise of systematic aerial detection in the 1960s rendered the towers technologically obsolete and economically impractical. The Parry Sound tower ceased to be used for fire detection at the end of the 1966 season. While 25 towers had been manned in the district in 1960, this number had dropped to four in 1968. By 1972, not a single tower remained in operation.[6]

Without regular maintenance, the unused towers deteriorated and all but the Parry Sound tower were dismantled. Thousands of tourists continued to climb the tower every year to enjoy the Georgian Bay scenery until engineering studies in the spring of 1973 revealed that it was dangerously overloaded and unsafe.

While the original tower where rangers sat for endless hours scanning the bush for fires has been replaced, the gardens that McEwen and his men so laboriously developed around it remain as a legacy of the fire tower days.

21

Hockey Heroes

BILL CARSON, A STAR PLAYER in the Ontario Hockey Association (OHA) during the early 1920s, turned down repeated offers from National Hockey League (NHL) teams before finally joining the Toronto St. Patricks in April 1926 for what was then the highest salary ever paid to a professional hockey player. Three years later, Carson scored the winning goal in the Boston Bruins' first Stanley Cup. Virtually unknown today, Carson was from Parry Sound.

For many years, travellers on Highway 69 were greeted by a billboard announcing Parry Sound as "The Home of Bobby Orr." Inducted into the Hockey Hall of Fame in 1979 after playing 12 seasons in the National Hockey League, Orr is a legend in his home town where he was honoured with "Bobby Orr Day" after scoring the winning goal for the Bruins in the 1970 Stanley Cup championship. The Bobby Orr Community Centre opened four years later and now there is the Bobby Orr Hockey Hall of Fame on the waterfront. Bill Carson, however, remains largely unrecognized by his home town, as are his younger brothers, Frank and Gerry, who also played on Stanley Cup-winning teams.

William James Carson was born in Bracebridge on November 25, 1900, the second son of lumberman Donald Melvin Carson and his wife, Elizabeth.[1] Shortly after the birth of Francis Reginald on January 12, 1902, the family relocated to Parry Sound, where George Gerald was born on October 10. 1903. Former Parry Sound High School teacher John Maddeford has operated the Carson House Bed & Breakfast with his wife, Donna, in the old Carson family home at

33 Church Street since 1999. "Since our surname is Maddeford, most of our guests are justifiably curious to know why our B&B is called the Carson House and not the Maddeford House," he says.[2]

In his 1974 book, *Bobby Orr: My Game*, Orr recounts how he and other boys his age used to skate for 30 hours or so on the Seguin River or the waterfront each and every week from the end of October until the middle of April. "Thinking back to those days in Parry Sound and comparing them to what I see nowadays, I realize how fortunate I was to have grown up when I did. And where I did. Everyone in Parry Sound took an active interest in hockey," Orr wrote. "Unfortunately for hockey, that type of interest no longer seems to exist ..., not even in Parry Sound. There are more diversions now for the kids and their parents. In Parry Sound, I suspect that kids spend more time on snowmobiles now than they do on ice skates."[3]

Bill Carson recalled his childhood in Parry Sound in a memoir published in 1960, which somewhat echoes Orr's sentiments. In the early days of the NHL, Parry Sound produced a number of professional players because boys in the community lived and breathed hockey for five months out of every year.

Bill Carson with his eldest brother, Leslie, and dog Jeff in 1910. Leslie, who remained in Parry Sound and worked with his father in family business, would die tragically from a heart attack in December 1938, when he was only 40 years old. *Courtesy of Ted Carson.*

In those days hockey was about our only sport and pastime. Radio and TV were still only a dream, the movies were a luxury and, of course, silent. Therefore, us kids had to make our own ice in order to play a little shinny and more than once a small rink was made on somebody's lawn for at least one season. We never got the same spot twice because when the spring came and the grass didn't grow, we had had it. One of our favourite rinks was the old creek that used to run through the field where now stands the high school. This was considered open territory and many a free-for-all would break out when one gang would try to capture the ice from the younger fry, including myself.[4]

Star hockey players Bill and Frank Carson left Parry Sound in 1918, along with Norman Shay, to attend Woodstock College and the *North Star* lamented that the community needed an Ontario Hockey Association team in order to give local boys something to which they could look forward. Two months later, the newspaper reported Clarence Wood and Ed Laird were playing for the Stayner

In the Carson family home at 33 Church St. during the winter of 1913–14. *Back row, left to right*: Leslie Carson, Melinda Carson, Elizabeth Carson, Bill Carson, Donald Melvin Carson, Maggie Hughes. *Front row*: Gerald Carson and Frank Carson. *Courtesy of Ted Carson.*

team. The editorials intensified after the Woodstock team visited Parry Sound and gave local fans the "best hockey game of this season" at the Palace Arena. By the end of 1919, Parry Sound had an intermediate OHA team for the first time since the 1906-07 season, largely due to the efforts of former mayor H.M. Purvis, who was president of the club.[5]

Just before the end of the First World War my father asked me my intentions. That is, what did I want to be—a doctor, lawyer, engineer or dentist. I was then going on 17 and like most lads of that era wasn't quite sure what I wanted to do. I do remember saying that I wanted to be a hockey player and my father replied that hockey players also have to have another vocation to follow during the off season, as they said in those days.

Somehow or other my dad seemed to instill in me the possibilities of being a dentist. It was a good profession—they were

Outside the Carson family home during the winter of 1913–14. *Back row, left to right*: Donald Melvin Carson, Melinda Carson, Elizabeth Carson, Maggie Hughes. *Front row*: Frank Carson, Leslie Carson, Gerald Carson and Bill Carson. *Courtesy of Ted Carson.*

considered the tops in their field and also reputable citizens in any man's town.

I can remember quite well thinking how a sign or shingle as they are commonly known, would look in front of my office when I graduated. Yes, there it was. 'Dr. William Carson, Dentist.' I can remember my enthusiasm to pass my exams and get that sign as soon as I could.[6]

Bill Carson began his studies in dentistry at the University of Toronto in September 1919 and graduated in 1923. During those four years, he played on the varsity hockey team, which won the intercollegiate title every year, the Allan Cup in 1921 and also was runner-up for the Allan Cup in 1920. "He is credited almost unanimously by the critics with being the shiftiest centre player in the amateur ranks," reported *The Daily Mail and Empire* in March 1921. "Against the Soo a week ago Bill scored eight of Varsity's 13 goals, a record for goal-getting in a single game of that calibre that will likely go unchallenged for a good many seasons.... Early in the season he was much sought after by St. Patrick NHL club, but refused the very flattering offer made him."[7]

After graduation, Carson moved to Grimsby, Ontario, where he played OHA Sr. hockey with the Peach Kings along with his youngest brother, Gerald. In March 1924, *The Globe* and the *The Daily Star* both reported that Carson would be opening a dental practice in Stratford, Ontario, and playing centre for the Stratford Indians, alongside brother Frank.[8] After the 1918–19 season with Woodstock College, Frank began playing with the OHA Jr. Stratford Midgets and then the OHA Sr. Indians. In 1920, Frank had purchased a men's clothing store in Stratford in partnership with Midgets teammate Ed Laird.

In December 1924, the manager of the Stratford Indians, Roy Brothers, told *The Globe* that Bill Carson had refused yet another bid to play for the St. Patricks and the Montreal Maroons had offered $4,000 a season for two years and a signing bonus of $1,000. "Carson turned down St. Pat's offer last year to please his father," Brothers said. "In fact, the two Carson brothers have an agreement with their father not to turn professional. Besides, Dr.

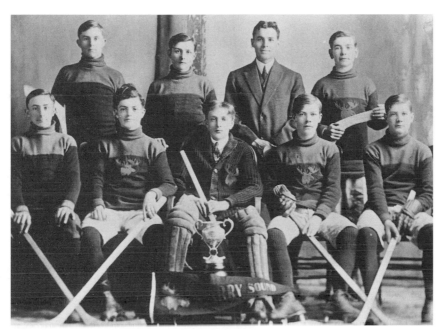

"The Elks," 1913. *Front, left to right*: Bill Carson, N. Keith, L. Biehn, C. Robinson, William Taylor. *Back*: Leslie Carson, Norman Shay, William Thorne (manager), H. Bottrell. After playing on the Woodstock Athletics with Bill and Frank Carson in 1918–19, Shay began a professional hockey career with the Port Colborne Sailors. He played 53 NHL games with the Boston Bruins and Toronto St. Patricks before being claimed on waivers in October 1926 by the New Haven Eagles of the Canadian-American Hockey League. *Courtesy of AO / David L. Thomas Collection, C253 Tray 11-36.*

Bill gave me his word of honour that he would not accept terms to play pro hockey under any circumstances."[9]

The St. Pats persisted in making offers to Bill Carson, who was the top OHA scorer in both 1925 and 1926, but *The Daily Star* reported in mid-January 1926 that he refused to sign a contract unless the club signed his brother Frank as well. "It is true enough that we would like to have Bill Carson for our team and it is true enough that Bill Carson and his brother Frank and their father were all down here yesterday discussing the matter, but we have not signed either of the Carsons and we have no immediate hope of doing so," St. Pats' manager Charlie Querrie said.[10] Things changed very quickly, however, when Frank signed a contract with the Montreal Maroons on January 23 and days later the OHA suspended

Bill for punching a referee.[11] On April 16, Bill signed a three-year contract with Toronto worth $22,000. To put this in perspective, no rookie received more than $8,000 per season until Bobby Orr signed his first professional contract with the Bruins in 1966, a deal that gave him a $25,000 per season salary and a signing bonus of at least $20,000.[12]

Carson proved himself to be well worth his hefty paycheque, scoring 16 goals during the 1926-27 season and 20 in 1927-28. In mid-January 1928, during his second season with Toronto, Carson was ranked third in the list of NHL goal scorers, behind Montreal Canadiens players Howie Morenz and Aurel Joliat, when he was hospitalized during a very physical game with the Detroit Cougars, after his head hit the ice and he was knocked unconscious. The injury proved more serious than first thought when X-rays revealed a fractured skull, which kept Carson out of the lineup until mid-March.[13]

In May 1927, Carson had been appointed by the Ontario Ministry of Health as a travelling dentist, providing free services to children in various northern communities that did not have resident dentists, a job he performed diligently before returning to the Toronto Maple Leafs for the 1927-28 season.[14] Carson again worked for the ministry during the spring and summer of 1928, apparently getting a lot of pleasure from interacting with youngsters. "To obtain the confidence of the pupils it is necessary to humour them at times and a good method, I found, was to carry a softball and a bat, and in that way show them that a dentist is human," Carson told a reporter. "When we got started to work in the chair, it seemed to be a lot of fun for them. The dental equipment I carried was all strange to them and they wanted to know all about everything. By keeping a child's mind on the instrument, I often had a cavity filled before he knew it."[15]

Bill Carson went back to the Toronto Maple Leafs for 1928–29, but his performance was nowhere near what it had been during the previous two years when he was the team's leading scorer. Then a serious elbow injury in November 1928 kept Carson out of several games. *The Evening Telegram* claimed Carson was "pouting" because Andy Blair, who replaced him at centre, had emerged as a star in his own right, leading the Leafs in assists during his 1928-29 rookie season. A road trip with games against Detroit, New York and Montreal "was the straw that broke the camel's back." Apparently, Carson argued with Leafs manager Conn Smythe prior to the Montreal game and "as a result Carson sat on the bench throughout the entire Canadiens game, something new for him." The Leafs sold Carson to the Boston Bruins on January 25, 1929.

"I will not have a player on this club that doesn't battle all the way. Carson was not giving us his best and a change was the only solution," Smythe told *The Evening Telegram*. "The boys battled in each of the three road games and it was indeed discouraging to see Bill doing the opposite."[16] *The Globe* later pointed out that the Toronto club owners were not within their rights in selling Carson because his three-year contract stated he could not be traded, sold or fined. Carson finally agreed to go to Boston after initially telling the newspapers that he would not.[17]

During the remainder of the 1928–29 regular season, Carson scored only four goals for the Boston Bruins in 19 games. The Bruins' investment paid off, however, when Carson slipped the puck past New York Rangers goalie John Ross Roach 18 minutes into the third period of Game 2 of the Stanley Cup finals, winning the series for Boston. But then, during the 1929–30 regular season, Carson scored a dismal seven goals in 44 games.

In October 1930, *The Globe* reported that "the Bruins, champions of the National Hockey League, have disposed of the services of Bill Carson, a man who could have been as great as he cared to be in the winter sport."[18] A month later, the newspaper reported that Carson had been picked up by the London Tecumsehs of the International Hockey League, a team headed by former Stratford Indians manager Roy Brothers. "Carson was with Brothers at Stratford when the present London pilot had a strong OHA senior team in the Classic City," *The Globe* said. "Carson is a young man yet, and under Brother's able handling he may regain the condition and cleverness that made him a brilliant player three or four years ago."[19] However, after playing just seven games for London, Carson retired from hockey, although he attempted a brief 33-game comeback with the New Haven Eagles of the Canadian-American League during 1933–34.

Bill Carson played 63 regular-season games and eleven
playoff games for the Boston Bruins, and made significant
contributions to the team's 1929 Stanley Cup win. Carson was released in October 1930, three weeks before
the start of the 1930–31 NHL season, when the team
was in Vancouver on an exhibition tour. *Courtesy of Hockey
History Inc. Archives, circa 1929.*

Ted Carson of Sudbury recalls that his great uncle Bill became a
dentist in Aurora after his hockey career ended, although he seems
not to have been listed in the Bell Telephone directories.[20] In September 1931, the former NHL star received severe head and face
injuries when his car crashed into a TTC standard on Lakeshore
Boulevard in Mimico and he was arrested on a charge of driving
while intoxicated.[21] Dr. Carson's name does appear in the Parry
Sound telephone directories for three years between 1939 and 1941.

Frank Carson, who had been signed as a free agent by the Montreal Maroons in January 1926, helped his team win the Stanley

Cup just a few weeks later. He played a further two full seasons with the Maroons before winding up with the minor-league Stratford Nationals. He made it back to the NHL with the New York Americans in 1930-31 after scoring 31 goals and 14 assists in 41 games the previous year with the Windsor Bulldogs of the IHL, his best season ever. He officially announced his retirement from hockey on October 15, 1934, after three NHL seasons in Detroit with the Falcons and Red Wings. He was then named coach of the Windsor Mic-Macs. He later represented the Industrial Acceptance Corporation at Windsor and Chatham, retiring to Cumlin, near London, where he operated a general store. Carson died suddenly from a heart attack on April 21, 1957, at age 55, only hours after a lengthy outline of his hockey career appeared in the *London Free Press*.[22]

Gerald Carson made his professional debut with the Philadelphia Arrows of the Can-Am League (joining Norman Shay of Parry Sound) after four seasons with the Grimsby Peach Kings. His first NHL year was 1928-29 when he played initially for the Montreal Canadiens before being loaned to the New York Rangers in February 1929. He returned to the Canadiens for 1929-30 to help the club win its second Stanley Cup and was then traded in October 1930 to the Providence Reds of the Can-Am League. A year after brother Frank made it back to the NHL ranks, Gerald also made a comeback and played three full seasons with the Montreal Canadiens, but his career was interrupted when he suffered a serious off-season injury and missed all of 1935-36 recovering from knee surgery. He spent his final year of professional hockey with the Montreal Maroons before retiring. He returned to Grimsby and worked as a salesman for the Dow Brewing Company until his death on November 9, 1956 at age 53.[23]

Days after Bill Carson's death in Parry Sound on May 29, 1967, at age 67, former Toronto Maple Leafs assistant general manager and former defenceman King Clancy told *Globe and Mail* columnist Dick Beddoes that Carson could have been the greatest hockey player there ever was.[24] Although Carson's stellar NHL career was ostensibly derailed by the serious head injury suffered in 1928, his later years were ruined by alcohol. In March 1956, Judge Francis Colenso Powell sentenced Carson to two months in jail for stealing $50 from a friend in McDougall Township and recommended that he be treated for alcoholism. "It grieves me very much, Bill, to find you guilty of this offence," Judge Powell told Carson. "This can be blamed entirely upon drink and anything that can be done to correct this situation will be to your advantage."[25]

Bill Carson's passing was marked with only a three sentence notice in the *North Star* and there were no tributes or obituaries in the Toronto newspapers.[26] He rests in an unmarked grave in the Carson family plot in Hillcrest Cemetery.

22

The Bulldozing of History

Iɴ Mᴀʀᴄʜ 1985, ᴀ ʙᴜʟʟᴅᴏᴢᴇʀ belonging to Maclaim Construction destroyed an irreplaceable piece of Parry Sound's history. The building was the last standing structure in the town tied directly to the lumber industry that had served as the prime reason for the community's existence in the 19th century.

Following the demolition, Britt resident and chairman of the Parry Sound Local Architectural Conservation Advisory Committee (LACAC) Stephen Wohleber attacked the town council for allowing the destruction of such an important piece of the town's past. Council showed no remorse for the action. Agitated at being rebuked, Councillor Barbara Sipila rudely remarked, "Do we go up to Britt and tell you how to run your affairs?"[1]

In most cases, buildings of importance to our past, such as the former Bank of Ottawa (Bank of Nova Scotia), cannot be preserved because they are privately owned. While the town council does have the power to protect buildings from demolition or modification, it is rarely exercised. Council passed two bylaws protecting the IOOF building and the former Kitchen house at 10 Ashwood Drive in February 1983.[2] Unfortunately, the remains of the Patent Cloth Board Company of Parry Sound Limited, located on property already owned by the corporation, were not so lucky.

The Patent Cloth Board Factory of Parry Sound Limited was incorporated under the Ontario Joint Stock Companies Act in 1897 with an authorized capitalization of $30,000.[3] The shareholders were William Walter Keighley and his wife, Fanny Maud Keighley; William Keighley's brother Lester John Keighley; and William

The Patent Cloth Board Factory buildings shortly after the
firm began operation. The sturdy stone building housing
the steam boilers stands beneath the smokestack. *Taken
from* The Parry Sound Directory, 1898–99.

Herbert Marcon and his wife, Amy Marcon. At the time of incorporation all of the parties lived in Toronto and, while William Keighley,
William Marcon and Lester Keighley were appointed as directors of
the company, the two women together held $24,000 in stock.

William Beatty Jr. sold the company 4.9 acres at the foot of
Prospect Street in August 1897. Construction presumably began
on the company's facilities shortly after, and a bylaw granted the
new company exemption from municipal taxation for ten years.[4]
In the factory, logs were steamed and rotated against a cutting edge
to produce thin strips of wood. These light boards were destined
for textile mills to roll bolts of fabric, as well as for veneers. The
facilities built by the company were quite extensive. Following a
common practice in the construction of sawmills, the boilers and
engines driving the machinery were enclosed in a stone building
so that the blast would be contained in the event of an explosion.[5]

The company began production in 1898 and the annual return
to the provincial-secretary of Ontario for the year ending December 1899 shows that William and Amy Marcon were both residing
in Parry Sound, as were William Keighley and his brother Lester.
While the two wives still held $24,000 in stock, a new stock-
holder, George Worthington, a Chicago capitalist and banker, now
held $2,000 worth of stock.[6]

The annual return of December 1900 indicates the first sign of trouble for the company as William Marcon had left Parry Sound to pursue mining in Vancouver, while his wife was residing in Guelph. Lester Keighley was working as an accountant in Chicago. The subsequent return shows that the Marcons had severed all connection with the venture and sold their shares to William Keighley, who was the only shareholder still residing in Parry Sound.[7]

The final annual meeting of the board of directors of the Patent Cloth Board Company of Parry Sound Limited, at which only William Keighley, Worthington and Lester Keighley were present, took place in February 1902. On May 6, 1903, Justice Thomas Ferguson of the Supreme Court of Ontario issued an order that the company be liquidated as per the provisions of Ontario's Winding Up Act. Edward Roger Curzon Clarkson of Toronto was appointed the liquidator and granted powers to dispose of all the company's assets and pay the creditors. He sold the facilities and the 4.9 acres to George Neibergall of Echo Bay, Ontario, for $3,000 in May 1906.[8]

Neibergall formed the registered partnership of George Niebergall & Son with his son William, who moved to Parry Sound as resident manager and purchased a dwelling on Waubeek Street. In the spring of 1911, the Niebergalls granted almost an acre to the Canadian Pacific Railway for the construction of a spur line across their property facilitating the transportation of their wood products by rail.[9]

On September 11, 1912, a fire raged through the buildings standing at the foot of Prospect Street and destroyed the structures erected by the defunct Patent Cloth Board Company of Parry Sound Limited, with the exception of the stone walls of the boiler shed and an unattached dryer house. George and William Niebergall subsequently sold the property with a six-acre water lot to Mark Rogers of Huntsville for $6,000 in November 1918 and the partnership of George Niebergall & Son was dissolved shortly afterwards.[10]

William Niebergall continued to live in his home on Waubeek Street until he passed away on September 4, 1935, at the age of 70.[11] He had suffered a stroke several months earlier and had been confined to his home, gradually growing weaker.

Insurance plans for Parry Sound prepared by the Underwriters Survey Bureau in October 1908 show the premises virtually

Enlarged by George Niebergall & Son, the wooden buildings originally erected by the Patent Cloth Board Factory
were destroyed by fire in September 1912. Only the stone
building survived to be utilized by the property's next
owner, Mark Rogers, who operated a sawmill. *Courtesy of
the Parry Sound Public Library Historical Collection, VF II.*

unchanged since the days of the Patent Cloth Board Company and
the boilers were still housed in the stone structure. Revisions of
August 1924, however, show very different facilities and the stone
building was now utilized for the storage of lumber. It was totally
isolated from the facilities of the sawmill and planing mill, which
were powered by electricity.

The property of the Patent Cloth Board Company of Parry Sound
Limited passed through the hands of successive owners and the buildings located there suffered repeated fires, but the stone boiler shed
withstood it all. Surviving numerous modifications and serving a
variety of uses, the structure remained the single enduring feature
on an ever-changing site. Eventually, the Corporation of the Town
of Parry Sound purchased the property for the new Waubuno Park
development. At a meeting in September 1984, Councillor Reg
Healey moved that council accept a $4,000 bid from Maclaim Con-
struction to remove the four buildings located there. The motion
was seconded by Councillor Sid McConnell and accepted.[12]

At the next council meeting Nancy Cunningham appeared on
behalf of LACAC to ask council to delay demolition of the stone
building until it could be assessed by experts. Museum curator

Peter F. McVey presented a written appeal from the executive of the West Parry Sound District Museum that the building be spared until it had been thoroughly examined. He stated that the Ontario Heritage Foundation had expressed an interest in the structure and grants for restoration were available.[13]

The resolution to destroy the building had been passed on a recommendation of the Waubuno Park Advisory Committee. The town's representative on the committee was Councillor Brian Bannerman, who apologized to Cunningham that LACAC, another committee of council, had not been consulted or informed before the tenders were announced. He admitted ignorance in not suggesting to council that the building might have been of historic or architectural significance. As a face-saving gesture, Bannerman made a motion calling for the postponement of demolition until the spring of 1985, which was seconded by Councillor McConnell and carried. While Councillor Healey was in favour of the delay, he remained adamant that the building conflicted with the corporation's plans for the shoreline.

At the November 20, 1984, council meeting, Cunningham introduced Mark Fram of the Ontario Heritage Foundation (OHF) and he presented a written report advising council not to demolish the building.[14] In his assessment, he described the building as a rare industrial type, notable for its rough and ready stone masonry. He said the masonry had been remarkably well laid and remained solid despite awkward openings cut into the walls and the weakness or absence of mortar. Given Parry Sound's historical development, Fram said, an opportunity to uncover artifacts associated with the waterfront milling industries ought to be very useful for local history, museum and tourism purposes, and demolition would destroy an irreplaceable opportunity.

He advised council that a program offered by the Ontario Heritage Foundation and the Ministry of Citizenship and Culture could provide a consultant to carry out a professional evaluation of the stone building within a fairly short time. While he could not be specific, he predicted it would be done before the end of December. Fram also offered a rationale for proceeding with an archeological survey of the site in the spring. He explained that these are generally carried out by students as summer works projects at the instigation of a graduate student interested in organizing such a dig and making the funding application.

With the frost still on the ground, the Maclaim bulldozer moved in and levelled the building in March 1985. There was no archeological dig conducted on the site, as LACAC and the OHF had hoped for at the very least. At the council meeting of April 2, 1985, Stephen Wohleber, chairman of LACAC, said that he could have understood such an occurrence in a larger environment where graft and corruption could form a monetary incentive for such an action. But in Parry Sound, as there was no discernible reward to be gleaned, he deemed the action must have been due to petty vindictiveness.[15]

He pointed out that LACAC is a committee of council, appointed by council and responsible to council, but it seemed to have no say. He found this disturbing and later expressed a good deal of sorrow that the region had lost a potential tourist attraction as well as an opportunity for students to experience an archeological dig. Councillor Healey was once again adamant that the building simply had to go. Mayor Wilfred Hall stated he hadn't been aware of the structure's removal.

There was no compelling reason to remove the building in March. Not until May 1985 did the Ministry of Municipal Affairs and Housing approve a grant of $47,125 for the construction of the parking lot and boat launch ramp at Waubuno Park.[16] The grant came under the ministry's Marina and Boating Facilities Program. Even more astounding, it was not until the council meeting of September 3, 1985, that Councillor McConnell moved that the corporation call for tenders to construct the parking lot and boat access ramp. At the October 1, 1985, meeting, council awarded a contract to Maclaim Construction to complete the work for a six-figure sum.[17]

The question of who gave the order to destroy the stone building in March remains unanswered, but it is clear that the structure stood in the way of corporation plans for the site and LACAC was gearing up for an all-out campaign to save it.

Parry Sound Today

P ARRY SOUND HAS PROBABLY UNDERGONE more changes in the last 25 years than in the any other similar time period in its history. The annexation of a portion of McDougall Township in January 1980 doubled the geographic area of the municipality to ten square miles and finally settled costly amalgamation attempts that had preoccupied and hamstrung Parry Sound councillors for more than a decade. Uncertainty over how far the municipality's borders would eventually extend had, for example, led to the indefinite postponement of important decisions about the construction of a new fire hall and enlarged police accommodations. Developing a detailed strategy to attract tourists and waterfront redevelopment were also not on the agenda.

In the beginning, the commercial core of the community centred around the general store owned by William Beatty at the intersection of James Street and Seguin Street. Virtually every other merchant operated along these two main streets. After the extension of a highway north from Parry Sound during the Depression, all cottagers and other automobile travellers to points beyond passed over the Seguin Street bridge and through the downtown. In his January 1949 inaugural address, Mayor Abe Adams commented on the congested traffic conditions and wondered if motorists couldn't be encouraged to use other streets to get through town.[1] The volume increased tremendously when the Trans-Canada Highway opened through to Sudbury. Back then there were more than a dozen gas stations along the Bowes Street/Seguin Street/Church Street artery.

In the east ward, a second commercial strip flourished for decades along Parry Sound Road, but the repeal of the Beatty Covenant in 1950 sounded its death knell, for both the liquor store and the beer store soon relocated across the river. Many of the east ward commercial establishments have been converted into residences although the century-old Shamess Block, which council had at one time designated a heritage building, sat empty for years and was demolished in September 2001.[2]

Shortly after the province constructed a highway bypass around Parry Sound in the early 1960s, the community's elected representatives began discussions with their counterparts in Foley and McDougall about amalgamation, discussions which began amicably but soon soured. "We can no longer continue to be strangled within our boundaries," Mayor George Saad wrote to McDougall Reeve Wilbert John Foreman in March 1969.[3] After first pursuing an amalgamation with just Foley and McDougall, Parry Sound council passed a bylaw in March 1970 requesting the Ministry of Municipal Affairs allow the municipality amalgamate with the townships of Foley, McDougall, Humphrey, Christie, McKellar, Hagerman, Carling and the village of Rosseau, as well as annex parts of the unorganized townships of Ferguson, Conger, Cowper, Croft, Spence and McKenzie. The Ontario Municipal Board convened a hearing at the Foley Agricultural Hall over several days in July and October 1972, but ultimately rejected the application.[4] However, David K. Martin's District of Parry Sound Local Government Study, released in August 1976, recommended that Parry Sound, Foley, McDougall and Carling be amalgamated to form a single municipality.

Parry Sound council established a five-member waterfront study coordinating committee in December 1981 chaired by Coun. Reg Healey, who declared the town was 20 years behind in getting started. The Toronto consulting firm of Marshall, Macklin and Monaghan spent nine months preparing a 200-page "conceptual" waterfront study aimed at transforming Parry Sound into a resort community over a long period of time with tourism becoming the area's primary industry. "At the present time, tourism is incidental and not the driving force behind the community," a

The Rotary and Algonquin Regiment Fitness Trail follows an
old railway right-of-way along Parry Sound's waterfront.
Courtesy of Adrian Hayes.

representative of the firm said in 1983. "Basically, the idea is to
attract tourists here and get them to spend money in this area."[5]

Several recommendations in the consultant's report became
realities fairly quickly. A new beach opened at Waubuno Park in
1986, as did a temporary museum in the old Mary Street fire hall.
The municipality also purchased the unused waterfront spur lines
from the Canadian Pacific Railway. Mayor Roy O'Halloran, who
served as a sergeant in the Algonquin Regiment until January 1943,
when he was accepted for training as an officer, saw to it that the
railway lands became the Rotary and Algonquin Regiment Fitness
Trail, which opened in 1991.

The Town of Parry Sound constructed a breakwater to protect
the inner harbour and the Big Sound Marina at Bob's Point in 1988.
Since it opened, the marina for transient boaters has been operated by the local Chamber of Commerce. Under the current
agreement, the Chamber pays the municipality five per cent of
the marina's gross revenue. The Chamber is responsible for paying for maintenance and repairs for the facility up to five percent
of the gross revenue and the municipality pays the rest.[6] In addition, the municipality has been trying for years to have the Ministry
of Natural Resources, the Ontario Provincial Police and the Ministry of Northern Development and Mines move from their
location just north of the marina. The town wants to purchase the

Between June and Thanksgiving Monday, the *Island Queen V* takes passengers on a three-hour cruise on Georgian Bay. For more than three decades, the ship has been one of Parry Sound's premier tourist attractions. *Courtesy of Adrian Hayes.*

land and then sell it to a developer for a hotel complex or resort. As the Ontario Realty Corporation is not permitted to deal with the private sector on the sale of property, the municipality must act as an intermediary for developers.[7]

In September 1919, council granted Imperial Oil permission to erect two storage tanks. Fuel oil, kerosene and other petroleum products from the company's refinery at Sarnia began coming into Parry Sound's harbour by tanker ships to be transported by rail as far north as Cochrane and south to Orillia. By 1941, the operation had grown to such an extent that Imperial Oil was the municipality's biggest taxpayer. However, in September 1950, the community became aware of how dangerous the operation was to both the environment and tourism when two million gallons of bunker oil escaped from one of the tanks and flowed into the sparking waters of the inner harbour.[8] Despite the best efforts contain the spill with a makeshift boom, oil eventually drifted as far south as Five Mile Bay and north to Nobel and Carling Bay. Some 38 islands suffered damage and cleanup efforts employing hundreds of men went on until April 1952.

Imperial Oil began to disassemble the storage tanks in August 1984, greatly improving the appearance of the harbour, but because the company knows the soil is contaminated it has not offered the 16-acre site for sale, although Parry Sound council would like to see redevelopment. In January 2004, council passed a resolution that if Imperial Oil is prepared to finance soil testing and clean up of the property, and sell it to the municipality for a nominal amount, then council will amend the official plan and zoning of the land to exclude residential uses. "They're worried about liability more than anything else," Councillor Conrad van der Valk told the *North Star*, "They realize that by removing the residential designation they are off the hook for a lot of it."[9]

For over three decades the 550-passenger Island Queen V tour boat has offered visitors a three-hour cruise introducing the natural beauty of Georgian Bay's 30,000 Islands region. The 65-foot M.V. Chippewa III, a former Niagara Falls Maid of the Mist, also offers a variety of daytime excursions and dinner cruises, while Georgian Bay Airways has air tours and sightseeing packages.

The jewel of the waterfront is the $12.5 million Charles W. Stockey Centre for the Performing Arts and Bobby Orr Hall of Fame, built on property purchased by the municipality in 1986 from Ultramar Canada. In addition to an acoustically perfect performance hall used by the world renowned Festival of the Sound, the multi-purpose facility also pays homage to the life and career

The $12.5 million Charles W. Stockey Centre for the Performing Arts and the Bobby Orr Hall of Fame opened in July 2003. *Courtesy of Adrian Hayes.*

Perhaps best known for his "glory days" with the Boston Bruins, Bobby Orr, Parry Sound's favourite son, ranks alongside Wayne Gretzky and Mario Lemieux when hockey experts are polled. *Courtesy of Canada's Sports Hall of Fame.*

of the Parry Sound-born hockey icon who started playing for the Boston Bruins in 1966 at age 18, as well as other notable professional and amateur athletes from the area. The Bobby Orr Hall of Fame plans to add a half-dozen or so new inductees each year.

Parry Sound has done much to develop tourism in the two decades since the Marshall, Macklin and Monaghan study. A new climate-controlled West Parry Sound District Museum opened in 1991 beside the 100-foot observation tower, which is now owned and maintained by the municipality. Annual events such as the Spring Jam Festival, Spring Fling, Sportbike Festival, Dragon Boat Festival, Tugfest, Native Awareness Days, Poetry Bash and the Parry Sound

Logging Days Festival draw thousands of visitors to the community. After one local resident recently wrote a letter to the editor complaining about visitors to town, a *North Star* editorial reminded readers how important tourists are to the local economy:

> No matter how you cut it, just about everyone in this area has a connection to the tourism industry. The more attractions there are, the more people want to be here and come back and the more money they spend, which is what makes every part of our world go 'round.
>
> So, if you're one of those people who gets upset when a 'visitor' almost knocks you down, while trying to get somewhere in the community, be polite, smile, and don't worry about it. They are helping to keep you, or someone you know, employed.[10]

Parry Sound has a vibrant community of artists and crafters who have staged the annual Art in the Park for three decades. A $150,000 restoration grant from the municipality allowed an energetic volunteer group headed by retired high-school teacher Ralph Smith to rehabilitate the old CPR railway station over a two-year period as a year-round showplace for the work of area artists and artisans. The Station Gallery Association leases the building, which is recognized as a heritage railway station by the Historic Sites and Monuments Board of Canada, from the municipality. For three days each October, area artists also open their homes to visitors during the Thanksgiving Studio Tour.

The 128-slip Big Sound Marina, operated by the local Chamber of Commerce, has laundry facilities and showers for transient boaters. *Courtesy of Adrian Hayes.*

The new Waubuno Park has replaced the unused buildings of
the former Jacklin Lumber Company. *Courtesy of Adrian Hayes.*

Over the last 15 years the real commercial growth in Parry Sound
has occurred along Bowes Street, starting with the opening of a
McDonald's restaurant in March 1989. Numerous fast-food
restaurants and coffee shops have sprung up along this strip, as well
as a Sobeys and a new Canadian Tire store. The traditional downtown area has changed as well. Years ago, there were hardware stores
and grocery stores, and residents of the community could do most
of their shopping by simply walking through the downtown core.

It was announced in April 2004 that a 72,000 square foot Wal-
Mart, scheduled to open in January 2005, will be constructed on
Bowes Street at the south entrance to town.[11] The first phase of the
development includes up to 15,000 square feet for smaller tenants
and a second phase on land not currently zoned for commercial use
will bring the total size of the project to about 240,000 square feet,
making it the largest project of its kind between Barrie and Sudbury. Although Mayor Ted Knight is enthusiastic about the
development, saying focus groups had identified the need for a
Zellers or Wal-Mart, reaction from the existing business community has been mixed. In early July 2004, the property management
arm of the A&P grocery store chain filed an application in Superior
Court to quash the municipality's zoning bylaw alleging a "secret

A view of downtown Parry Sound, looking north on James Street. After 14 decades, the William Beatty Company Limited is still a fixture at the town's main intersection. *Courtesy of Adrian Hayes.*

scheme" existed between the Town of Parry Sound and the owners of Oastler Park Plaza Limited.

In many communities where a Wal-Mart-type development is built on the edge of town, the commercial core suffers irreparable damage. To help maintain the viability of Parry Sound's downtown, council has budgeted for a facade improvement program to provide loans to business owners to help cover the costs of improving storefronts. It will be interesting to see how merchants along James Street and Seguin Street will meet the challenges presented by the new Wal-Mart plaza.

As well, it is anticipated the new $24 million West Parry Sound Health Centre will be ready for business in April 2005 to replace the old hospitals on Bay Street and Church Street. Over the years the community has supported numerous initiatives that have raised over $5 million towards the West Parry Sound Health Centre Foundation's $6 million goal. Following the end of the Give-in-a-Heartbeat capital campaign in August 2005, fundraising efforts will continue through annual events. It's a testament to Parry Sound's growing importance as a vacation destination that 51.7 per cent of emergency room visits during August 2003 were made by patients residing outside of the West Parry Sound area.

Notes

INTRODUCTION

1   "The future of Parry Sound," *Parry Sound North Star*, Sept. 29, 1892, 2. Hereafter the newspaper is simply referred to as *North Star*.
2   Archives of Ontario (hereafter AO), RG 55-1, MS 7162, Lib. 40-36, Letters of incorporation for the Parry Sound Electric Light Company Ltd. dated Nov. 7, 1895.
3   "Houses wanted," *North Star*, May 9, 1907, 9.
4   "Editorial briefs," *North Star*, May 9, 1907, 5.
5   "That bylaw," *North Star*, Oct. 31, 1907, 3.
6   "Another bonus bylaw," *North Star*, Sept. 12, 1907, 5; "The board of trade," *North Star*, Oct. 3, 1907, 3; "Wood alcohol factory," *North Star*, March 12, 1908, 6; "Shortells Limited," *North Star*, March 26, 1908, 6.
7   "The smelter is coming," *North Star*, Feb. 27, 1908, 1.
8   Parry Sound Bylaw #347 passed Sept. 7, 1909.
9   Parry Sound Bylaw #388 passed Feb. 20, 1912. Whereas *North Star* editor William Ireland had been gung-ho on the bonuses, a new editor was much more critical. "Truly this granting of bonuses is a pernicious system and no town knows that better than Parry Sound," John Schofield Dick wrote in the Aug. 21, 1919, *North Star*. "It holds out inducements to weak or bankrupt companies, leading them to locate in a town where local conditions are not at all conducive to their special requirements. The consensus is the industries last just as long as the bonus lasts, and they collapse and the town has a big debenture to pay for an empty and useless factory."
10   "Canadian Explosives," *North Star*, Jan. 16, 1913, 5; "Closed down," *North Star*, Dec. 18, 1913, 5.
11   Manuscript on Nobel by Shirley Graham, written in March 1959 for C.C. Johnson of the Parry Sound Historical Society. Reprinted in Sam Brunton (compiler), *Notes and Sketches on the History of Parry Sound* (Parry Sound: Parry Sound Public Library, 1969) 99-106.
12   "Nothing doing at Nobel plants," *North Star*, May 22, 1919, 8.
13   AO, RG 19-142, Boxes 1022, 1023 and 1700, Municipal financial information returns for the Town of Parry Sound, 1887–1968. All population figures quoted also come from these returns.

14 "Notes and comments," *North Star,* Aug. 21, 1919, 4.

15 "Roadwork commences," *North Star,* Jan. 10, 1935, 1; "Sudbury-Parry Sound highway to be started within year," *Sudbury Star,* June 3, 1936, 1.

16 AO, RG33-6, Ontario Municipal Board file C1980.

17 "CIL will close Nobel works at end of April," *North Star,* Feb. 7, 1985, 1.

18 "Mayor Hall—'Winds of change are blowing in Parry Sound, '" *Parry Sound Beacon Star,* Feb. 25, 1982, C3.

1 – WILLIAM BEATTY JR.: THE FOUNDER OF PARRY SOUND

1 "William Beatty Sr.," *Thorold Post,* Feb. 7, 1881, 3.

2 The word "berth," as used in this context, is a Canadian forestry term meaning a specified area of timberland in which a company, or an individual, is entitled to fell trees (according to *The Canadian Oxford Dictionary,* 1998).

3 AO, RG 1-131-1-1, Western timber district timber licence register, 1855–68, Licence No. 45 issued to William Milnor Gibson on Nov. 10, 1856; AO, RG-1-189-0-3, Woods and Forests Branch returns of timber licences and timber dues, Huron and Superior territory (Western timber district), 1861–63.

4 *Ontario Sessional Papers,* "Statement of timber licenses granted in the Huron and Superior Territory from the year 1860 to the 1st July, 1867, inclusive," Return No. 6, Session 1868–69, Volume 1, Part 1, 198–9; AO, RG 1-546-5-4, Woods and Forests Branch outgoing correspondence, Letter book No. 6, Department of Woods and Forests to J. & W. Beatty and Company of Thorold dated March 30, 1864.

5 Library and Archives Canada (hereafter LAC), RG 31, Reel C-10023, 1871 Ontario Manuscript Census for The Sound (A)1, Schedule 6: Return of industrial establishments.

6 AO, RG 55-17-51-5, MS 3596, #5,421 Simcoe County partnership declaration for J. & W. Beatty and Company registered May 25, 1871.

7 *Canada Gazette,* Vol. XXIV, No. 37, Sept. 16, 1865, 3226.

8 William Beatty Jr. to Isabella Eliza Bowes, Aug. 16, 1872. When the author saw the Beatty correspondence in 1985, it was all in the possession of Frances Marion Beatty. Hereafter references to material held by Mrs. Beatty is indicated by FMB.

9 *Northern Advocate,* Jan. 18, 1870, 1.

10 FMB, Election poster from the 1867 federal election promoting William Beatty Jr. as MP for Algoma, printed by James H. Little of Owen Sound, 1867.

11 Legislative Assembly of Ontario, *Hansard,* Jan. 11, 1868, Reel No. 1.

12 FMB, William Beatty Jr. to Isabella Eliza Bowes, Sept. 6, 1872.

13 McDougall #1, Deed dated Dec. 21, 1871, Transferring ownership of the J. & W. Beatty and Company mill facilities to H.B. Rathbun & Son, Registered Jan. 15, 1872, at Parry Sound.

14 McDougall #49, Deed dated June 1, 1872, Transferring ownership of the former J. & W. Beatty and Company mill facilities from H.B. Rathbun & Son to Anson G.P. Dodge, Registered Dec. 19, 1872, at Parry Sound

15 "Death of James H. Beatty," *Thorold Post,* Jan. 31, 1902, 1; "Death of Henry Beatty, prominent vesselman," *The Globe,* April 11, 1914, 8.

16 McDougall Bylaw #9 passed Sept. 11, 1872.

17   Parry Sound #172, Deed dated Oct. 31, 1881, Transferring the Seguin Steam
      Mills from William Beatty Jr. to John Clauson Miller, Registered Nov. 18, 1881,
      at Parry Sound.

18   AO, RG 55-1, MS 6736, Liber 5 Folio 42, Letters of incorporation of the Geor-
      gian Bay Transportation Company Limited dated June 22, 1877.

19   AO, RG 8-1-1, Box 292, #187 of 1885, Return to the Provincial Secretary
      regarding winding up of operations of the Georgian Bay Transportation Com-
      pany Limited.

20   AO, RG 55-1, MS 6738, Liber 14 Folio 37, Letters of incorporation for the
      Parry Sound Hotel Company dated Dec. 15, 1881.

21   "Mill burned," *North Star*, July 27, 1893, 3; Beatty's card of thanks appeared in
      the same edition.

22   "Death of Wm. Beatty, MA, LLB; founder of Parry Sound passes away," *North
      Star,* Dec. 8, 1898, 1.

23   AO, RG 22-399, MS 887, Reel 77, Grant #98. Estate file of William Beatty Jr.

24   FMB, John D. Beatty to Isabella Eliza Bowes Beatty, May 2, 1899.

25   Ontario Ministry of Consumer and Business Services, Companies and Personal
      Property and Security Branch, Corporation file for #C4171 William Beatty
      Company Limited incorporated June 15, 1904.

26   Corporation file for C-12284 William Beatty Lands and Timber Limited incor-
      porated April 8, 1914.

2 – THE MILLER FAMILY, MORE TIMBER RIGHTS AND A TRAGIC EVENT

1   Donald W. Wilson, *Lost Horizons: The Story of the Rathbun Company and the Bay of
      Quinte Railway* (Belleville, ON: Mika Publishing Company, 1983).

2   AO, RG 1-191-0-1, Auction sales of timber berths Muskoka sale of Nov. 23,
      1871, Muskoka and Parry Sound Districts sale of June 6, 1877.

3   *Statutes of Canada, 1872,* "An Act to naturalize Anson Greene Phelps Dodge," Vic.
      35, Cap. 118, 522–3; *Return on the Second General Election for the House of Com-
      mons of Canada* (Ottawa: I.B. Tayor, 1873) 56–7. For more on Anson G.P. Dodge
      see James T. Angus, *A Deo Victoria: The Story of the Georgian Bay Lumber Company,
      1871–1942* (Thunder Bay, ON: Severn Publications, 1990) and Mary Byers, Jan
      Kennedy and Margaret McBurney, *Rural Roots: Pre-Confederation Buildings of the
      York Region of Ontario* (Toronto: University of Toronto Press, 1976) 170–2.

4   Simcoe County Archives (SCA), Acc. 987-45, E12 B2 R2A S8 Sh.2, Georgian
      Bay Lumber Company Papers, Agreement concluded on Nov. 30, 1871, between
      Anson G.P. Dodge and H.B. Rathbun & Son.

5   Ibid, Georgian Bay Lumber Company Papers, Agreement concluded on Nov.
      30, 1871, between Anson G.P. Dodge and John Clauson Miller.

6   "J.C. Miller, Ex-MPP; The late member for Muskoka dies in California," *The
      Globe*, April 14, 1884, 6.

7   Florence B. Murray, "John Clauson Miller," in *Dictionary of Canadian Biography*,
      Vol. XI (1881–1890) (Toronto: University of Toronto Press, 1982), 594; C.H.
      Mackintosh, ed., "John Clauson Miller," *Canadian Parliamentary Companion and
      Annual Register* (1878) 229.

8   *Ontario Sessional Papers*, "Report to the Commissioner of Crown Lands for 1869," 1870–71, Return No. 7, Vol. 3, Part 2, 1; and "Report of the Commissioner of Crown Lands for 1870," 1871–72, Return No. 1, Vol. 4, Part 1, Appendix 1.

9   *Statutes of Ontario*, "An Act to incorporate the Parry Sound Lumber Company," 1871–72, Vic. 35, Chap. 98, 330–7.

10 SCA, Georgian Bay Lumber Company Papers, John Bell to Dalton McCarthy, Sept. 5, 1872; Edward Wilkes Rathbun to John Bell, Sept. 6, 1872; John Bell to Dalton McCarthy, Sept. 7, 1872; John Bell to Dalton McCarthy, Sept. 11, 1872.

11 McDougall #79, Deed dated May 16, 1873, Transferring ownership of the former J. & W. Beatty and Company mill facilities from Anson G.P. Dodge to the Parry Sound Lumber Company, Registered June 5, 1873, at Parry Sound.

12 SCA, Acc. 987-45, E10 B2 R2A S8 Sh2, Georgian Bay Lumber Company Papers, Agreement between William Earl Dodge and the Royal Canadian Bank dated Dec. 15, 1874. For more on William Earl Dodge see Robert Glass Cleland, *A History of Phelps Dodge, 1834–1950* (New York: Alfred A. Knopf, 1952).

13 SCA, Acc. 987-45, E13 B2 R2A S8 Sh.2, Georgian Bay Lumber Company Papers, Power of Attorney by which W.E. Dodge empowered Dalton McCarthy to act on his behalf in Ontario, sworn and witnessed on May 17, 1873.

14 *North Star*, Nov. 16, 1874, 3 and Nov. 30, 1874, 2. The reader will note frequent references to dates before March 14, 1879, which is the first issue currently available on the microfilm. The earlier copies were in the possession of FMB.

15 AO, RG 49-39, Box 26, Original Bill #74 of the 2nd Session of the 3rd Parliament, "An Act to amend the Free Grant and Homestead Act." First reading Jan. 11, 1877; defeated Jan. 22 on 2nd reading.

16 *Ontario Gazette*, Vol. IX, No. 2, Jan. 8, 1876, 36.

17 AO, RG 8-1-1, #1334 of 1875, Annual return for the Magnetawan Lumber Company Incorporated March 2, 1872. Includes minutes of the Parry Sound Lumber Company board of directors meeting held on Jan. 29, 1878.

18 AO, RG 55-1, Libre 7 Folio 6, MS 6737, Letters of incorporation of the Parry Sound Lumber Company dated April 1, 1876; *Ontario Gazette*, Vol. IX, No. 5, April 8, 1876, 462.

19 "Burial of D'Alton McCarthy," *Barrie Northern Advance*, May 19, 1898, 1.

20 W.E. Hamilton, John Rogers and Seymour Richard Penson, *Guide Book & Atlas of Muskoka and Parry Sound Districts* (Toronto: H.R. Page, 1879) 31 and A. Kirkwood and J.J. Murphy, *The Undeveloped Lands in Northern and Western Ontario: Information Regarding Resources, Products and Suitability for Settlement* (Toronto: Hunter, Rose, 1878).

21 AO, RG 8-1-1, #351 of 1880, Annual return for the Parry Sound Lumber Company to the provincial secretary of Ontario.

22 "Local news," *North Star*, Sept. 10, 1880, 2.

23 B.M. Greene, ed., "John Bellamy Miller," in *Who's Who and Why, 1919–1920*, (Toronto: International Press Limited, 1920), 528 and Henry James Morgan, ed., "John Bellamy Miller," *Canadian Men and Women, 1912* (Toronto: William Briggs, 1912), 803.

24 "Lt.-Col. Miller, veteran, dies," *The Globe*, Sept. 3, 1941, 5.

25 Parry Sound #172, Deed dated Oct. 31, 1881, Transferring the Seguin Steam Mills from William Beatty Jr. to J.C. Miller, Registered Nov. 18, 1881, at Parry Sound.

26 *The Globe*, April 14, 1884, 6; AO, MS 396, D.F. Macdonald diaries, May 18, 1884.

27 D.F. Macdonald diaries, Feb. 2, 1884.

28 Parry Sound #298, Deed dated April 29, 1984, Transferring Parry Sound Lumber Company sawmill at the bottom of Bay Street from J.C. Miller's estate to William Henry Pratt and Augustus Nathaniel Spratt, Registered Feb. 15, 1884, at Parry Sound.

29 Parry Sound #327, Mortgage dated Dec. 2, 1884, Covering Parry Sound Lumber Company properties used as security on notes held by the Ontario Bank, Registered Jan. 8, 1885, at Parry Sound.

30 Parry Sound #932, Mortgage dated Nov. 7, 1893, Covering Parry Sound Lumber Company properties used as security on notes held by the Ontario Bank, Registered Feb. 2, 1894.

31 AO, RG 55-1, MS 6740, Libre 18 Folio 61, Letters of incorporation for the Polson Iron Works of Toronto Limited dated Oct. 16, 1886; *Ontario Gazette*, Aug. 25, 1888, Vol. XXI, No. 34, 831; *Ontario Gazette*, Vol. XXI, No. 45, Nov. 10, 1888, 1179; AO, RG 8-1-1, #432 of 1892, Annual return to the provincial secretary for the Polson Iron Works of Toronto Limited.

32 "Terrible calamity, double drowning accident," *North Star*, Aug. 31, 1893, 8.

33 "The double drowning," *The Globe*, Aug. 28, 1893, 8.

34 Dr. Kenneth Andrew Denholm, *History of Parry Sound General Hospital* (printed privately, 1973) 5.

35 Greene, ed., *Who's Who and Why, 1919–1920*, 528.

36 "Lt. Col. J.B. Miller dies in Toronto," *North Star*, Sept. 4, 1941, 1.

37 Ministry of Consumer and Business Services, Companies and Personal Property and Security Branch, Corporation file for #TC-13877 Parry Sound Lumber Company incorporated April 1, 1876.

38 *Canada Lumberman*, Oct. 15, 1910, 25.

39 "Local news," *North Star*, Jan. 10, 1918, 7.

40 Corporation file for #TC-13877 Parry Sound Lumber Company.

41 Greene, ed., *Who's Who and Why, 1919–1920*, 528.

3 — PATRICK MCCURRY: JUDGE AND ENTREPRENEUR

1 *Statutes of Ontario*, "An act to provide for the organization of the Territorial District of Parry Sound," Vic. 33 Cap. 24, 1869, Assented to Dec. 24, 1869, 53–7.

2 Mary Ellen Perkins (compiler), *Discover Your Heritage: A Guide to Provincial Plaques in Ontario* (Toronto: Natural Heritage, 1989) 209.

3 "Judge McCurry passes," *North Star*, Aug. 14, 1919, 1.

4 Foley #38, Deed dated Dec. 24, 1872, Transferring lot 150, concession A from Joseph Hunt to Patrick McCurry and Robert Pauncefort Carrington, Registered Dec. 24, 1872, at Parry Sound.

5 Foley #75, Deed dated June 18, 1873, Transferring mill site from Patrick McCurry and Robert Pauncefort Carrington to John Hogg and the Guelph Lumber Company, Registered Feb. 16, 1874, at Parry Sound.

6 Hamilton, Rogers and Penson, *Guide Book & Atlas of Muskoka and Parry Sound Districts*, 34.

7 *Canada Gazette*, Vol. X, No. 21, Nov. 18, 1876, 643.

8 Edgar J. Boland, *From the Pioneers to the Seventies: A History of the Diocese of Peterborough, 1882–1975* (published privately) 353.

9 Foley #211, Mortgage dated Dec. 16, 1875, Registered Jan. 3, 1876.

10 Foley #285, Mortgage dated Jan. 4, 1876, Registered Jan. 29, 1880.

11 Foley #250, Assignment of mortgage dated Jan. 13, 1880, Transferring Guelph Lumber Company held by the London and Canada Loan and Agency Company to the Ontario Bank, Registered Feb. 7, 1880.

12 *North Star*, June 10, 1880, advertisement for auction, 3; "Local news," *North Star,* July 1, 1880, 3.

13 Foley #487, Deed dated May 31, 1883, Transferring former Guelph Lumber Company properties to the Midland and North Shore Lumber Company, Registered Nov. 29, 1883.

14 *Statutes of Ontario*, "An Act respecting Muskoka and Parry Sound," Vic. 60 Chap 61, 1888, Assented to March 23, 1888, 23–30.

15 LAC, MG26 A, Vol. 27, Reel C-1497, John A. Macdonald Fonds, William Rabb Beatty to Macdonald, May 19, 1888, 10723–4.

16 *Canada Gazette*, Vol. XXI, No. 52, June 23, 1888, 2641; "Death came to Judge Mahaffy in England," *The Daily Star*, July 13, 1917, 23.

17 AO, RG 22-399, MS 887, Grant #867, Estate file of Patrick McCurry.

4 – THE BEATTY COVENANT AND THE FIGHT AGAINST BOOZE

1 McDougall Bylaw #9 passed Sept. 11, 1872, To prohibit the sale of intoxicating liquor; FMB, William Beatty Jr. to Isabella Eliza Bowes, Sept. 6, 1872.

2 "Bill to delete Beatty Covenant passes the committee with ease," *North Star*, March 30, 1950, 1.

3 "Private bill slated for Monday," *North Star*, March 23, 1950, 2.

4 Foley Bylaw #4 passed Dec. 4, 1872, To allow for two licensed taverns. See also Bertha Clare, *You, Me and Foley, 1872–1972* (Bracebridge, ON: Herald-Gazette Press, 1972) 1–4.

5 Foley Bylaw #5 passed Jan. 15, 1873, To repeal Bylaw #4.

6 Foley council minutes, June 10, 1873.

7 *Statutes of Ontario*, "An Act to amend and consolidate the law for the sale of fermented or spirituous liquors," Vic. 37, Chap. 32, 1874, Assented to March 24, 1874, 239–57.

8 The law was amended by *Statutes of Ontario*, "An Act to amend the Acts respecting the sale of fermented or spirituous liquors," Vic. 40, Chap. 18, 1877, Assented to March 2, 1877, 138–58.

9 Foley council minutes, Nov. 19, 1874.

10 "Local news," *North Star*, July 15, 1880, 2.

11 Parry Sound council minutes, Aug. 23, 1887.

12 Ibid, Feb. 28, 1888.

13 Ibid, June 26, 1888.

14 Ibid, Nov. 25, 1890.

15 Ibid, Jan. 20, 1891; Parry Sound Bylaw #70 passed March 24, 1891.

16 Parry Sound Bylaw #165 passed Dec. 28, 1897, To repeal Bylaw #70; *North Star*, Jan. 13, 1898, Notice of meeting of board of licence commissioners, 5; "Tavern licenses," *North Star*, Jan. 20, 1898, 5.

17 Parry Sound Bylaw #165.

18 *North Star*, Dec. 14, 1905, Advertisement, 4.

19 "The hotel question," *North Star*, June 20, 1918, 4.

20 "Council asked to support move to quash Beatty clause in deeds," *North Star*, Nov. 7, 1940, 1.

21 "More beverage rooms for Parry Sound," *North Star*, Letter to the editor by C.C. Johnson, Oct. 11, 1945, 1; "Beverage room licences refused," *North Star*, Letter to the editor by William S. Beatty, Nov. 22, 1945, 6.

22 "Electors turn out for near record municipal vote to delete covenant," *North Star*, Dec. 8, 1949, 1; "Parry Sound asks Ontario to cancel teetotal pact of 1873," *Globe and Mail*, March 4, 1950, 15.

5 — PROHIBITION AND THE PRESS

1 Biographical information comes from Florence B. Murray, "Thomas McMurray," in *Dictionary of Canadian Biography*, Vol. XI, 1881–90, 580–1.

2 Thomas McMurray, *The Free Grant Lands: From Practical Experiences of Bush Farming in the Free Grant Districts of Muskoka and Parry Sound* (originally published 1871; reprint Huntsville, ON: Fox Meadow Creations and B. Hammond, 2002) 32.

3 McMurray, *The Free Grant Lands of Canada*, 33.

4 Ibid, 34.

5 AO, N-300, Reel 1. A history of the newspapers in Bracebridge, Huntsville and Gravenhurst appears at the start of the *Northern Advocate* microfilm.

6 McMurray, *The Free Grant Lands of Canada*, 46–7.

7 *North Star*, Oct. 6, 1874.

8 Ibid, July 18, 1879, 2.

9 *Northern Advocate*, Jan. 4, 1870, 2; *Christian Guardian*, Sept. 24, 1879, 308 and Oct. 29, 1897, 349.

10 The *Christian Guardian*, April 4, 1883, 109.

11 "Thomas McMurray dead," *North Star*, Aug. 23, 1900, 1.

6 — DIRTY POLITICS 1887

1 *North Star*, Jan. 7, 1875, 2.

2 "Looking backward, The story of the Corporation of Parry Sound," *North Star*, Feb. 26, 1903, 1.

3 *Statutes of Ontario*, "An Act to incorporate the Town of Parry Sound," Vic. 50, Chap. 61, Assented to April 23, 1887, 260–5.

4 LAC, MG A, Volume 518, Part 1, Reel C-29, John A. Macdonald Fonds, Macdonald to William Beatty Jr., Jan. 23, 1871, 154...LTB 15; *The Globe*, Dec. 9, 1922, 18.

5 AO, MS 229, Thomas Walton Papers; John Macfie, *Now and Then, More Footnotes to Parry Sound History* (published privately: 1985) 3–9.

6 "First town nomination," *North Star*, May 13, 1887, 2.

7 "Sudden death of J. W. Fitzgerald," *North Star*, June 25, 1908, 1.

8 *North Star*, May 13, 1887, 2.

9 "The first town election," *North Star*, May 20, 1887, 2.

10 "The late Thomas S. Walton, MD," *Parry Sound Canadian*, Jan. 12, 1902, 1, included with the Thomas Walton Papers. All copies of the *North Star* for 1902 are missing from the microfilm.

7 – RUNNING WATER, FIRE BELLS AND A LAWSUIT

1 *North Star*, Sept. 28, 1893, 2.

2 "Looking backward, The story of the Corporation of Parry Sound," *North Star*, March 19, 1903, 1

3 Ibid, Council minutes, Dec. 17, 1889; Bylaw #45 passed Dec. 17, 1889.

4 Council minutes, Jan. 21, 1890; Bylaw #47 passed Jan. 21, 1890, which repealed Bylaw #45.

5 AO, RG 80-8, MS 935, Reel 58, Vol. D, #11339, #11340 and #11341 of 1890, Death certificates of Melinda Robinson, Ida Amelia Robinson and Cornelius Benjamin Robinson; Council minutes, March 6, 1890.

6 Council minutes, March 18, 1890.

7 Ibid, May 20, 1890; *North Star*, March 13, 1903, 1.

8 Council minutes, May 27, 1890.

9 Ibid, July 8, 1890.

10 Ibid, Dec. 2, 1890.

11 "Looking backward, The story of the Corporation of Parry Sound," *North Star*, March 12, 1903, 1.

12 Council minutes, April 7, 1891.

13 Ibid, July 16, 1891.

14 Ibid, May 10, 17 and 24, 1892; "Waterworks," *North Star*, May 26, 1892, 3.

15 "Town and district news," *North Star*, June 2, 1892, 2 and "Town and district news," *North Star*, July 21, 1892, 3; Council minutes, July 20 and Aug. 30, 1892.

16 "Town and district news," *North Star*, Oct. 20, 1892, 3; "Town council," *North Star*, Jan. 26, 1893, 2.

17 "Waterworks," *North Star*, Jan. 19, 1893, 3; "Town council," *North Star*, March 2, 1893, 3.

18 "Town parliament," *North Star*, Feb. 9, 1893, 2.

19 Ibid.

20 "Town council," *North Star*, Jan. 26, 1893, 2.

21 Council minutes, May 1, 1893 and May 15, 1893.

22 Ibid, June 26, 1893.

23 "Waterworks test," *North Star*, June 8, 1893, 3.

24 Council minutes, July 3, 1893.

25 Ibid, July 4 & 5, 1893.

26 "Town and district news," *North Star*, July 27, 1893, 3.

27 Council minutes, Jan. 22, 1894.

28 Ibid, Dec. 29, 1893, and Feb. 26, 1894.

29 "Reflections on current topics," *North Star*, Dec. 21, 1893, 2.

30 "Looking backward, The story of the Corporation of Parry Sound," *North Star*, April 2, 1903, 1.

31 AO, RG 80-8-0-206, MS 935, Reel 85, Vol. H, #19802 of 1897, Death certificate of Solomon Byron Purvis, MS 935 reel 85.

32 Council minutes, Jan. 15, 1894 and Feb. 8, 1894.

33 AO, RG 19-142, Auditors report of the receipts and expenditures, assets and liabilities of the Town of Parry Sound for the year 1894.

8 — ARTHUR STARKEY: ADVENTURER OR REMITTANCE MAN

1 G.R. Pimlett, senior librarian at the Crewe Library in Crewe, England, to R.A. Smith, director of the Algonquin Regional Library in Parry Sound, Dec. 16, 1976, Enclosing Starkey family genealogy from George Ormerod, *History of Cheshire* (1883).

2 LAC, RG 31, Reel C-10023, 1871 Ontario Manuscript Census for The Sound (A)1, Schedule 1: Nominal return of the living, 11 #16 and Schedule 4: Return of cultivated land, of field products and of plants and fruits, 6.

3 AO, MU 2736 F 1023-5-1, Duncan Fraser Macdonald Papers, Biographical information about D.F. Macdonald and his family.

4 Carling #11, Free grant to Arthur Starkey of 200 acres, lot 41 of concession D and lot 42 of concession 12 in Carling Twp, Recorded May 1, 1876, at Toronto and registered Jan. 12, 1877, in Parry Sound; Carling #12, Deed dated April 29, 1876, Transferring 74 acres from the Crown to Arthur Starkey.

5 Macdonald diaries, entry for Dec. 25, 1876; *North Star*, Jan. 8, 1877, 2.

6 AO, RG 55-17-42-5, MS 5506, #6 District of Parry Sound partnership declaration for the Parry Sound Brick Manufacturing Company dated March 26, 1877.

7 *North Star*, Nov. 12, 1880, 2; LAC, RG 31, Reel C-13244, 1881 Ontario Manuscript Census for Parry Sound, Parry Harbour and Parry Island, Schedule 1: Nominal return of the living, 41 #2.

8 Parry Sound #446, Deed dated Feb. 22, 1882, Transferring The Cedars from William Beatty Jr. to Arthur Starkey.

9 One chain is the equivalent of 66 feet or about 20 metres.

10 D.F. Macdonald diaries, Aug. 18, 1882.

11 McDougall council minutes, Oct. 6, 1884.

12 D.F. Macdonald diaries, Sept. 11, 1912.

13 Ibid, Dec. 2, 1884.

14 Minutes of McDougall Township nomination meeting held Dec. 28, 1885, Recorded in council minute book.

15 AO, RG 75-57, Order-in-council 16/384 appointing Arthur Starkey as registrar of deeds for the District of Parry Sound, Approved July 19, 1883.

16 "Charges against the registrar," *North Star*, Nov. 19, 1886, 3.

17 *North Star*, Dec. 8, 1898, 5.

18 FMB, Arthur Starkey to Frances Margaret Beatty, Dec. 22, 1899.

19 FMB, Arthur Starkey to Rose Beatty, Jan. 21, 1910.

20 Parry Sound #4908, Transferring The Cedars from the estate of Arthur Starkey to Kenneth Vere Starkey, Registered Feb. 16, 1914, at Parry Sound; AO, MS 887, Reel 1787, #1787, Estate file for Arthur Starkey. English probate granted Dec. 21, 1912, and ancillary probate by Judge Patrick McCurry in Parry Sound on Aug. 20, 1913. The *North Star* reported on Jan. 30, 1913, that Starkey had left an estate of £44,518 or $222,590.

21 Parry Sound assessment books, 1904–3?.

22 Parry Sound #8050, Tax deed transferring The Cedars to the Town of Parry Sound, Registered Nov. 19, 1930, at Parry Sound.

23 "Town council rescinds the resolutions asking resignations," *North Star*, Feb. 19, 1931, 1.

24 "Close file on Starkey Point," *North Star*, Feb. 21, 1963, 1; Parry Sound resolution #63-55 passed Nov. 19, 1963.

9 – DR. WALTON: SCOUNDREL OR VICTIM OF POLITICAL PATRONAGE

1 AO, MS 229, Thomas Walton Papers. Biographical information appears at the beginning of the microfilmed material, which includes deeds, birth and marriage records, as well as personal correspondence and newspaper clippings.

2 Thomas Walton Papers, Thomas Smith Walton to James Walton, March 1870.

3 LAC, RG 10, Vol. 2210, File 42205, Reel C-11180, "Parry Sound Agency—Correspondence regarding an agent for the Parry Sound Band, 1883–1901," Thomas Smith Walton to Prime Minister John A. Macdonald, undated. Hereafter, this Department of Indian Affairs file is referred to by the microfilm reel number C-11180.

4 LAC, RG 10, Vol. 9178, Reel T-1778, Indian Affairs Establishment Book, 1850–1890, Appointment of Thomas Smith Walton as of April 1, 1884, p.111.

5 C-11180, William Henry Pratt to Secretary General of Indian Affairs Clifford Sifton, April 7, 1897.

6 Ibid, Sifton to the Governor General in Council, April 15, 1897. Sifton gives a lengthy summary of events starting with Chief Nebenayanequod's complaint.

7 Ibid.

8 Ibid.

9 Ibid.

10 C-11180, Acting secretary of Indian Affairs J.D. McLean to Walton, June 2, 1897.

11 LAC, RG 10, Vol. 9180, File 42205, Reel T-1778, Indian Affairs Establishment Book (outside service), 1870–1920, Appointment of William Brown Maclean as of May 28, 1897, 143; C-11180, J.D. McLean to Sifton, June 28, 1897.

12 C-11180, Walton to deputy minister James A. Smart, June 4, 1897 and Aug. 31, 1897.

13 C-11180, Clipping from the Oct. 28, 1897 *North Star*. All 1897 copies of the newspaper are missing from the microfilm.

14   C-11180, Order of the House of Commons calling for all letters, telegrams and correspondence, undated.
15   C-11180, Smart to J.D. McLean, June 1, 1899; Reginald Rimmie to Smart, June 15, 1899.
16   C-11180, Smart to J.D. McLean, July 21, 1900.
17   C-11180, Sifton to Governor General in council, July 24, 1900.
18   C-11180, Report of the Committee of Privy Council approved by the Governor General on June 6, 1901.

10 — THE STRUGGLE FOR A RAILWAY

1   McDougall Township council minutes, Dec. 1, 1884; Foley Township council minutes, Dec. 13, 1884.
2   *Statutes of Ontario*, "An Act to incorporate the Parry Sound Colonization Railway Company," Vic. 48, Chap. 78, 1885, assented to March 30, 1885, 365–74.
3   McDougall council minutes, March 2, 1885.
4   Foley council minutes, Jan. 23, 1886; McDougall council minutes, Feb. 1, 1886.
5   Statutes of Canada, Vic. 49, Chap. 10, 1886, Assented to June 2, 1886, 72.
6   Parry Sound council minutes, March 19, 1889.
7   *Statutes of Ontario*, "An Act respecting aid to certain railways," Vic. 52, Chap. 35, 1889, assented to March 23, 1889, 128–32; *Statutes of Canada*, "An Act to authorize the granting of subsidies in aid of the construction of the lines of railway therein mentioned," Vic. 52, Chap. 3, 1889, Vol. 1, assented to May 2, 1889, 49.
8   LAC, RG 12, Vol. 1880, File 3268–73, Parry Sound Colonization Railway chief engineer S.R. Poulin to president Patrick McCurry and the company directors, June 18, 1890.
9   Ibid, James Marcus Ansley to Minister of Railways and Canals John Haggart, Sept. 15, 1892. Information comes from an enclosed petition dated Sept. 15, 1892, to extend time for completion.
10   *Statutes of Ontario*, "An Act to amend the Act to incorporate the Parry Sound Colonization Railway Company," Vic. 54, Chap. 92, 1891, assented to May 4, 1891, 337–9.
11   LAC, RG 12, Vol. 1880, File 3268-73, Ansley to Haggart, June 3, 1892, and Order-in-council 1597 dated July 14, 1891, that earned portion of subsidy not be paid.
12   Ibid, Parry Sound Colonization Railway general manager William G. Reid to Haggart, June 15, 1892.
13   Ibid, Reid to Prime Minister Sir John Abbott, June 24, 1892.
14   Ibid, Railways and Canals chief engineer Collingwood Schreiber to T. Trudeau, acting secretary of Railways and Canals.
15   Ibid, Order-in-council granting extension to Oct. 16, 1891.
16   Ibid, Ansley to Haggart, April 26, 1893.
17   Doris French, "The Booths of Ottawa," in *Chatelaine*, December 1963.

18 G.R. Stevens, *Canadian National Railways,* Volume II (Toronto: Clarke, Irwin and Company, 1962) 365.

19 Ibid.

20 *Statutes of Ontario,* "An Act to incorporate the Ottawa, Arnprior, and Renfrew Railway Company," Vic. 51, Chap. 71, 1888, Assented to March 23, 1888, 195–209; *Statutes of Canada,* "An Act to incorporate the Ottawa and Parry Sound Railway Company," Vic. 51, Chap. 65, Assented to May 4, 1888, 66–72; *Statutes of Canada,* "An Act amending the Ottawa and Parry Sound Railway Company, the Ottawa, Arnprior and Renfrew Railway Company under the name of the Ottawa, Arnprior and Parry Sound Railway Company," Vic. 54–55, Chap. 93, 1891, Vol. II, Assented to July 31, 1891, 122–30.

21 *North Star,* June 8, 1893, 3; "Railway meeting," *North Star,* June 15, 1893, 2.

22 LAC, RG 12, Vol. 1880, File 3268-70, Canada Atlantic Railway secretary-treasurer Andrew W. Fleck to J.H. Balderson, Aug. 18, 1894; LAC, RG 12, Vol. 1880, File 3268-73, Schreiber to Balderson, Sept. 10, 1894.

23 LAC, RG 12, Vol. 1880, File 3268–70, Francis Lynch to Schreiber, Dec. 17, 1894.

24 LAC, RG 10, Vol. 7663, File 22022-5, Reel C-11608, "Parry Sound Agency, Right of Way for Ottawa, Arnprior and Parry Sound Railway Company through a portion of the Parry Island reserve," Indian Affairs to Thomas Smith Walton, March 20, 1895.

25 *North Star,* May 2, 1895, 3.

26 LAC, RG 10, Vol. 7663, File 22022-5, John Rudolphus Booth to T. Mayne Daly, Sept. 30, 1895.

27 Ibid, Commissioner James J. Campbell's report of Oct. 16, 1895, George Lang Chitty's report of Oct. 14, 1895, and Indian Affairs to Walton, Oct. 18, 1895.

28 *Parry Sound Directory, 1898–1899* (Parry Sound: Ireland & Bundy, 1898) 38.

29 LAC, RG 10, Vol. 7663, File 22022-5, Superintendent General Clifford Sifton to Governor General in council, Aug. 19, 1899.

11 — MINING FEVER: BOOM AND BUST

1 *North Star,* July 27, 1899. The newspaper printed 4,000 copies of this special mining issue, most for free distribution outside of Parry Sound.

2 "The North Star has been continuously published in Parry Sound for 63 years," *North Star,* July 8, 1937, 1; "We celebrate a birthday today—North Star starts 81st year," *North Star,* Nov. 19, 1953, 1.

3 *The Parry Sound Directory, 1898–99* (Parry Sound: Ireland & Bundy, 1898), Publisher's preface.

4 "Our mining boom," *North Star,* June 15, 1899, 1.

5 "A rich find in gold, Judge McCurry discovers a bonanza," *North Star,* Aug. 10, 1899, 1; and July 27, 1899, 16.

6 "Latest mining news, One million dollars refused," *North Star,* July 13, 1899, 1; and Aug. 31, 1899, 1.

7 "'The McGowan' dead—The third white settler in Parry Sound," *North Star,* July 30, 1903, 1.

8 Foley #279, Free grant dated June 7, 1877, To Thomas McGowan Sr. for lots
   20 and 21 on concession 12, as well as lot 146 on concession B, Registered Aug.
   20, 1878, at Parry Sound; Foley #280, Deed dated June 10, 1872, Transferring 130 acres at lot 145 on concession B from the Crown to Thomas McGowan
   Sr., Registered Aug. 20, 1878; Foley #775, Deed dated Jan. 17, 1889, Transferring 18 acres at lot A, concession B from James and Pheobe Badger to Thomas
   McGowan Sr., Registered April 13, 1889, at Parry Sound.

9 *North Star*, July 30, 1903, 1.

10 Ibid.

11 AO, RG 55-1, MS 7163, Liber 44 Folio 44, Letters of incorporation of the
   McGowan Gold Mining Company of Parry Sound Limited dated April 7, 1897.

12 Foley #1001, Deed dated March 14, 1898, Transferring 59 acres at lot A concession B and lot 146 concession B from Thomas McGowan Sr. to the McGowan
   Gold Mining Company of Parry Sound Ltd., Registered March 17, 1898.

13 *Ontario Sessional Papers*, "Report of the Bureau of Mines for the year 1899," Return
   No. 5, Session 1900, Volume 31, Part 2, 100.

14 Foley #1199, Deed dated Feb. 1, 1900, Transferring 162 acres at lot 146 concession B, lot A concession B and lot 146 concession A from the McGowan Gold
   Mining Company of Parry Sound Ltd. to the Parry Sound Copper Mining Company Ltd., Registered March 2, 1904, at Parry Sound; "Mining boom, McGowan
   gold mine sold," *North Star*, March 9, 1899, 1.

15 AO, RG 55-1, Liber 56, Folio 28, Letters of incorporation of the Parry Sound
   Copper Mining Company Limited dated March 23, 1899.

16 *North Star*, July 27, 1899, 1.

17 *Ontario Sessional Papers*, "Report of the Bureau of Mines for the year 1900."

18 "Spur railway line needed," *North Star*, April 20, 1899, 1.

19 *North Star*, Aug 24, 1899, 1.

20 Ibid, July 27, 1899, 1,

21 Ibid, July 2, 1903, 1.

22 Foley #1201, Quit claim deed dated Feb. 6, 1904, by which Robert Forbes,
   William Foulkes and Frank Johnson surrender all rights to mining properties
   in the Parry Sound Copper Mining Company Ltd., Registered March 17, 1904,
   at Parry Sound; Foley #1200, Mortgage dated Feb. 13, 1904, for the mining
   properties held by Eleanor R. Elkinton, Registered March 12, 1904, at Parry
   Sound.

23 D.F. Macdonald diaries, May 7, 1906; Foley #1660, Assignment of mortgage
   dated Sept. 30, 1914, Transferring from Eleanor R. Elkinton to William E. Jones
   of Ottumwa, Iowa, Registered Oct. 13, 1914, at Parry Sound.

12 — RAILWAYS: DIVISION AND DISHARMONY

1 Council minutes, Jan. 8 and 10, 1898; "$3,000 a mile for a railway from Parry
   Sound to Sudbury," *North Star*, Jan. 13, 1898, 1.

2 Council minutes, April 17, 1899; *North Star*, April 20, 1899, 1.

3 Council minutes, June 14, 1899; *Statutes of Ontario*, "An Act respecting aid to
   certain railways," Vic. 63 Chap. 29, 1900, Assented to April 30, 1900, 93.

4   Council minutes, July 12 and Aug. 16, 1900; Parry Sound Bylaw #202 passed Aug. 22, 1900, To issue debentures to be able to provide a $20,000 bonus to the James Bay Railway.

5   Council minutes, June 5 and Aug. 29, 1901.

6   *Statutes of Ontario*, "An Act respecting aid to certain railways," 2 Edw. VII, Chap. 25, 1902, Assented to April 17, 1902, 79–80; Council minutes, Feb. 25, 1903. Council authorized payment of the balance of the $20,000 bonus at the Aug. 2, 1904, meeting.

7   *North Star*, July 21, 1904, 1.

8   Ibid, July 28, 1904, 1; and Aug. 11, 1904, 1.

9   Ibid, May 3, 1905, 4.

10 "Canadian Northern Ontario Railway opened between Toronto and Parry Sound," *North Star*, Nov. 21, 1906, 1.

11 Ibid, April 12, 1905, 1.

12 Council minutes, June 6, 1905.

13 *North Star*, Aug. 2, 1905, 4; Council minutes, April 6, 1906.

14 Council minutes, April 17, 1906; *North Star*, April 18, 1906, 1.

15 *North Star*, Oct 12, 1906, 1; Nov. 21, 1906, 9; and Dec. 5, 1906, 1

16 Council minutes, Sept. 11, 1906; *North Star*, Sept. 12, 1906, 1; "Canadian Pacific Railway," Oct. 24, 1906, 1.

17 *North Star*, Oct. 17, 1906, 1.

18 Ibid, Dec. 5, 1906, 1.

19 Council minutes, Dec. 18, 1906.

20 Ibid, Jan. 15, 1907; Feb. 19, 1907; March 5, 1907; and March 7, 1907.

21 Council minutes, March 13, 1907; Parry Sound Bylaw #306 passed March 13, 1907, Closing a portion of James Street in the east ward; Parry Sound Bylaw #307 passed March 13, 1907, Closing portions of Melissa St., Fleck St. and Railway Ave. in the east ward; Parry Sound Bylaw #308 passed March 13, 1907, Closing Victoria Ave., Margaret St., Cascade St., Marion Ave., Adelaide St., Armstrong St., Church St., Melvin St.

22 "Criminal libel, The Burk's Falls Beacon in trouble," *North Star*, Sept. 22, 1898, 1; Astrid Taim, *Almaguin: A Highland History* (Toronto: Natural Heritage, 1998) 49–51.

23 *North Star*, Jan. 24, 1907, 8; Feb. 14, 1907, 8; Feb. 28, 1907, 1; and Aug. 1, 1907, 9.

24 "The new agreement with the CPR," *North Star*, Nov. 7, 1907, 1.

25 "First train on CPR," *North Star*, June 17, 1908, 1; Bylaw #329 passed June 16, 1908, Authorizing clerk and mayor to execute conveyance to transfer property to CPR; council minutes, Oct. 22, 1908.

26 AO, RG 19-142, Box 1022, Municipal financial information return for the Town of Parry Sound, 1908.

27 Bylaw #594 passed May 18, 1926, To issue debentures to finance Armstrong Street subway; "12-year-old killed by CP freight train," *North Star*, Oct. 22, 1997, 1.

13 – VIOLENCE AND MURDER

1   "Murder and then suicide," *North Star*, Aug. 22, 1906, 1; "Verdict of murder and suicide," *North Star*, Aug. 29, 1906, 1.

2   AO, RG 20-86-1-1, MS 5183, Parry Sound jail register, 1908–1916.

3   AO, RG 22-392-0-4918, Box 117, Supreme Court Central Office criminal assize indictment file for Rex. v. Louis Peterson AKA Louis Young, 1910.

4   "Murder in Burpee, two Italians stab four men, one fatally, another seriously," *North Star*, Dec. 26, 1906, 1; "The Whitestone murder, alleged murderer and accomplice captured," *North Star*, Jan. 2, 1907, 1; "Parry Sound assizes, Two Italians charged with murdering William Dow," *The Globe*, May 29, 1907, 7; "Expect verdict today for murderous attack unfinished," *The Globe*, May 30, 1907, 8; "Capelle found guilty; Marano, his companion, acquited by jury," *The Globe*, May 31, 1907, 7; "Escape from gallows, Capelle after facing death twice, is not to hang," *North Star*, Nov. 14, 1907, 1.

5   "Witness is missing, Louis Young must wait till autumn assizes for trial," *North Star*, April 28, 1910, 1.

6   "Young gets life sentence for manslaughter," *North Star*, Oct. 20, 1910, 1.

14 – THE NORTHERN PIONEERS IN THE FIRST WORLD WAR

1   D.F. Macdonald diaries, Jan. 19, 1904.

2   LAC, RG 24, Vol. 197, Regimental history of the 23rd Northern Pioneers.

3   Ibid, List of officers who commanded the 23rd Northern Pioneers.

4   D.F. Macdonald diaries, Aug. 20, 1914.

5   LAC, RG 9 III-D-3, Vol. 4912, File 350, Reel T-10704, War diary of the 1st Battalion, CEF. See also John Macfie, *Letters Home* (published privately: 1990) and Adrian Hayes, *Pegahmagabow: Legendary Warrior, Forgotten Hero* (Huntsville, ON: Fox Meadow Creations, 2003). *Letters Home* is a collection of correspondence by three brothers from the Parry Sound-area—Roy, Arthur and John Macfie—who served with the 1st Battalion. *Pegahmagabow* is a biography of Parry Sound-area Aboriginal Francis Pegahmagabow, who also served for four years with the 1st Battalion.

6   War diary, Appendix I of April 1915, Narrative of operations April 23–30, 1915; G.W.L. Nicholson, *Canadian Expeditionary Force, 1914–1919* (corrected edition) (Ottawa: R. Duhamel, Queen's Printer, 1964) 67–71.

7   AO, MU2736 F1023-5-2, Duncan Fraser Macdonald papers, Lieut. Aubrey White Calquhoun Macdonald to Alexander Fraser Macdonald, dated April 4, 1916.

8   *North Star*, Sept. 1, 1916, 5; D.F. Macdonald diaries, Sept. 3, 1916.

9   AO, MU 2735 F1023-5-1, Duncan Fraser Macdonald papers, Biographical information about members of the Macdonald family.

10 "James Arthurs," *Canadian Dictionary of Parliament, 1867–1967*, (Ottawa: Public Archives of Canada, 1968) 14; "Late senator paid tributes," *The Globe*, Oct. 11, 1937, 5.

11 *North Star*, Aug. 31, 1916, 5.

12 Ibid, Sept. 28, 1916, 5.

13 Ibid, Oct. 16, 1916, 5.
14 Ibid.
15 Ibid, Oct. 12, 1916, 5.
16 Ibid, Sept. 1, 1916, 5.
17 Ibid, Dec. 7, 1916, 5.
18 Ibid, Nov. 14, 1918, 1.
19 Ibid, Feb. 6, 1919, 1.

15 – THE DAY THE DAM BURST

1 "Host of candidates for municipal honors," *North Star*, Dec. 30, 1920, 1.
2 *North Star*, Jan. 8, 1920.
3 Ibid, Mar. 24, 1921, 1.
4 Ibid, Aug. 18, 1921, 1.
5 Ibid, Dec. 15, 1921, 1.
6 AO, RG 55-1 MS 7162, Lib. 40–36, Letters of incorporation for the Parry Sound Electric Light Company Ltd. dated Nov. 7, 1895; Parry Sound Bylaw #143 passed Jan. 13, 1896, Allowing the Parry Sound Electric Light Company Ltd. to regulate, erect and maintain electric light poles and wires.
7 *North Star*, July 11, 1906, 11.
8 "The Late R.R. Hall," *North Star*, Feb. 25, 1932, 1; "Richard Reece Hall," *Canadian Parliamentary Guide, 1923*, 320.
9 *North Star*, Feb. 13, 1919, 1.
10 Ibid, Mar. 13, 1919, 1.
11 Richard White, *The Skule Story: The University of Toronto Faculty of Applied Science and Engineering, 1873–2000* (Toronto: Faculty of Applied Science and Engineering, University of Toronto, 2000).
12 *North Star*, May 15, 1919, 1.
13 Ibid, June 26, 1919, p. 1; and July 10, 1919, 1.
14 Ibid, Aug. 14, 1919, 1.
15 Ibid, Jan. 8, 1920, 1; "Liberal candidate has big majority," *North Star*, Oct. 23, 1919, 1.
16 *North Star*, Jan. 15, 1920.
17 Ibid.
18 Ibid, June 23, 1898, 1.
19 Ibid, Feb. 19, 1920, 1.
20 Ibid, Oct. 7, 1920.
21 Parry Sound Bylaw #415 passed Jan. 20, 1914, To authorize and provide for the purchase of the property and capital stock of the Parry Sound River Improvement Company.
22 Harry Roland Reed was born Feb. 16, 1892, at Markham, Ontario. He entered the University of Toronto's Faculty of Applied Science and Engineering in September 1911, but discontinued third year studies to volunteer for overseas service with the Canadian Expeditionary Force. Reed sailed from Halifax on June 2, 1917, as a lieutenant in the Huntsville-based 122nd Infantry Battalion, which was disbanded in England. He was reassigned to the 75th company, Cana-

dian Forestry Corps and reached France in September 1917, where he contracted pulmonary tuberculosis. Invalided back to Canada, Reed spent time convalescing at the Muskoka Cottage Sanatorium in Gravenhurst before being discharged as medically unfit on Sept. 28, 1918. Reed received his degree on June 4, 1920, at the recommendation of Prof. T.R. Rosebrugh, head of the electrical engineering department. Library and Archives Canada (LAC), RG 150, Acc. 1992-93/166, Box 8164-18, Personnel record of Lt. Harry Roland Reed; University of Toronto Archives (U of T), A69-0008/003, Admission application for Harry Roland Reed, U of T, A98-0003/007, Student transcript card for Harry Roland Reed.

23   *North Star*, May 20, 1920, 1.
24   Ibid.
25   "Public meeting held on Tuesday night—Some citizens wanted explanations about power plant," *North Star*, June 24, 1920, 1.
26   Ibid, Sept. 16, 1920.
27   Ibid, Feb. 5, 1920, 1.
28   "Elec. superintendent monthly report," *North Star*, Dec. 9, 1920, 1.
29   *North Star*, Oct. 7, 1920.
30   Ibid, March 3, 1921, 1.
31   "Mayor and council by acclamation," *North Star*, Dec. 29, 1931, 1.
32   *North Star*, Apr. 7, 1921, 1, and June 2, 1921, 1.
33   Harry Roland Reed married Bernice Wiggins of Parry Sound in a March 1922 ceremony at St. James Methodist Church in Parry Sound: "Reed-Wiggins," *The Daily Star*, Mar. 9, 1922, 14.
34   "W.J. Lockhart retires after 40 years," *North Star*, Nov. 12, 1959, 1.

16 – A TRAIN ROBBERY, GUNPLAY AND THE INEVITABLE MURDER

1   "Pursued mail car bandits slay farmer," *The Evening Telegram*, Aug. 18, 1928, 1; "Mail robbers kill farmer, wound two men," *The Daily Star*, Aug. 18, 1928, 1.
2   "Witness says he saw Burowski fire three shots," *The Daily Star*, Sept. 26, 2.
3   "Witness tells how man was captured," *The Daily Star*, Sept. 27, 1928, 3.
4   Statement of John Burkowski, undated. Contained in the 477-page OPP file on the murder of Thomas Jackson and the mail train robbery, a copy of which the author obtained through the Ontario Freedom of Information and Protection of Privacy Act. Burowski would later claim that he signed "Burkowski" because he was "very weak."
5   "Sons of slain farmer take up hunt, swear to get bandit," *The Evening Telegram*, Aug. 20, 1928, 23.
6   "Jail is now jammed with many suspects," *The Daily Star*, Aug. 22, 1928, 5.
7   "Burowski officially named as slayer of Thomas Jackson," *The Evening Telegram*, Aug. 21, 1928, 26; "Burowski is named murderer of farmer after investigation," *The Globe*, Aug. 21, 1928, 1; "Thos. Jackson killed when bandit fires at pursuers," *North Star*, Aug. 23, 1928, 1.
8   "Commit Burowski on murder charge," *The Daily Star*, Aug. 25, 1928, 3.
9   "Refuses to delay Burowski's trial," *The Daily Star*, Sept. 26, 1928, 3.

10   Ibid.

11   "Burowski on stand in his own defence," *The Globe*, Sept. 27, 1928, .2.

12   "'I didn't shoot Jackson,' Burowski tells court," *The Daily Star*, Sept. 27, 1928, 18.

13   "Self defence plea offered for Burowski," *The Daily Star*, Sept. 27, 1929, 1.

14   AO, RG 4-32, File #2319 of 1928, Rex v. Burowski, Harold Polkinghorne to Attorney General William H. Price, Sept. 6, 1928.

15   Ibid, Walter L. Haight to deputy attorney general Edward Bayly, Aug. 25, 1928.

16   Note 14, OPP Commissioner V.A.S. Williams to Attorney General William H. Price, Aug. 30, 1928.

17   AO, RG 75-57, Order-in-council 168/19 authorizing rewards for Walter Laird, Haughton Laird and Harold Joseph Rolland, approved Sept. 24, 1928.

18   AO, RG 4-32, file #2319 of 1928, Attorney General W.H. Price to Walter Laird, Haughton Laird and Harold Joseph Rolland, Nov. 19, 1828; "Presentations made at council meeting," *North Star*, Nov. 22, 1928, 1.

19   Ibid.

20   AO, RG 4-32, file #2319 of 1928, Application to the Minister of Justice for executive clemency, either by way for a new trial or commutation of the death sentence, in the case of Rex v. Burowski, undated.

21   Ibid, Affidavit of John Burowski to sheriff James E.T. Armstrong, Dec. 6, 1928.

22   Ibid, Telegram from Attorney General W.H. Price to sheriff James E.T. Armstrong, Dec. 6, 1928.

23   Ibid, Attorney General W.H. Price to John Rolland Hett, Dec. 18, 1928.

24   "Burowski to hang, Attorney General says province is not further concerned with case," *The Daily Star*, Dec. 20, 1928, 1.

25   "Official hangman busy buying gifts," *The Daily Star*, Dec. 22, 1928, 2.

26   OPP file, Report of Sgt. Eric Hand to Insp. Arthur Moss, Sept. 26, 1928.

27   OPP file, Report by Const. Robert G. Beatty to OPP Commissioner William H. Stringer, Nov. 29, 1950 and Report by Insp. Ralph L. Taylor to Chief Insp. Albert H. Ward, Dec. 8, 1950.

17 – THE POLITICS OF POLICING

1   Parry Sound Bylaw #325 passed Feb. 4, 1908, To establish a board of commissioners of police; Parry Sound Bylaw #329 passed Jan. 9, 1909, To dissolve police commission for the Town of Parry Sound.

2   Philip C. Stenning, *Police Commissions and Board in Canada* (Toronto: Centre of Criminology, University of Toronto, 1981) I.17.

3   *North Star*, April 7, 1938, 2.

4   "Do we need a police commission?" *North Star*, Jan. 14, 1954, 7

5   *North Star*, March 20, 1958, 1.

6   "Committee chairman a key witness at hearing," *Parry Sound Beacon Star*, March 29, 1988, 7.

7   *North Star*, Dec. 15, 1921, 1.

8   Parry Sound council minutes, Aug. 23, 1887.

9 Ibid, Dec. 29, 1891.
10 Bylaw #192 passed Jan. 18, 1900, To regulate and define the duties of the town constable.
11 *North Star*, Dec. 13, 1900, 4.
12 Robert Dunlop to Parry Sound council, April 3, 1906.
13 Council minutes, June 5, 1906.
14 Octave Julien to Parry Sound council, undated.
15 Francis Ronan Powell to Parry Sound clerk Errol Everard Armstrong, Aug. 3, 1909.
16 *North Star*, June 2, 1910, 1.
17 Bylaw #416 passed Feb. 3, 1914, To regulate and define the duties of the town constables.
18 Council minutes, June 20, 1916.
19 Ibid, Dec. 8, 1916.
20 "Town council," *North Star*, Dec. 14, 1916, 4; "Another judicial investigation and chief of police suspended," *North Star*, Dec. 21, 1916, 1.; and "Civic investigations," *North Star*, Dec. 28, 1916, 5.
21 Council minutes, Feb. 13, 1917.
22 Council minutes, Feb. 20, 1917; June 4, 1918; and Nov. 2, 1920.
23 Council minutes, Aug. 16, 1921; and Oct. 18, 1927.
24 "Council demands resignation of police force and assessor," *North Star*, Feb. 5, 1931, 4.
25 *North Star*, Feb. 26, 1931.
26 Council minutes, Nov. 20, 1934 and Dec. 4, 1934. "Cornwall man chief of police at Parry Sound," *The Cornwall Standard-Freeholder*, Nov. 28, 1934, 1.
27 Council minutes, June 7, 1938; *North Star*, June 9, 1938.
28 Council minutes, Aug. 6, 1940.
29 Ibid, Nov. 21, 1944; Norina D'Agostini, Toronto Police Service, to Adrian Hayes, Aug. 23, 1999.
30 Council minutes, Aug. 1, 1944.
31 Ibid, Oct. 7, 1947.
32 Ibid, Nov. 15, 1949
33 Ibid, Oct. 19, 1948.
34 *North Star*, March 21, 1963, 8; Council minutes, Jan. 28, 1964.
35 A Survey of the Adequacy of the Parry Sound Police Force, May 31, 1973. Prepared by Walter F. Johnston and John S. McLaren, advisors to the Ontario Police Commission.
36 Mark Bourie, "Parry Sound votes to disband police," *Globe and Mail*, Aug. 22, 1987, A-13.
37 *North Star*, March 6, 1958, 1; April 3, 1958, 5; and May 8, 1958, 1.
38 Ibid, Oct. 17, 1963, 6.
39 Council minutes, July 21, 1964.
40 OPC report, 1973.
41 *Annual Report of the Parry Sound Police Department for the year ending Dec. 31, 1975.*
42 "No large savings expected but more policing for dollar," *North Star*, Aug. 20, 1987, 1.

43   "Staff changes sink official police report," *Parry Sound Beacon Star*, Jan. 24, 1989, 1.

44   *Annual Report for the Parry Sound Police Department for the year ending Dec. 31, 1987.* Accepted by council on March 1, 1988.

45   Town of Parry Sound executive assistant Rebecca Johnson to Adrian Hayes, Nov. 22, 1999.

46   Ontario Minister of Finance Ernie Eves, QC, to Adrian Hayes, Nov. 16, 1999.

47   "Study group to assess police service," *Parry Sound Beacon Star*, Dec. 4, 1999, 1; "Policing costs increasing for province," *Parry Sound Beacon Star*, Sept. 29, 2001, 1.

18 – THERE WERE ONCE THREE THEATRES

1   "Sweating ends, as Festival moves into cool new digs on waterfront," *North Star*, July 23, 2003, 1.

2   "The municipal building," *North Star*, March 1, 1934, 1.

3   "Council purchase site for proposed building; architect is also engaged," *North Star*, March 15, 1934, 1; "Auditorium in proposed building would practically double cost," *North Star*, Feb. 22, 1934, 1.

4   "Council and utilities commission discuss municipal building plans," *North Star*, Sept. 30, 1945, 1.

5   *North Star*, March 14, 1879, 1.

6   "Fire destroys Gibson garage," *North Star*, Dec. 28, 1933, 1.

7   Tish Hannon, "Ice sports in Parry Sound," *East Georgian Bay Historical Journal*, 1985, Vol. IX, 122.

8   "Local rink is prey to flames," *North Star*, Jan. 27, 1927, 5; "Skating rink soon ready," *North Star*, Nov. 24, 1927, 1.

9   "Curling rink," *North Star*, Sept. 28, 1899, 5; "The new curling rink," *North Star*, Jan. 18, 1900, 5.

10   "The Lyric Theatre," *North Star*, April 28, 1910. 1.

11   All issues of *North Star* between Dec. 11, 1913, and Sept. 17, 1914, are missing from the microfilm. A copy of this article was provided to the author by Alicia Ryder Nesbitt.

12   "No hard times," *North Star*, Oct. 1, 1914, 5.

13   "Skidoo party," *North Star*, Oct. 15, 1914, 5.

14   "At the Princess," *North Star*, Aug. 24, 1916, 5.

15   "Quality counts," *North Star*, Nov. 23, 1916, 5.

16   "Recruiting meeting," *North Star*, Dec. 7, 1916, 5.

17   "Large attendance at soldiers' meeting," *North Star*, Apr. 11, 1918, 1.

18   "E.J. Groves takes over Quinn Motors," *North Star*, Mar. 14, 1929, 1.

19   AO, RG 56-10-28-5, Architectural drawings of the Royal Theatre; "Royal Theatre to equip for talkies," *North Star*, Jan. 9, 1930, 1; "G.W. Spence passes suddenly," *North Star*, June 23, 1932, 1; "The Theatre Holding Corporation takes over the Royal Theatre," *North Star*, Feb. 9, 1939, 1; "John Campbell bids goodbye to show business after many years," *North Star*, Feb. 16, 1939, 8; "John Campbell dies in Kentucky," *North Star*, May 18, 1939, 1; "A tribute to Mr. John Campbell," *North Star*, June 1, 1939, 5.

20 AO, RG 56-9-54-9, Theatre regulatory file on Parry Sound; AO, RG 56-9-54-11, Theatre regulatory file on the Strand Theatre; AO, RG 56-10-105-4, Architectural drawings of the Strand Theatre.

21 "Rink company is now formed," *North Star*, April 15, 1948, 1; "Lions Club to raise funds for a new skating rink," *North Star*, Oct. 21, 1948, 1; "Memorial Arena opened last week," *North Star*, Jan. 20, 1948, 1.

22 AO, RG 56-9-54-10 and RG 56-9-113.22, Theatre regulatory file on the Parry Sound Drive-In.

23 Ibid.

24 "Building permit issued for new shopping plaza," *North Star*, Nov. 8, 1973, 1.

25 "Outdoor theatre seeks 'fund to raise a fund, '" *North Star*, Jan. 15, 1963, 1.

26 "Outdoor theatre called 'bolder than Stratford, '" *North Star*, May 30, 1963, 1.

27 "Death of a dream," *North Star*, Jan. 26, 1965, 1.

19 — HMCS *PARRY SOUND*

1 LAC, RG 24, Vol. 7721, Deck log of HMCS *Parry Sound*, entry for Aug. 18, 1945. The author met with Joe Burnie at his home in Ailsa Craig, Ontario, during the summer of 1990.

2 LAC, RG 24, Vol. 5832, file 8000-332/74, General information file for HMCS *Parry Sound*; "Corvette HMCS Parry Sound due here in six weeks," *North Star*, May 18, 1944, 1; "Corvette arrival has been delayed," *North Star*, June 22, 1944, 1.

3 "Purchase piano for HMCS Parry Sound," *North Star*, June 15, 1944, 1; "Donations to the corvette committee," *North Star*, July 6, 1944, 1.

4 "More about the corvette arrival," *North Star*, June 22, 1944, 1; "Complete plans to receive corvette," *North Star*, Aug. 31, 1944, 1.

5 "Huge crowds inspect corvette HMCS Parry Sound; entertain the officers and crew of adopted ship," *North Star*, Sept. 14, 1944, 1; "Commander of corvette thanks the Rotary Club," *North Star*, Oct. 19, 1944, 1.

6 LAC, Deck log, Aug. 30, 1944, to July 10, 1945.

7 LAC, General information file for HMCS *Parry Sound*.

8 Ken Macpherson and John Burgess, *The Ships of Canada's Naval Forces 1910–1981: A Complete Pictorial History of Canadian Warships* (Toronto: Collins, 1981) 101.

20 — A MEMORIAL TO THE FOREST RANGERS

1 "Parry Sound observation tower is officially opened," *North Star*, Aug. 21, 1975, 1.

2 Murray Meldrum, "Removal of old forestry fire tower signalled end of an interesting era," *North Star*, Aug. 21, 1975, 13.

3 "Will erect forestry tower at Parry Sound," *North Star*, March 3, 1927, 4; "New tower being erected," *North Star*, June 30, 1927, 5; "Many visitors to fire tower," *North Star*, July 7, 1927, 1.

4 Murray Meldrum, *North Star* Aug. 21, 1975, 13; "Forestry Branch make improvements," *North Star*, April 24, 1930, 1.

5 "Child meets tragic death in fall from forestry tower on Sunday," *North Star*, May 27, 1937, 1.

6   Murray Meldrum, *North Star*, Aug. 21, 1975, 13.

21 — HOCKEY HEROES

1   Jim Carson, the only son of Frank Carson, has read this chapter and noted, from his perspective, some discrepancies in the names of all three brothers. The author took the names from the birth certificates of the brothers and, in the case of Bill, his University of Toronto records. For example, while Bill's U of T records and yearbook entries say "William James Carson," Jim says he was "William Joseph Carson," as does www.legendsofhockey.net.

2   Telephone conversation with John Maddeford, May 3, 2004.

3   Bobby Orr with Mark Mulvoy, *Bobby Orr: My Game* (Boston: Little, Brown & Company Limited, 1974) 40.

4   "Hockey of Yesteryear," *North Star*, Nov. 24, 1960, 10.

5   "Let us have hockey," *North Star*, Nov. 28, 1918, 1; "Parry Sound boys can play hockey," *North Star*, Jan. 23, 1919, 1; "Pleasant hockey supper," *North Star*, March 6, 1919, 1; "OHA hockey for Parry Sound," *North Star*, Sept. 18, 1919, 1; "Hockey meeting for organization," *North Star*, Oct. 9, 1919, 1.

6   "Hockey of yesteryear," *North Star*, Dec. 1, 1960, 10.

7   "University of Toronto beat Brandon in final game 8 to 1 and lift Allan Cup," *The Daily Mail and Empire*, March 22, 1921, 8.

8   "Grimsby team's star moves to Stratford," *The Globe*, March 26, 1924, 8.

9   "Bill Carson declines to turn professional," *The Globe*, Dec. 11, 1924, 8.

10 "The Carsons have not accepted terms," *The Daily Star*, Jan. 19, 1926, 10.

11 "Carson of Stratford suspended by OHA," *Daily Mail and Empire*, Feb. 10, 1926, 8.

12 "Dr. Carson is signed by St. Pat's owners," *The Globe*, April 17, 1926, 12; *The Daily Star*, April 17, 1926, 12, Craig MacInnis, *Remembering Bobby Orr, A Celebration* (Toronto: Stoddart Publishing Co. Limited, 1999) 88.

13 "Bill Carson leads Leafs in Points with Day second," *The Daily Star*, Dec. 7, 1927, 12; *The Daily Star*, Jan. 20, 1928, 13; "Carson suffered concussion of brain in fall," *The Evening Telegram*, Feb. 6, 1928, 28; "Bill Carson will be out for three weeks," *The Daily Star*, Feb. 9, 1928, 12; "Dr. Bill Carson rejoins Leafs this evening," *The Evening Telegram*, March 13, 1928, 32.

14 "Dental officer appointed for free clinical service," *The Globe*, Oct. 28, 1927.

15 University of Toronto, A73-0026/1053(12). Press clipping file on William James Carson. This particular article is of uncertain origin.

16 "Poor playing on road trip hurried the Carson sale," *The Evening Telegram*, Jan. 26, 1929, 37.

17 "Bill Carson opposes former teammates," *The Globe*, Jan. 30, 1929, 10.

18 "Bill Carson parts company with Boston Bruins," *The Globe*, Oct. 17, 1930, 10.

19 "Dr. Bill Carson is signed by London," *The Globe*, Nov. 25, 1930, 8.

20 Taped telephone conversations with Ted Carson, June 3 and June 20, 2004.

21 "Hockey Player hurt as car crashes pole," *The Evening Telegram*, Oct, 1, 1931, 3; "Boston player hurt," *The Evening Telegram*, Oct. 1, 1931, 3.

22 "Amateur, pro hockey great of former years,"*Globe and Mail*, April 22, 1957, 22; "Nothing wrong with hockey today says Frank Carson, former NHL great," *London Free Press*, April 20, 1957, 25; "Puck star R.F. Carson victim of heart attack," *London Free Press*, April 22, 1957, 5.

23 "Was hockey star with Canadiens,"*Globe and Mail*, Nov. 10, 1956, 30,

24 *Globe and Mail*, June 1, 1967, 24.

25 "Gets 2 months for theft of $50 in Parry Sound," *Sudbury Star*, March 27, 1956, 3.

26 "Former hockey great dies," *North Star*, May 30, 1967, 1.

22 – THE BULLDOZING OF HISTORY

1 "LACAC chairman upset over sudden removal of stone building," *North Star*, April 4, 1985, 5.

2 "IOOF Hall and 'Kitchen house' are intertwined in history of the town," *North Star*, Feb. 10, 1983, 12.

3 AO, RG 55-1, MS 7164, Liber 48 Folio 23, Letters of incorportion for the Patent Cloth Board Factory of Parry Sound Ltd. dated May 20, 1897.

4 Parry Sound #1373, Deed dated Aug. 10, 1897, Transferring ownership of 4.9 acres from William Beatty Jr. to the Patent Cloth Board Factory of Parry Sound Ltd; Parry Sound Bylaw #166 passed Dec. 28, 1897, Granting the Patent Cloth Board Factory of Parry Sound Ltd. exemption from taxation for ten years.

5 John Macfie, "Then as it is now, progress gives impetus to local industry," *North Star*, June 30, 1999, 3.

6 AO, RG 8-1-1, #841 of 1899, Annual return to the Provincial Secretary for the Patent Cloth Board Factory of Parry Sound Ltd.

7 Ibid, #733 of 1900, Annual return to the Provincial Secretary for the Patent Cloth Board Factory of Parry Sound Ltd.

8 Note 6, #2327 of 1902, Annual return to the Provincial Secretary for the Patent Cloth Board Factory of Parry Sound Ltd.; #5549 of 1904, Liquidation file for the Patent Cloth Board Factory of Parry Sound Ltd.

9 Parry Sound #4314, Deed dated March 14, 1911, Transferring 9/10 acre from George and William Niebergall to the Canadian Pacific Railway.

10 D.F. Macdonald diaries, Sept. 11, 1912; *North Star*, Feb. 20, 1913, 4; AO, RG 55-17-42-5, MS 5506, #402 District of Parry Sound partnership dissolution for George Niebergall & Son dated Sept. 16, 1919.

11 "Wm. Neibergall passes away," *North Star*, Sept. 5, 1935, 1.

12 Council minutes, Sept. 11, 1984; Council resolution #84-298 passed Sept. 11, 1984.

13 Council minutes, Sept. 18, 1984; Council resolution #84-319 passed Sept. 18, 1984. A photo of the building appeared in the *North Star* on Sept. 20, 1984.

14 Council minutes, Nov. 20, 1984; "Heritage Foundation official urges retention of historic building," *North Star*, Nov. 27, 1984, 1.

15 "LACAC chairman upset over sudden removal of stone building," *North Star*, April 4, 1985, 5.

16 "Grant for Waubuno Park," *Beacon*, May, 11, 1985, A-3.

17 Council minutes, Sept. 3, 1985 and Oct. 1, 1985; Resolution #85-328 passed Sept. 3, 1985, Corporation tender for construction of parking lot, boat access ramp, etc.; Resolution #85-371 passed Oct. 1, 1985, Awarding contract #85-3 to Maclaim Construction.

23 — PARRY SOUND TODAY

1 Council minutes, Jan. 5, 1949.
2 "Now you see it… now you don't," *Parry Sound Beacon Star,* Sept. 15, 2001, 1.
3 AO, RG 37-6, Case P9302-69, Box 1143, Mayor George Saad of Parry Sound to Reeve Wilbert John Foreman, March 20, 1969.
4 "Board turns down application for amalgamation into maxi town," *North Star,* Nov. 14, 1972, 1.
5 *Parry Sound Beacon,* May 11, 1983.
6 "Big Sound Marina first-season success," *North Star,* Sept. 5, 1989, 1; "Town will study feasibility of running transient boater marina, instead of contracting to Chamber of Commerce," *North Star,* Feb. 11, 2004, 1.
7 "Town inches toward purchase of 7 Bay Street," *North Star,* Jan. 28, 2004, 1.
8 "50 years ago—Bunker oil slick spreads from harbour," *Parry Sound Beacon Star,* Sept. 16, 2000, 1.
9 "Wheels in motion to clean up another part of waterfront," *North Star,* Jan. 14, 2004, 1.
10 *North Star,* editorial, July 28, 2004.
11 "Walmart comes to Georgian Bay country," *Parry Sound Beacon Star,* May 1, 2004, 1; "Mixed reaction to having our own Walmart," *North Star,* May 5, 2004, 1.

Bibliography

Angus, James T., *A Deo Victoria: The Story of the Georgian Bay Lumber Company, 1871–1942* (Thunder Bay, ON: Severn Publications, 1990).

Brunton, Sam (compiler), *Notes and Sketches on the History of Parry Sound* (Parry Sound, ON: Parry Sound Public Library, 1969).

Byers, Mary, Jan Kennedy and Margaret McBurney, *Rural Routes: Pre-Confederation Buildings of the York Region of Ontario* (Toronto: University of Toronto Press, 1976).

Cleland, Robert Glass, *A History of Phelps Dodge, 1834–1950* (New York: Alfred A. Knopf, 1952).

Greene, B.M., ed., "John Bellamy Miller," in *Who's Who and Why, 1919–1920* (Toronto: International Press Ltd., 1920).

Hamilton, W.E., John Rogers and Seymour Richard Penson, *Guide Book & Atlas of Muskoka and Parry Sound Districts* (Toronto: H.R. Page, 1879).

Kirkwood, A. and J.J. Murphy, *The Undeveloped Lands in Northern and Western Ontario: Information Regarding Resources, Products and Suitability for Settlement* (Toronto: Hunter, Rose, 1878).

Macpherson, Ken and John Burgess, *The Ships of Canada's Naval Forces 1910–1981: A Complete Pictorial History of Canadian Warships* (Toronto: Collins, 1981).

McMurray, Thomas, *The Free Grant Lands: From Practical Experiences of Bush Farming in the Free Grant Districts of Muskoka and Parry Sound* (originally published 1871; reprint Huntsville, ON: Fox Meadow Creations and B. Hammond, 2002).

Murray, Florence B., "John Clauson Miller" in *Dictionary of Canadian Biography*, Vol. XI (Toronto: University of Toronto Press, 1982).

Nicholson, G.W.L., *Canadian Expeditionary Force, 1914–1919* (corrected edition) (Ottawa: R. Duhamel, Queen's Printer, 1964).

Perkins, Mary Ellen (compiler), *Discover Your Heritage: A Guide to Provincial Plaques in Ontario* (Toronto: Natural Heritage, 1989).

Stenning, Philip C., *Police Commissions and Boards in Canada* (Toronto: Centre of Criminology, University of Toronto, 1981).

Taim, Astrid, *Almaguin: A Highland History* (Toronto: Natural Heritage, 1998).

White, Richard, *The Skule Story: The University of Toronto Faculty of Applied Science and Engineering, 1873–2000* (Toronto: Faculty of Applied Science and Engineering, University of Toronto, 2000).

Wilson, Donald, *Lost Horizons: The Story of the Rathburn Company and the Bay of Quinte Railway* (Belleville, ON: Mika Publishing Company, 1983).

Index

About the Author

A graduate of Parry Sound High School, Adrian Hayes developed an interest in the community's past while studying for a Bachelor of Arts in history from Laurentian University. In the fall of 1986, just prior to the town's centennial celebrations, he began writing a column on local history for the *Parry Sound North Star* while still a student. *Parry Sound: Gateway to Northern Ontario* is the result of his continuing curiosity about the days of old in his hometown.

Hayes received a Bachelor of Applied Arts in journalism from Ryerson Polytechnic Institute in 1991 and accepted his first job as a reporter at the *North Star*. He has since worked for *Orillia Today*, *The Barrie Examiner* and *The Uxbridge Times-Journal*, and is currently employed by Transcontinental Publishing. He is the author of *Pegahmagabow: Legendary Warrior, Forgotten Hero*, a biography of former Wasauksing First Nation chief and Aboriginal rights activist Francis Pegahmagabow, a First World War veteran who had been awarded the Military Medal and Two Bars for valour, published in 2002.

Adrian Hayes lives in Newmarket, Ontario, where he is president of the Newmarket Historical Society.